# LOST IN
# KATRINA

# LOST IN
# KATRINA

## MIKEL SCHAEFER

**Foreword by Douglas Brinkley**

**PELICAN PUBLISHING COMPANY**
Gretna 2007

**Library of Congress Cataloging-in-Publication Data**

Schaefer, Mikel.
  Lost in Katrina / by Mikel Schaefer ; foreword by Douglas Brinkley.
    p. cm.
  Includes index.
  ISBN 978-1-58980-511-8 (pbk. : alk. paper)  1.  Hurricane Katrina,
2005. 2.  Hurricanes—Louisiana—Saint Bernard Parish. 3.  Disasters—
Louisiana--Saint Bernard Parish. 4.  Disaster victims—Louisiana—
Saint Bernard Parish--Interviews. 5.  Rescue work—Louisiana--Saint
Bernard Parish. 6.  Saint Bernard Parish (La.)  I. Title.
  HV6362005.L8 S33 2007
  976.3'36064--dc22
                              2007022326

Printed in the United States of America

Published by Pelican Publishing Company, Inc.
1000 Burmaster Street, Gretna, Louisiana 70053

Dedicated to all victims of Katrina because St. Bernard's story is your story — our story.

I also dedicate this book to my entire family, especially my wife, Jaye, and sons, Connor and Aidan, whose support and sacrifice during a difficult time helped preserve a story near and dear to my heart.

# CONTENTS

# FOREWORD

Anyone who lived through Hurricane Katrina knows what an all-encompassing tragedy it was. There was disaster on a mythic scale, with three breached levees in New Orleans, the wall of water in St. Bernard Parish, and the Lake Borgne surge in Bay St. Louis. Randomly pick a Gulf South city on a map (pin-the-donkey fashion) and you will automatically land on a community that was in desperate peril on August 29, 2005. The ache was—and still is—palatable. Nowhere else in America is storytelling still a high-art form than in Louisiana. So from the minute the hurricane made landfall, it was clear that Blues tales would come tumbling out of survivors.

Now, on the second anniversary of Katrina, eyewitness Mikel Schaefer has written a lament filled with anguish and uplift. Written by a WWL-TV New Orleans journalist, *Lost in Katrina* is a heartfelt, deeply personal recounting of the worst storm to ever hit the United States. Every line rings true, which is not necessarily a good thing.

Schaefer writes so vividly about his beloved St. Bernard Parish—and what it has endured—that I felt my pot boiling up with rage all over again. To read those harrowing tales of survival, of people axing their way through rooftops, and hanging onto trees for dear life is unsettling. His reporting of the St. Rita's Nursing Home tragedy is particularly horrific, enabling the reader to relive the moments before the water filled the lungs of the thirty-five patients who died.

During the storm, Schaefer was in Baton Rouge, keeping his TV news station on the air. Three weeks after Katrina, he began interviewing victims with a small micro-recorder. He literally drove around and asked everybody he could what he or she saw and experienced in the storm. In St. Bernard Parish, he heard of floating corpses, no dry land, and a small jail turned into a triage

9

station. The stench of floodwater permeates every page of this important book.

Then the community rose. In heroic, epic fashion the people of St. Bernard Parish saved themselves. With no U.S. Calvary coming down in chariots from the sky, locals rescued locals. It all makes for dramatic, true-life stories that are unforgettable.

Which brings us to those shoddily constructed levees. Reading Schaefer's work reminds us that the U.S. Army Corps of Engineers was the outfit most responsible for the loss of human lives during Katrina. In my book, *The Great Deluge,* I called them Lego-levees, but that was far too generous. They were nothing more than miles of flimsy, half-baked, grotesquely awful slabs of engineering abomination writ large. Just imagine the national uproar if the Hoover Dam or the St. Lawrence Seaway had been built on the cheap, using construction firms' sub-par materials, putting a major metropolitan area at risk. Every time a talented writer like Schaefer publishes a book—and we relive the widespread suffering all over again—I am haunted by this simple, basic, essential post-Katrina point: that the U.S. federal government was responsible for the flooding. That fact sticks in my craw. It makes me quake. There really is no point in debating the future of St. Bernard Parish. If the U.S. Army Corps of Engineers screwed up, then they need to fix their humongous errors.

If *Lost in Katrina* drives only one point home, it is that Chalmette, Arabi, Poydras, and Reggio will rise up again through sheer grit. This book is a tribute to the fortitude and perseverance of a parish determined to defy odds time and time again.

DOUG BRINKLEY

# LOST IN
# KATRINA

CHAPTER ONE

# The Call


## Sunday, August 28

### Day One


*There's an energy that circulates around hurricanes when they're in
the Gulf. You can feel it; there's an excitement; it's a force of nature.
It's an odd sort of thing but you feel that high energy and anticipation
and the hurricane parties start. It's a strange sort of reaction to something as deadly as these storms, but in this one, particularly locally,
you could sense a much more solemn attitude about this storm. I think
people knew this might have our name on it.*

—Jack Stephens
St. Bernard Parish Sheriff


Sunday morning, August 28, less than twenty-four hours to
landfall, Hurricane Katrina's track was one of the most threatening
this parish had ever seen. By 6:00 A.M. the hot water of the Gulf of
Mexico helped cook Katrina into a monstrous category five storm
with sustained winds of 175 miles per hour and gusts reaching 215
mph. The conditions were so conducive for a direct hit that the
threat set off some unprecedented phone calls. A fast talker placed
a call to Stephens at his home in Yscloskey around 8:30 A.M.

"'Is this Sheriff Stephens?'"

"Yea."

"'This is the National Hurricane Center in Miami.'"

"What can I do to help you?" Stephens said.

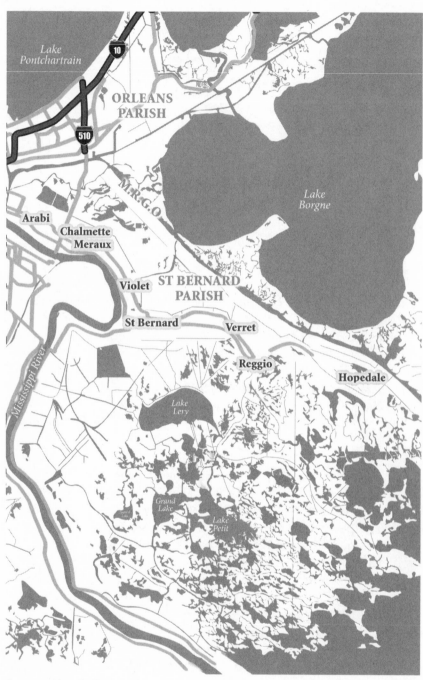

*Courtesy Mariella Pariente*

"'I'm really sorry to have to make this call, but I felt compelled to make it. I just want you to know you're going to have a thirty-foot sheer wall of water that's going to slam into your parish. You're going to have flooding levee-to-levee. The property damage is going to be catastrophic, and you're going to have serious loss of life. God bless you and good luck.'"

Stephens, stunned by the numbing message, does not even recollect who called. Stephens, who spent twenty-two years as St. Bernard sheriff and ten years prior as parish manager and director of planning, mindlessly put the phone down. A gut wrenching realization set in that Katrina was going to be the worst-case scenario for his parish. He turned to his wife, Desiree.

"Take the pictures off the walls and pack the insurance papers, this is the last time you're gonna see this place."

Sheriff Stephens grew up in Shell Beach, a lower St. Bernard fishing hamlet where within minutes you're in the marshes of south Louisiana, minutes from redfish and speckled trout, and if you want to hit the Gulf of Mexico, you're less than a tank of gas to the oil rigs. It's where you feel you're in the middle of nowhere but somewhere so special your heart beats with the rhythm of the waves, and you know you're where you want to be for the rest of your life.

The son of immigrants from Spain, Stephens built his dream home about a year before, near his childhood home, a stones throw away, in Yscloskey (pronounced Y-clas-key, the first s is silent), in Fort Beauregard Marina Estates. However, Stephens's new home was nothing like where he grew up; this home sits on pilings twenty-one feet above sea level in a brand new, exclusive, upscale, gated development to accommodate the fast growing group of weekend fishermen who want a getaway pad. They have enough cash and a burning fever to be near the water whenever possible, and these homes give them the ability to launch a boat from their private dock. You can idle into the man-made canal that leads to the shipping channel called the Mississippi River Gulf Outlet or MR-GO, and from there you can almost start counting the fish you'll haul into the boat, with fresh, live shrimp or live cocahoe minnows as bait.

Stephens's beautiful new home was worth hundreds of thousands of dollars and a quantum leap from the old, wooden homes that line Florissant and Hopedale Highways. Owned mostly by fishermen, who make their living dredging oysters, shrimping, or fishing, these homes sit along the bayous. The area had seen an emergence of new development of fancy, fishing homes, also called camps, for the white-collar elite, semi-elite, and blue-collar men who had saved their money well.

His house was built to withstand a category three hurricane, because the structure is outside of the hurricane protection levee system. There's nothing between those homes and a storm, except the constantly disappearing St. Bernard Parish coastline that can no longer slow down hurricanes like it once could.

With Katrina's gears shifted towards the Louisiana coast, Stephens called his two sons, Justin and Barrett, on Saturday and told Desiree to start preparing their home for the storms wrath. While he dealt with the duties of preparing the parish for the storm, his family picked up and tried to secure the house the best they could.

"I knew I was in trouble when Sunday morning I got the call from the National Hurricane Center."

—Larry Ingargiola
St. Bernard Parish director of Homeland Security and Office
of Emergency Preparedness

The severity of the threat prompted another morning call from the National Hurricane Center, this time to Ingargiola, who was stationed at the government complex and recalls the conversation.

"I got some bad news for you," the man on the other end of the phone said.

Ingargiola asked, "Who's this?"

"'Dr. Max Mayfield, director of the National Hurricane Center in Miami.'"

"You don't have to tell me no more. This is the first time y'all have ever called me to warn me of a storm. What am I looking at?"

"'The worst-case scenario.'"

"O.K."

"'If I was y'all, I'd try to do your evacuation as soon as possible, start getting your people out.'"

"We already did a recommended evacuation; we tried to get as many people out."

the medical needs of parish President Henry "Junior" Rodriguez who had recently been released from a long stay in the hospital.

"He just recently got discharged from the hospital in ICU, and I took care of him while he was in ICU," said Brenda. "I knew what his condition was, so I had to make sure he was O.K. I had to do dress and changes on him also."

Ingargiola, who served more than three decades with the St. Bernard Parish Sheriff's Department, once saved a child's life. He and another deputy responded to a call of an accidental hanging. Ingargiola performed mouth-to-mouth resuscitation during the frantic ride to Chalmette General Hospital and is credited with saving the boy's life. With Katrina, he feared the deaths of many of his fellow St. Bernardians.

"This is what they call a hundred year storm. This was no hundred year storm; this was a five hundred year storm."
—Henry "Junior" Rodriguez
St. Bernard Parish president

Rodriguez was hot and bothered as he drove the near deserted road past miles of uninhabited land towards his home in the tiny town of Verret. He thought about what effect the Mississippi River Gulf Outlet (MR-GO) shipping channel would have on St. Bernard, as Katrina's projected storm surge of twenty plus feet promised to flood streets and homes. Rodriguez is the unequaled opponent of the MR-GO, which opened in the mid 1960s, and has been for years. He has ranted and raved to just about anyone who would listen and that includes senators, congressmen, and the guys at Meraux Food Store, anybody!

For decades Rodriguez has complained about the seventy-six mile long shipping channel's destruction of the wetlands. Created to give ships a shorter route to New Orleans than going up the Mississippi River, the MR-GO has also had the undesired effect of allowing salt water to creep into the freshwater marsh-lands; thus killing precious cypress trees and marsh grass that act as a critical buffer between storms and the people.

"We had ten miles of swamp, at least five to ten miles in depth with hard grove and cypress trees," said Rodriguez. "When the

"'Y'all are gonna get hit pretty good unless ᵢ and we don't see a change.'"

Ingargiola dialed his wife, Brenda, who was stᵢ

"Get the young ones out; tell them to leave, clothes, and come up here."

The young ones he is referring to are two of their sᵢ twenty-three-year-old Christina, who left for Houstoᵣ husband, and their youngest, twenty-year-old Nichoᵢ went to Monroe with his girlfriend, who is going to there. Ingargiola's three oldest children would stay: his ᵢ ter Lisa, a nurse who works at Chalmette Medical Center; ᵢ Jr.; and Michael, who is a deputy with the St. Bernard Sheᵢ Department. Their son Steve, also a seasoned deputy, had leᵢ June to train Iraqi officers in the Middle East.

The phone's now ringing constantly at the sheriff's house aᵢ the forecast track stays dead on its path toward St. Bernardᵢ Several friends phoned still wondering if they should ride this storm out. His cousin and general counsel for the sheriff's department Sal Gutierrez called.

"You think we ought to stay?"

In the most serious way he could the sheriff shot back, "If you love your family, then you need to get out of here, because if you stay, you're gonna die."

For the rest of that day Stephens's nervous energy turned to excitement, then to a more negative state of being. He pondered how much water the parish was going to take on; who's going to get it; and how many lives could the parish lose.

Ingargiola's wife Brenda, a nurse, who happened to be off that weekend, packed three suitcases and hauled them into his second floor office. Larry raised his voice when she strolled in with the two suitcases full of clothes and one packed with important papers.

"What in the hell are you gonna do with three suitcases?"

"He fussed at me," said Brenda. "I knew for every hurricane he stayed for seven days after. He wouldn't come home to bathe; he would do everything at work; so I was making sure he had enough clothes, but he didn't know that at the time."

Brenda had spent nearly thirty years with Chalmette Medical Center, and her primary objective during Katrina was attending

MR-GO was put in, it wasn't but one to two years, the salinity had started to kill the trees. That destroyed our buffer."

MR-GO was on the mind of almost every official in St. Bernard. They knew they did not have protection from anything that was capable of pushing that amount of water toward the levees.

"We could see where the levee dipped," said Ingargiola. "My parish president took many a people on tours of the MR-GO. And the thing that you noticed [was that] the levees were supposed to be sixteen to seventeen feet high; it doesn't take a genius or an engineer to see [that] when a levee does this [moves hand in a sloping down u shape], there's something wrong there, and there was several sections for two, three, four hundred feet that dipped like that. When you get to the New Orleans' section on this side of Bayou Bienvenue, the levee was only ten to twelve feet."

As Rodriguez drove towards the far eastern edge of the levee where everything beyond is outside of the levee protection system, he saw the water had already risen higher than normal. He thought of the water topping those levees as he went to pick up his wife, Evelyn, at their home.

Rodriguez is a lifelong resident of St. Bernard and traces his roots in the parish back to 1776. He is a part of a long line of descendents from the Canary Islands who emigrated to St. Bernard. He served as parish president for the last two years and before that spent thirty years as a juror or a councilman.

It had been a tough summer for Rodriguez; he was only a month removed from the hospital. In early June, he had gallbladder surgery, and after complications that required him to be put on a ventilator, he had an angioplasty, which kept him in Chalmette Medical Center for weeks. With the help of a cane, he is able to walk around, but while the will to move is strong, the struggle to make it happen is equally as tough. If you're wondering whether his hardship has muted his wicked sense of humor, get too close to that cane and you may feel a goose to your backside.

When he left the modest home that his family had finished remodeling off of Bayou Road, on his way to the Parish Complex to ride out Katrina, he looked around at his neighbors' houses and turned to Evelyn.

"You take a good look cause if this thing hits, the only thing you're gonna have left is memories."

"I don't believe you," she replied.

"Well I'm just telling you it's all we're gonna have left are memories."

## Chalmette High, Shelter of Last Resort

Chalmette High Principal Wayne Warner received the call he figured he'd get and one he's answered many times in the past. This time school system superintendent Doris Voitier informed Warner that the school would open as a shelter of last resort. It would be one of two schools, along with St. Bernard High School in the St. Bernard community, opened in the parish as last resort shelters.

Shelters of last resort were opened for those people playing hurricane roulette. They are places for residents who wait too late to leave; are without transportation; or are diehards, those people who think they can handle anything, to go if Katrina forces them out of their homes.

This was Warner's gift to St. Bernard, as if he owed the parish any more than he had already given. His calming, steady guidance over the decades has provided the public school with much more than just a leader but with a father figure for thousands of St. Bernard Parish teens to look up to.

The shelter welcomed everyone, including those with special needs and the elderly, despite the fact that the school was not equipped with any special facilities to handle these needs. The only exception is the "severe and profound room," which has been used for Chalmette High students with serious disabilities.

Watching Katrina truck towards the area, Warner was overcome with a strange sense of safety. When Hurricane Betsy hit in September of 1965, just four years after the school was built, the building did not take on any water, and he had heard over the years that the school sat on what some called the "Chalmette ridge" and was the highest point in the parish.

Warner and his wife packed up their three dogs and drove to the school. In the past, the Red Cross would not allow animals in evacuation shelters; however, volunteers didn't want to work unless they could bring their pets along. Now that the Red Cross only opens shelters north of Interstate-12, it's up to the locals to decide how they handle the shelters, and Chalmette High would have a place for animals. The pets were housed in the shop area and band room, a series of rooms detached from the main school building.

One of the first things Warner and some of his staff, like long-time assistants Carole Mundt and Debbie Gaudet and custodian Walter Barcelona, did was go into the classrooms and line up the desks along the walls underneath the windows, clearing out space for evacuees to lay down blankets, pillows, or sleeping bags and providing a barrier between the people and the windows.

When the evacuees arrived, they signed in and received a set of rules and a garbage bag. Evacuees were not allowed to smoke in the classrooms; they needed to keep their children with them at all times, and there was a curfew. Not long after Warner got to the shelter, around 10:00 A.M., residents accustomed to coming to the school for shelter were already arriving.

One gentleman, the father of two very fragile, paraplegic, young men, was familiar to Warner and those at the school. The two men were placed in the "severe and profound room." It is a place they spent time in growing up, because they attended Chalmette High. Not long after that another regular, a man who is on oxygen, came in and looked for a comfortable spot with his oxygen tank in tow. These men are just a few of the special needs patients who sought out the high school for shelter.

## Chalmette Medical Center

The morning started off contentiously at Chalmette Medical Center when Dr. Bryan Bertucci, the parish coroner and family practitioner, asked the hospital administrator, Tim Coffey, when he was going to have the hospital hurricane evacuation meeting for the medical staff; Coffey told him six o'clock in the evening. When Dr. Bertucci said that was too late, Coffey just walked off. In short the hospital was open for business.

Dr. Lee Domangue practiced medicine in the parish for twenty-nine years and was the director of the emergency room department at the hospital. He did not see much sense in the hospital still admitting patients that morning, either. Meantime, Dr. Bertucci was saying to people coming in, "If you're sick, go somewhere else. Don't go to this hospital and get admitted and then have to be evacuated."(All of Dr. Bertucci's quotes are taken from a court deposition from the following lawsuit: *Raymond Cousins and Bernard Reyes* vs. *The Mangano Corp., St.*

*Rita's Nursing Facility, Salvador A. Mangano, and Mabel Buffone Mangano.)*

The hospital evacuated the critical care patients, sending them to Methodist Hospital in New Orleans East a few miles north but still very much in the strike zone area. All ambulatory patients, people able to leave the hospital, were sent home. The hospital had fifty-three patients who couldn't be sent home, because they were chronically ill and could only be transported by ambulance. Many were older patients with ailments such as uncontrolled hypertensive issues, kidney failure, and coronary disease.

Despite the hospital's decision not to evacuate everyone, according to Dr. Domangue, there was a full complement of staff, from around seventy nurses, X-ray techs, and support employees dealing with house keeping, dietary, and maintenance. They only had three doctors on staff Dr. Domangue, the chief-of-staff, Dr. Bong Mui, and another emergency room physician, Dr. Al Lemerande.

Dr. Bertucci headed to the government complex where he and other officials participated in a press conference held on government cable access channel 76, which was broadcasted to residents. The announcements included the latest on the storm and advice from local officials. At 8:45 A.M., they stepped in front of the microphone and sounded the alarms on a storm barreling across the Gulf of Mexico as a category five juggernaut.

"At this point, I guess I'm gonna speak from the heart and tell the people of St. Bernard Parish this is the big one. This is the one we've always been told if it comes it could be devastating. You must leave. I would say it's mandatory at this point; you must leave St. Bernard Parish."

—Joey DiFatta
St. Bernard Parish councilman chairman,
St. Bernard Parish cable channel 76

When the press conference had ended, someone brought up the question about the evacuation of the nursing homes and someone answered, "All the homes are evacuating."

Dr. Bertucci responded, "Well I don't think that St. Rita's is evacuating."

He was asked to call the owners of the facility Sal and Mabel Mangano and said he reached Mabel by phone.

Dr. Bertucci asked if they were evacuating and said Mabel told him they had five special needs patients, five nurses, and a generator and had spoken to most of the families, and they seem to be comfortable with them staying. "Well, do you think they'll be mad?"

"The Council? Well, to be honest, it doesn't make any difference if they're mad or not," Dr. Bertucci informed. "I have two buses that will take you wherever you'd like to go. Do you want the buses or not?"

Dr. Bertucci said she paused and answered, "No."

The Mangano's attorney, Jim Cobb, states, "Mabel's recollection is fairly clear that she did not have this conversation with Dr. Bertucci. We believe Dr. Bertucci had it with a staff member who was a staff member that he always called and talked to, and that's confirmed by that staff member that she spoke with Bertucci not Mabel about the buses."

Ingargiola says around 11:00 A.M. on Sunday the parish issued a mandatory evacuation, and they held off on it, because they wanted to wait until the last possible moment to shut down everything. He believes by Sunday morning a good seventy to eighty percent of the parish had evacuated. Saturday and Sunday, parish officials had been on cable channel 76 with live broadcasts warning people to get out. As time went on, the warnings became more dire, especially for anyone outside of the hurricane protection levee.

"If you're outside the levee protection system, you have no business being there believe me," President Rodriguez implored. "This is no time for heroics, no time to say I'll be able to tell 'em this story cause you may not be able to tell this story."

## Checking St. Rita's

St. Bernard Fire Captain Steve Gallodoro reacted to the mandatory evacuation by running to St. Rita's Nursing Home in the lower end of the parish to help them evacuate. The day before, Gallodoro said he went to the facility and talked to the Manganos about their plan to leave, moving his father Tufanio Gallodoro and the others out of town.

"They assured me that they had contracts with a bus service," said Gallodoro. "They had two sites, one facility in Alexandria and one in North Baton Rouge that were going to take the residents, and if a mandatory evacuation was called that they were going to bus the residents to those locations."

He also said they told him his eighty-three-year-old father would be in better hands with them instead of moving him in a private vehicle.

"My father had been paralyzed with a couple of strokes, it would have been difficult or impossible to transport him in a regular vehicle; his needs were greater than what we could provide. I was assured by Sal Mangano that the plan was in place, services were ready; he was bringing his entire staff in, and that he would be safer with them and not us."

Speaking for the Mangano's, Cobb said, "Who's in the best position to know who can provide what; I find it unlikely that we would have said that to him." A year before, when Hurricane Ivan forced an evacuation, Gallodoro's sister Cheryl Emmons took Tufanio with her to Mississippi. He wore a catheter, was paralyzed on the left side, and confined to a wheel chair.

"Sixteen hours into the trip, he physically could not take any more of the trip," said Gallodoro. "They were rescued by a resident of Jackson [Mississippi] who brought them to his own house, and they stayed there until the storm had passed and then came back."

With this in mind and his father's condition being worse than it was a year before, he told his family letting St. Rita's handle Tufanio was the best thing, and the home was evacuating. Sunday morning his family left St. Bernard for Shreveport, Louisiana, and Philadelphia, Mississippi. Gallodoro said with a mandatory evacuation called, he went to the nursing home and met up with Sal Mangano, asking him what he needed.

"I was in uniform, so I figured he kind of knew what I was asking."

"'What do you mean what do I need?'" Gallodoro remembered Mangano saying.

"Just tell me how many men you need and I'll have that many firemen here, and we'll load the buses and assist you in getting the residents out."

"'Well we've decided that we're not gonna leave that we're going to shelter in place, the levees are gonna hold, and it's never flooded in this area.'"

"That's unacceptable."

"'If I move these residents, if I bus these residents to Alexandria, there'd be a possibility that one or two of 'em not surviving the ride.'"

Time was running out; his family had already hit the road; he hadn't made alternate plans for his father, based on the conversation he had with the Mangano's the day before; and he was activated at the fire department and had a job to do.

"At that time my radio sounded, it was a call for me to go to the Wal-Mart parking lot and assist in loading seven buses of residents who had no transportation out of the parish. I had to leave, go to Wal-Mart, [and] take care of that."

Gallodoro left without seeing his father, but he had spent time with him on Saturday; he would have to see him after the storm now. When he drove into the Wal-Mart parking lot in Chalmette he saw Councilman Craig Taffaro.

"I just left St. Rita's; Sal Mangano advised me they were not leaving; that's unacceptable," said Gallodoro.

Mangano's attorney Cobb said, "If in fact there was a mandatory evac in effect at ten thirty to eleven o'clock Sunday morning and an official with the parish, a sheriff, someone with authority goes up and says we are ordering you to leave, at that point in time, try getting a bus. The things were in chaos, if the civilian authorities said we want you to go, and we're gonna give you some school buses, and we're gonna help load them up, we would have done it. If he [Gallodoro] thought it was unacceptable, all he had to do was go back to the EOC and say St. Rita's says they're staying; that's unacceptable to me. Now did that happen? Absolutely not."

Cobb also questioned the parish's contention they called a mandatory evacuation.

"They did not as a matter of law," said Cobb. "DiFatta doesn't have the authority to declare a mandatory, number one; number two, we've asked for a copy of the mandatory evacuation order; they don't have one."

Parish Chief-of-Staff Charlie Reppel disagreed, saying, "We have a copy of the mandatory evacuation, and we have a fax, which reflects the time the notice was sent to the State."

Gallodoro went into fireman mode; he had to help people walking from the surrounding neighborhoods and the special needs individuals who were brought to the buses.

"We had handicapped people, wheelchair bound people that we put on two buses, [and] sent them out," said Gallodoro. "We had five other busloads of people who didn't have transportation out."

## Fire Department

As chief of the St. Bernard Fire Department, Thomas Stone was taking care of countless tasks, including getting his men to help load buses, before the tropical storm force winds reached the parish. They pulled in all of their platoons with a mandatory call back. He sent two of their newest pumpers and two rescue HAZ-MAT squads north to Holden, Louisiana, near the Mississippi Border. He pulled everyone out of the fire stations and called his chiefs together to come up with a plan to set up task forces at safe areas around the parish. He stationed firefighters at the government complex, next door at the civic center, and at Domino Sugar Refinery in Arabi, while others hunkered down at shelters at Chalmette and St. Bernard High Schools.

Using information from a GPS system, Stone said the St. Bernard Port area was twenty-nine feet above sea level, and since the area, which was the former site of Kaiser Aluminum, didn't flood during Hurricane Betsy, they parked all their personal vehicles there. They worked out a deal to put a lot of the department's apparatus inside the sugar silo at Domino, on top of mounds of sugar. They parked three boats at the complex including a Zodiac fireboat and two rubber boats like the Navy SEALS use. It was a lot to manage in a short period, and it took up all of Stone's time.

As fire chief of the parish for the past fifteen and a half years and twenty-seven in the department total, Stone used his experience and that of his chiefs to set a plan in motion that would place his department in a position to respond quickly after the storm roared through. What Stone's experience as chief couldn't provide an answer for was what to do with his family. Stone admittedly forgot about getting his most precious assets out of the storm's way, his wife, Lauren, eighteen-year-old son, Chad, and eight-year-old daughter, Nikki. He told them to hunker down with the rest of the parish's essential personnel at the complex. Stone's oldest son, twenty-two-year-old Thomas, Jr., was away in Lake Charles at McNeese State University.

One of Stone's most experienced men, Captain Gallodoro, may have been consumed with his job but his goal was to get back to the government complex and find someone who could force St. Rita's to leave. As time marched on and Katrina marched toward the parish, those desires faded with reality.

"The wind started picking up and the rain, and we were busy

trying to set up staging areas for the firefighters," said Gallodoro. "The opportunity for me to get back down there didn't happen."

## The Final Bus Call

Brenda Ingargiola's role to take care of the recovering parish president and help out at the government complex expanded, and she quickly morphed into a phone operator for the Office of Emergency Preparedness. People who desperately needed transportation were calling to get picked up and brought to the buses or to anywhere but their homes. Many had not registered for special needs transportation and were now trapped without a ride.

"What was happening [was that] people had designated family members to come pick them up and take them away," Brenda said. "Because contraflow [where all lanes of the interstate at designated areas were heading one way out of town] was already activated, these people were not allowed to come back in to pick up their relatives. They were either working out in Metairie or the airport and the contraflow was the other way. All these people were actually stranded even though they had a plan."

Some asked if they were under a mandatory evacuation did they really have to go.

"My husband told my family to leave, which he has never done before; this means he's serious; this is a bad one," Brenda told one caller. "Some of them took it with a grain of salt and some didn't."

One mother, in particular, took it with a box of salt.

"This one particular lady really upset me cause she said when was the next bus leaving, because she couldn't get ready in two hours."

This was eleven o'clock in the morning and the buses were set for pickup at 1:00 P.M.

"This was the last bus," said Brenda. "They weren't leaving after this; you're on your own."

"'You have to come and get me if I stay,'" the woman said indignantly.

"Mam it all depends on the weather if we can come and get you."

"'Well I can't get ready in two hours.'"

"Why can't you?"

"'I have two children.'"

"O.K., how old are they?"

"'Nine and twelve.'"

"Well you tell them to get whatever they value with them in a bag, and you get to the bus; this is the last bus."

"'I just can't do it,'" she told Brenda.

"Mam, then your life is in your own hands right now. We can't help you any further than that."

CHAPTER TWO

# Blood Is Thicker than Seawater

## Sunday, August 28

### Day One

Gene Alonzo is a fisherman, a hardened man with tough sun beaten skin, a tiger tattoo on his left arm, and forearms that remind you of what Popeye's might look like if he were in his mid-fifties. He grew up in "da Parish" as it is affectionately referred to. Like many raised in Yscloskey, the green-eyed Alonzo comes from a long lineage of Spanish heritage fishermen, like his father and grandfather, who migrated to Louisiana from the Canary Islands.

Hurricanes like Katrina send fishermen in the lower end of St. Bernard Parish scrambling to save their women. Not the flesh-and-bone kind, they've already been sent away, but their beloved water vessels; their lovers away from home and for most, probably more like wives. They live, breathe, and worship the water, and their means to embark on nearly daily journeys are their boats. Big or small they are built mostly for the manly trade of dredging oysters, shrimping, and fishing, whichever is more plentiful and the most profitable at the time.

Alonzo like dozens of other fishermen boarded his thirty-two-foot skiff, the *Captain Alex,* with a little cabin, and sailed down the bayous outside of the flood protection levees, headed for safe harbor inside man-made levees. A caravan of Alonzo's fishing family and friends took their boats out of the bayous into the MR-GO shipping channel. As they reached the Bayou Dupre control locks, which are concrete and steel structures that block water from entering the Violet Canal, they turned left through the locks and docked inside the levee system. This had to happen before the locks were closed, because once they're closed that's it; if you're too late, you are left to fend for yourself, riding out the storm with no levee protecting you, just ask Charles Inabnet.

The Inabnet family doesn't live far from Alonzo, just a few miles farther southeast in the fishing town of Hopedale at 4917 Hopedale Highway, a two-lane road that drives like a straight shot into nowhere. There's Bayou La Loutre on one side and there's mostly homes and fishing camps built up on concrete and wooden pilings as high as ten or twelve feet on the opposite side of the bayou. Behind the Inabnet home is a vista of marshland spanning as far as you can see; all down the waterway are oyster vessels, flatboats, shrimp boats, and just about anything that will float in the water, and Inabnet had a big one in Bayou La Loutre.

On Saturday, Inabnet turned on the television and tuned in to the local government cable access channel 76, where St. Bernard officials were on a full-court press to get people out.

"We strongly urge, we are strongly urging all residents of St. Bernard Parish, all residents now to move from this area. As it shows now, most parts of St. Bernard parish will be in the direct path of the eye of the storm. This is a critical situation."

—Joey DiFatta
St. Bernard Parish councilman,
4:00 P.M., Saturday, August 27

The local officials' warnings to get out caught the attention of his wife, Terry, and their only daughter, Charity. Some warnings were tempered with an even tone, but the message was clear.

"It had 'em a nervous wreck," said Inabnet.

It was all part of his plan, plant the seed, fertilize the fear, and watch them run.

"You're two days from the storm, so won't you leave and beat the traffic," Inabnet told his wife and daughter.

It wouldn't take much more prodding once he got their antennas up.

"I brain washed 'em," he laughed. "I psyched them up; I got them out."

So Inabnet's head game worked; his wife and daughter set out for Bossier City, in the northwest corner of Louisiana, Saturday afternoon. Inabnet had to figure out his plan; when Hurricane Ivan threatened to slam St. Bernard in 2004, he took his fifty-foot oyster boat and headed for safe harbor. He didn't time his escape very well because when he made it to the Bayou Dupre locks, it was closed. He was forced to ride out Ivan in Lake Borgne, a large body of water sitting on St. Bernard's northeastern border. Thankfully for him that storm made a late turn to the east, more than likely sparing his life.

However, the experience of Ivan wasn't enough to convince Inabnet to leave for Katrina. He pulled the ropes out of his red shipping container that sat on a forty-five-degree angle next to the highway, dipping slightly to the back toward his house. He spun a spider web of strong coarse rope in order to tie down his boat, stretching it around nearby telephone polls, across Hopedale Highway, and wrapping it as tight as he could around the wooden pilings holding up one his neighbors' home.

His ID may say Charles Inabnet but the slender weather worn fifty-nine-year-old likes to make the joke that if you drop the "b," his last name would sound like "In a net," quite fitting for a commercial fisherman. But if you want to find him, you need to call him by his nickname, Charlo, like Char-lou.

There have been people who've asked for him down in Hopedale, "Where can I find Charles Inabnet?" They're more than likely to get the same answer, "There's no one down here by that name."

Charlo, sometimes pronounced Char-low, is his calling card. It is a name his grandfather gave him as a kid growing up in Plaquemines Parish, and he doesn't have a clue whether or not it has special meaning. But it's infamous in these parts for a man's deep drawn facial lines to signify years of hard work and the dangers that come with making a living on the water. With his wife and daughter safe, Charlo weighed his options: ride out Katrina on his precious oyster vessel or inside of his home?

Gene Alonzo called his girlfriend, Eloise Terry.

"Come pick me up," he bellowed in his thick slow Cajun-like drawl.

"I'm scared; my daughter's going to Texas, and I'm going with her," she said.

So Alonzo, knowing his ride back home was now on her way out of town, said goodbye. He figured why shouldn't she leave;

his daughters Gina and Tammy and their families were on the road to Texas as well. Now he had to catch a ride back to the home he grew up in; the home that was left to him by his mother Irene. Carefully gripping the ropes and putting the final slips into place, Alonzo secured the *Captain Alex*, named in honor of his father, brother, and grandson, and hitched a ride back into the danger zone with a fellow fisherman. Alonzo's home wasn't your typical raised on wooden or concrete pillars bayou home. It sat on regular cinder blocks a couple of feet off of the ground.

He loaded up his brown Ford Explorer with as much as he could, knowing his home would flood. But as he's done many times before, his house flooded for prior storms, he grabbed a few of his weapons, including sentimental shotguns belonging to his father and brothers, and placed them on the bed. Some he packed in his SUV along with important papers and clothes. Everything was pretty and green outside of his home as he pulled off in his Explorer.

Alonzo's plan for Katrina was to go to St. Rita's Nursing Home to be with his younger brother Carlos. Alonzo says that Carlos can be a handful, and he expected many of the staff to evacuate with their own families, so help would be at a premium. Carlos suffered brain damage after a fishing accident nearly sixteen years ago. Alonzo wanted to be there if they evacuated the facility, so he could help move Carlos out; if they did not evacuate, then he would stay put with his brother. It is a sense of duty he has fulfilled ever since Carlos went into the nursing home, spending other hurricanes at the facility.

He pulled his SUV into St. Rita's parking lot and looking around the facility, which is surrounded by acres of large trees; Alonzo noticed the weather was still pleasant, not a hint of being just hours away from a menacing killer storm was evident. Then he came across Jimmy Martinez, who was there with his wife, inside St. Rita's.

"Man, I guess we gonna be all right here?" said Alonzo. "The storm according to the news [is] gonna be a bad storm."

The news reports were now on 24/7 and Alonzo's instincts kicked in. He felt that he should put his brother in the car and just take off. But those same news reports that made him want to leave also convinced him to stay. He just couldn't see hitting the road with the traffic on I-10 heading out of town.

"I don't know where you gonna go with all this traffic. You

might get blocked on the highway," Martinez said to Alonzo.

"Yea, I guess I'm just gonna stay," replied Alonzo. "I'm gonna be in a car with him by myself."

The thought of having to pull off of a crowded highway to find a bathroom, in the event Carlos needed to relieve himself, or change him, in case he didn't make it to the restroom in time, was too much for Alonzo; Carlos can be "more than a one person job at times."

The nursing home served dinner and everyone ate before nightfall. The news just played and played, while eyes stayed glued to Katrina's path. The satellite radar showed just how big she was, covering a huge chunk of the Gulf of Mexico. Residents, families, and workers gathered around the TV and talked, as Katrina never wavered on its path toward St. Bernard Parish.

Carlos's room had two single beds and he shared it, like most in the home did, with an elderly man named Harold Kurz. He's a skinny, elderly man Alonzo said, who liked to color in a coloring book all the time "like a little kid." Alonzo, his brother Carlos, and many others tried to get a little sleep but they could not get much, since the wind and rain created enough of a stir to keep those at St. Rita's in an uneasy state.

## Modern Day Viking

Never uneasy is "Doogie" Robin, the most recognizable seafood man in the parish. If you could ever get Doogie to give you a straight answer on his real age he would tell you "seventy-nine or eighty, something like that," with a devilish smirk on his face. And if you try to pry his real name out of him he might say Edward, almost matter of factly. However, if you try to get the octogenarian to leave the parish when a hurricane is coming, you've got a better chance of coaxing Fidel Castro to give up his dictatorship of Cuba, because when it comes to hurricanes and Doogie, he's not leaving.

He's never left, not for Betsy, Camille, Georges, or Ivan, and he wasn't going to leave his fleet of boats with anyone else without him being in command of one of them. Not much more than five feet tall, his family knows better than to say to their larger-than-life father, "don't you think you're a little old to ride out a possible category five storm on an oyster boat in a canal?" Even they know you don't go there with him.

Doogie's family name, Robin, is like saying seafood in St. Bernard, and like many of the area fishermen, he knows no other life and has prospered in the name of Louisiana seafood. Doogie's father settled in St. Bernard from the Canary Islands, as did many Isleños that came from the Spanish-speaking archipelago of seven islands. They fished and helped create the rich heritage lower St. Bernard has become known and cherished for.

Doogie carried on the family legacy and opened his first seafood shop after spending, not so ironically, some time on the ocean in the navy, fighting in the Pacific campaign in World War II. He had seven invasions and ran the Higgins boats, created and built in New Orleans, onto the beach during invasions.

After the war, Doogie, never far from the sea, returned to lower St. Bernard and took up fishing, and in 1947, he started his seafood business and after nine children and "twenty-four grandchildren, I think," he's spent the rest of his life providing oysters, fish, and you name it to the rest of the state and country.

Like his fishing comrade Gene Alonzo, Doogie took one of his boats from Yscloskey to the Violet Canal. Saturday, Doogie and his crew guided his flotilla inside the levee protection system, and even he will tell you in his charming, aged accent, "It's not too much protection, but it's the best that we got." They tied the boats together along with five or ten other fishermen. Big oyster boats were locked with ropes in an effort to keep them together when Katrina hit.

Sunday morning, Doogie went down to Yscloskey and Shell Beach with his buddy he calls Judge, Guy Costanza, because of his white hair. What they saw made the tough-as-nails fisherman think hard about the destructive possibilities of Katrina. He saw the water coming over the marshland and it looked like the Gulf of Mexico had already taken over lower St. Bernard.

"Judge, you see these houses in Shell Beach, it won't be here tomorrow," said Doogie.

He and Judge went looking for a bite to eat around 10:00 A.M. and everything was closed except R.C.'s lounge. Not ones to shy away from a few drinks, Doogie and some friends had a few stiff ones. Before he left to ride out Katrina on his oyster boat, the bar crowd pleaded with him to stay.

"Man, won't you stay here with us tonight; this is the highest part of the land," they chimed in.

R.C.'s is at the corner of Paris Road and St. Bernard Highway, cater-corner from the St. Bernard Jail, which is directly in front of Chalmette Refining. The refinery backs up to the Mississippi River levee, which has some of the highest land in St. Bernard. As you get closer to the Mississippi River levee, the land rises so much that many people in this area are considered outside of the flood plain and aren't required to have flood insurance.

Those in R.C.'s should have known better than to try to persuade Doogie to stay off of his boats.

"Let me tell you something," said Doogie. "I'm not staying in my house. I'm not staying in nobody else's house. Anyplace I'm gonna stay is gonna be in my boat."

### No Room for Error

Lorenzo "Bubby" Bodden, a high school quarterback at Chalmette, baseball player, track star, class president, and nearly professional cyclist, once rode his bike across the United States of America. Like Doogie, no one knows Bubby by his real name, Lorenzo. Bubby is so ingrained in the minds of those that know him that it doesn't sound like a nickname.

He's a special athlete, and if you've ever had the pleasure of knowing him, then you would know he's a special man. He sets the standard for the good guy. He's everybody's all-American, and it's not just the athletics that set him apart; he breaks the mold on the clichéd high school quarterback.

If you can find anyone who dislikes Bubby then you may have the ability to find the Holy Grail, because I'm not sure that person exists. He gets along with anyone and everyone, and he can make you feel like you're as important as any person in the room.

Sunday, Bubby and his wife, Connie, left a work related retreat in Destin, Florida, for their Chalmette home. The storm, once projected to go that way, forced Bubby and Connie off the beach. Bubby planned to prepare his California ranch-style home for Katrina by boarding up the windows and such. Like many watching the news, the traffic influenced a crucial decision for Bubby. Believing contraflow out of town would force him to sit on the interstate for hours, Bubby told his wife to head to Mississippi with her family; he would stay behind with his cat, Neo.

About four o'clock the well conditioned, nearly six-foot tall, forty-one year old left his Buccaneer Villa South home on Colonel Drive and drove to his brother-in-law's house. He observed a "very, very eerie sight;" no one was on the roads and few people had boarded up their homes and businesses. Soon after Bubby returned home, he opened the white, wooden, front door to go outside and welcomed an unlikely visitor, a yellow Labrador retriever on his front porch.

"It was just sitting there like saying something's coming," Bubby said. "So I let it come in, and it stayed in my house a little while. I went back out; he came out with me and boom it was gone, just disappeared. Never seen the dog in my neighborhood at all; I found that a little odd."

The potential wrath of Katrina didn't measure up to Bubby's expectations; he thought he would just get high wind and rain. He hadn't quite factored in the extent of the storm surge possibilities. He also didn't feel comfortable leaving his home unattended. For a former quarterback whose decisions need to be strong, bold, and calculated, there's the occasional gut throw that gets you the big score or the big mistake. Bubby would find out if the excitement of experiencing a potential category five storm would be the touchdown pass or the interception that lost the game.

## CHAPTER THREE

# Here Comes the Night

## Sunday, August 28

### Day One

The St. Bernard Parish Government Complex is ground zero for all essential personnel, the parish president, the parish council, the fire department, and many of their family members. They brought suitcases, bags of food, and ice chests with drinks. People's moods ranged from calm to intense. As Hurricane Katrina roared across the Gulf of Mexico, the 10:00 P.M. National Hurricane Center advisory listed her as a "potentially catastrophic" category five storm with maximum sustained winds of 160 mph. The storm was very large with hurricane force winds extending as far as 105 miles from the center.

The prayers of the people riding out Katrina inside the government building consisted of "please turn east." It happened during Hurricane Ivan in 2004, and it happened during Hurricane Georges in 1998, but while many prayed for that last minute jog, there was also the sense that this was the one that would take out St. Bernard.

Parish government officials continuously broadcasted on their cable channel, warning residents that this was their last chance to get to higher ground. The final warning came Sunday night with a somber and resigned President Rodriguez summing up all of their feelings, after seeing the 10:00 P.M. bulletin and having a final conference call with the other parishes in the path of Katrina.

"I hope I'm not talking to a lot of people right now; I hope

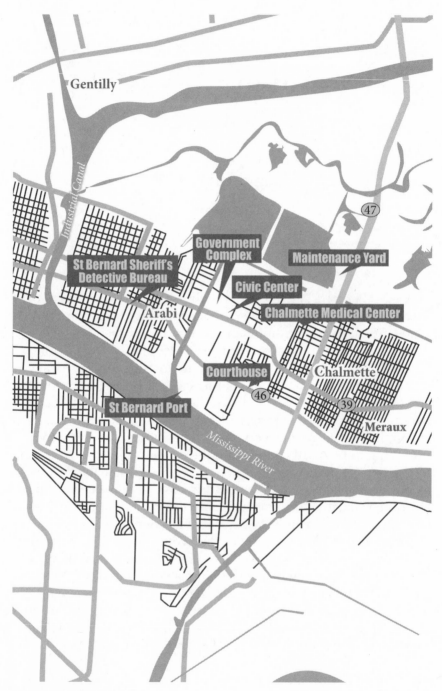

*Courtesy Mariella Pariente*

everybody's in a safe place. Those of you that's still at home, hunker down, and get ready cause it's gonna be a long night, tomorrow's gonna be a long day. I hope you've done the best you could, got everything protected."

—President Henry "Junior" Rodriguez,<br>St. Bernard cable channel 76, 10:45 P.M.

But with the roads quiet under the glow of the shimmering and swaying streetlights, nightfall brought the realization that if anyone wanted to leave, it was too late. Those who had not jumped on Judge Perez Drive, Paris Road, or St. Bernard Highway with a destination out of town needed to get to one of the two shelters of last resort or batten down the hatches.

The heavy lifting had been done for the Lake Borgne Levee District employees. They completed their visual inspections of the levees, sandbagged some areas that are normally open, closed the locks at Bayou Bienvenu and Bayou Dupre, took care of the floodgates at Carnarvon and Verret, and held workers at the pumping stations as long as possible.

From the government complex the head of the Levee District, Bob Turner, monitored the situation and knew it would be too dangerous to leave his men at the pumping stations; so, after President Rodriguez's speech, Turner let everyone watching the emergency channel know of his plans to pull the men back but only until it was safe enough to return.

"The weather service has been telling us now for most of the day to anticipate storm surges in the magnitude of approximately eighteen feet on our hurricane protection system. The hurricane levee was designed to handle surges up to twelve feet; the levee itself is built up to seventeen and a half. The weather service has been telling us there's a good possibility that our levees will be overtopped. The winds are so high with this storm we're not gonna be able to leave our crews at the pumping stations for the entire duration of this storm. What that means is we can anticipate that we're gonna get some street flooding during the period of time that some of those pumps are off. Right now we're looking at a window of approximately nine hours where we'll be under hurricane force winds, and we're gonna try to keep the pumps going as long as we possibly can."

—Bob Turner, Lake Borgne Levee District chief,<br>St. Bernard cable channel 76

Days of conference calls with all of the parishes in Southeast
Louisiana had come to an end, and everyone was on their own
until after Katrina. When the press conference ended, a weary
President Rodriguez knew he better get some rest before the
break of dawn, so he went into his second floor office and took
a nap with his wife, Evelyn.

Around midnight the winds reached near hurricane force and
Turner pulled his crews back to pre-designated safe areas as close
to the pump houses as possible, such as the school shelters and
the civic center. The threat of flooding was on Turner's mind, and
he wanted to get the pumpers back to the stations as soon as he
could after the storm.

Turner had the heavy equipment on standby so his crews
could clear the roads as soon as they got back to the stations.
Troy Douglas, Sr. shut down station #8 in Verret and headed
toward St. Bernard High School to meet up with some of his
crews from pumping station #4, behind Guerra Drive in Violet,
and station #5, near St. Bernard High School. The others went to
Chalmette High from station #7, in Meraux, while the men from
stations #1 and #6 went to the civic center, just down the street
at the end of Jean Lafitte Parkway in the Buccaneer Villa North
subdivision.

The guys were having trouble closing the floodgates near station #4, so Douglas, Sr. drove through the increasing squalls to
help them complete the task before finally making his way to the
high school.

Russell Gelvin is a St. Bernard Sheriff's deputy, who was
assigned to the Lake Borgne Levee District, and all around his
station he could hear the timber crashing and loud snapping
noises, but it was so dark that he couldn't see a thing. He was
ready to leave for Chalmette High when the word came to evacuate the pumping stations.

**Medical Center Countdown**

At nightfall people were still coming to Chalmette Medical
Center for medical attention. Dr. Domangue knew these patients'
doctors wouldn't be making it back to the hospital. There were
two emergency room physicians and the chief-of-staff. Three
doctors for more than fifty patients, and under storm conditions,
this scenario was a recipe for a bad night. The nursing staff just

kept working, resigned to the fact that their fates were sealed in this hospital. They concentrated on the patients, rotated staff, and tried to get the little breaks they needed as Sunday night turned into Monday morning.

Around ten o'clock, Dr. Domangue called his longtime friend and colleague Dr. Bertucci to return to the hospital to help care for the patients.

"He called me at ten o'clock and I had a meeting to go to," said Dr. Bertucci, "He said he had seven admits to the hospital and no physicians there, would I come and admit the people to the hospital."

Still bewildered by the hospital's reluctance to evacuate everyone, Dr. Bertucci returned around midnight and "worked on admitting patients from midnight till about six in the morning."

Dr. Domangue tried to get some rest. After ending her shift, nurse Barbara Warren couldn't sleep, so she stayed around helping the others. They tried to ignore the rush of the wind and the rain slapping the windows.

Waking a few hours later, Dr. Domangue discovered patients still in the observation area and not yet admitted. He wondered how much longer it would be before they lost power and the generators kicked on, or maybe they had already kicked on. The hospital had two backup generators on the ground floor.

### Shaking The Complex

Councilman Kenny Henderson invited his son-in-law, Troy Guerra, and his father, Constable Tony Guerra, to bunk in his first floor office at the government complex. They set up cots, but it didn't matter, because they decided sleep would have to wait. Guerra and his son left all their clothes in their respective car and truck. Not comfortable with the idea that they would escape flooding, they moved their vehicles onto the sidewalk underneath the complex overhang next to the large circular concrete columns.

Looking out across Torres Park, which sits behind the complex and the civic center, the tall oak and cypress trees were bending in the wind, and with each passing minute, the rattling of the storm protection over the complex's windows grew stronger. Henderson could feel the building move beneath his feet as the gusts increased. Everyone in the building could hear the rocks shooting off the flat roof and striking the rectangle shaped atrium glass that makes up part of a wall that stretches from the base of the second floor ceiling to the roof. Looking up and hearing the loud pops, he wondered if the glass was going to crack, and if it did, would the roof eventually go with it.

Councilwoman Judy Hoffmeister and her husband, Lloyd, crated their pet boxer, Caramel, and set her up in the downstairs office at the government complex. Hoffmeister spent time on the phone doing an interview for her daughter Heidi's television show "Daily Buzz Live" out of Orlando, Florida. She described the frightening scene while her daughter knowing she was getting great television, could only pray her mother wasn't threatened by inescapable danger.

Those same rocks zipping like gunshots across the parking lot, shattered the windows in Tony Guerra's car and his son Troy's truck. Mad as hell, Guerra, through the large windows downstairs, could see their clothes getting soaked, but there was nothing he could do about it, certainly not with projectiles, capable of taking your head off, ripping through the air.

Around three o'clock Monday morning, "POW," the window shattered in the office of C.A.O. Danny Menesses.

"Shit!" screamed President Rodriguez. His semi-peaceful sleep came to an abrupt end as he jumped up. At this point, rest for anyone would be a chore. The outer bands of Katrina were turning into triple digit gusts and trees snapped, signs blew down, light poles swayed and toppled, power poles fell to forty-five degree angles, while power lines popped like giant bullwhips in the wind. They could see that part of the civic center's roof next to the government complex was beginning to shred.

## St. Bernard High School

Katrina's threat sent dozens, from places like Kenilworth, Toca, Reggio, Verret, and Poydras, to St. Bernard High School, a two-story building in the shadow of the St. Bernard water tower and resting between the Judge Perez extension and Bayou Road. Like Chalmette High, St. Bernard High has a football stadium and a baseball stadium directly behind the campus. The school is a large complex that houses hundreds of boys and girls.

The only shelter in the eastern end of the parish by midnight, St. Bernard High housed about one hundred people who had trickled in throughout the day. With pets being the main reason many stayed behind, those seeking safety dragged their furry loved ones to the school. Parish personnel Mitch McDaniel, along with firemen Rodney Ourso and Michael Lebeau and Sheriff's Department Sergeant Greg Hauck, helped oversee the shelter and gathered evacuees into the school cafeteria. People marked their territory on the floor, with little more than what they carried into the school. Blankets, pillows, and bags of clothes became the boundaries of their temporary homes.

The fire department set up down the hall in an office away from the cafeteria. If there was any sense of calm in the cafeteria, the howling winds changed all that when the hum turned to shrieking crashes just after midnight, as windows blew out in the cafeteria. No longer safe in this part of the school, Ourso and Lebeau helped move the evacuees out of the cafeteria. In the back of their mind the fear of rising water influenced those running the shelter to forget housing on the first floor. Amidst the organized rush they moved everyone upstairs into one wing of the second floor.

Safer upstairs, the school along with the rest of the parish went dark around four o'clock. The firemen went outside in the swirling winds and rains to crank up the generator set up for the school. After a half hour the school still did not have power, and they couldn't get the generator started. Then the smell of gas permeated the school.

Ourso and Lebeau suited up to head outside again to find the leak; this time the winds felt like "one hundred miles per hour." The thought of an explosion was their first concern; they didn't want something to ignite the leak, and with heavy objects skirting around outside, just one spark could pose a huge problem. They grabbed flashlights and pushed the doors against the wind to get outside of the cafeteria to see if they could find the source. They found the main gas line and shut it down.

**Like Old Times but Worse**

With about one hundred evacuees at Chalmette High it felt like any prior Hurricane. The evening meal was better than most had that night, the head-of-the-cafeteria, Kathy Barbier, had brought shrimp from home, she wasn't going to let it rot in her freezer if the power went out, and made shrimp stew. But the meal had to be stretched to feed more personnel than in previous storms, because they had more firemen and policemen than ever at the school, a sign this was the most convincing threat St. Bernard faced since Betsy.

Not only were the able bodied showing up to Chalmette, but increasingly, people who needed special attention and medical treatment arrived, and the school did not have the facilities or staff to attend to these needs.

"It was a guy that came with his mother who was bedridden, I don't remember the ailments, she couldn't speak," said fireman Charles Liccardi, Jr. "He had her and his elderly father, and they were supposed to be taken away by ambulance somewhere, the ambulance never did show up, and he shows up by us. At the time, we thought the Superdome had facilities for that, and we said he'd be better off over there; we really can't take care of her here. We gave them directions, and he went there."

Liccardi was surprised when about an hour and a half later the man came back to the school, saying they were rejected at the Superdome.

"We loaded her up and got her inside. They had a blow-up mattress that she was on in the back of his van," said Liccardi. "We transported her with, I think it was a salad bar that we found somewhere; we . . . got her set up in one of the rooms by herself."

With a mixture of nerves and calm, some evacuees bedded down for the night. The smokers sat near the front of the school by the office lobby, so they could go outside and smoke when the urge hit, while others curious about the storm and unable to sleep watched Katrina kick up, swinging the red lights on Palmisano Boulevard and Judge Perez Drive. The illuminated school sign with a large letter C, a fighting owl mascot logo, and the word Owls spelled out on the sign's base was taking a whipping. Lacoste Elementary School directly across the street from Chalmette was dark, quiet, and suffering from the increasing wind speeds as well.

With every hour ticked off and Katrina one hour closer to moving directly over St. Bernard, more and more people, especially those who lived near the school, traded bravery, carelessness, or stupidity for the shelter. As they tried to come through one of three doors that opened up to the hall next to the front office, the wind caught the door, shoving the people and the door inward. The force was so strong that the firemen had to move in to help shut the doors.

The evacuees walked in soaking wet; some walked, some came in cars, and others peddled to the school on bikes. Many gathered around the television as the shelter tuned to the only local television broadcast to survive Katrina, WWL-TV channel 4, the local CBS affiliate. For the first time in nearly fifty years on the air, the news broadcast was forced out of its North Rampart Street studios. Dozens of WWL-TV's staff headed to LSU's Manship School of Communication in Baton Rouge, where anchors Eric Paulsen and Sally Ann Roberts and reporter Bill Capo kept the broadcast alive late Sunday night and into the morning hours. Most of the remaining crew evacuated to the Hyatt Regency in downtown New Orleans awaiting Katrina's departure, so they could get back into their French Quarter studios.

It seemed, as morning passed, those at the high school measured the storm minute by minute, and with every new evacuee the force of the wind outside grew exponentially. The driving rain soaked the hallway in the main school lobby, shooting underneath the doors and coming through a broken window that curved around the arched ceiling above the door.

"You didn't need Nash Roberts, a beloved local hurricane expert and retired meteorologist for WWL-TV, telling you how bad it was; you were feeling it," said longtime school administrator Carole Mundt.

Someone manned the desk and logged everyone coming in. A fireman woke Warner from a brief nap, and when he saw the water in the hallway, Warner thought to himself, "This was gonna be different." The terrazzo floors became very slick, but no matter how much cardboard was laid down, it didn't hold the amount of water coming in, so they stopped using the main entrance.

## Courthouse

The hub of all things legal in St. Bernard centered around the sixty-six-year-old, art deco designed courthouse, with ornate ironwork and adorned with images of magnolias and the blindfolded Lady Justice protecting some of the windows facing St. Bernard Highway. The sheriff's office complex, which sits right behind the courthouse, also bustled with officers and their family members. The concrete building swelled to nearly three hundred people

*View from the courthouse Monday morning, minutes before the floodwater arrived. Photograph by Errol Schultz*

Sunday night, with many wandering up either side of the curved, marble staircases and going inside one of Louisiana's largest and most beautiful courtrooms. The room is lined with deep, dark, wooden benches and walls that engulf the entire courtroom. From the ceiling, hang three large glass fixtures, which soak the room with opaque light.

"We felt pretty safe there," said Major James Pohlmann. "There were some sleeping accommodations in the old jail. We knew the building was three levels in the event of flooding."

Captain Chad Clark was out on a roadblock until "they said it's dangerous." When the signs started to fly, it was time to get to the courthouse. The wind threatened to shatter the courthouse's two beautiful stained-glass windows that stretched from the ceiling to several feet above the floor. One of the brightly colored windows depicts the famous Battle of New Orleans fought in Chalmette, displaying the vibrant redcoats of the British as they are defeated on St. Bernard's rich soil.

The other stained-glass honors the arrival of St. Bernard's settlers from the Canary Islands. Los Isleños, the islanders, ride high above the window hugging a coat of arms, while below, signs of their life, fishing boats on dark blue water with nets of speckled trout. The rattling and coarse sound of the winds forced everyone to flee the massive room. Colonel Forrest Bethay couldn't get over how the wind sounded outside the courthouse.

"Brrrrruuuuuuu—sounded like a freight whistle coming through," said Bethay. "The wind was unbelievable. We got everybody out of the courtroom and put them on the balcony, around 150 deputies and 150 civilians. We thought that was all gonna come in, and you would have had flying pieces of glass slicing everybody up; so that was real dangerous; so we got everybody out of there."

### St. Rita's Restless

Gene Alonzo and the rest of the nursing home ate supper before sitting down to watch the coverage of Katrina on TV.

"Everybody was talking and watching the weather," said Alonzo.

Hunkered down with his brother, Carlos, Alonzo managed to get a little shuteye before windows began to break, and the rising gusts of wind began jostling the ceiling inside, like an airplane gliding right above St. Rita's rooftop.

"It would suck the acoustic up; you could see it was making some kind of vacuum pressure or something," said Alonzo. "Lord man, I hope this roof don't start flying off with all these people. I thought the roof was gonna start letting go."

Then his cell phone rang and one of his daughter's was on the other end. She wanted to know how he and Carlos were doing at the nursing home.

"We're alright," he told her. "I didn't want to let on that it was scary; it was bad, cause I knew they was gonna be worried more."

### Saving Energy

Never taking his mind off the game, Bubby Bodden, lying down around midnight, figured he'd get whatever sleep he could until nature's alarm clock went off. The drive home from Destin, Florida, and the constant preparation wore him down, and he didn't want to be tired when the worst hit. His instincts were right, because around 4:00 A.M. the rattling of the house woke him up, and he knew he wouldn't need a snooze button.

He looked at the television and that anxious feeling hit him, "Whoa, this is eighty miles away." Then the power went out. Like a stowaway on a deserted island, Bubby plotted his next move.

"The only thing you can do is hunker down and take every thing you think you're gonna need in a catastrophic situation and put it to where if something happens, you can utilize it. I had all the necessary tools."

He pulled on the thin rope that brought down the folding attic stairs in his hallway and began stocking his attic with tools to cut the roof with. He filled a green laundry basket with flash-lights, batteries, and a can of cat food for Neo. He threw up an extra set of clothes, expecting to have to seek higher ground.

"Constantly thinking of the next step to getting out if the water was to rise or if there was a flood or the roof blows off," Bubby noted.

He had first-aid, water, and a number of different power bars, so he could carry as many as possible in a small bag.

"Basic survival skills I guess I never knew I had, but all along I've had 'em, just a gamut of things going through your mind, plus you're thinking of your family."

Everyone stayed on their cell phones as long as they could and Bubby was no exception. His sister called soon after the lights went out and wanted to know what it was like outside.

"The winds are picking up; the water's not even up to my driveway or my sidewalk; I'm thinking I'm pretty good; I'm hearing a couple of shingles fly off, which I pretty much expected."

He grabbed a small, white, battery-operated television and handheld Sony Walkman® radio. Although the reception for his TV wasn't very good, he could keep up with the impending storm.

"Not really panicking, but knowing something was coming, the cat in the house was definitely kind of freaky. I figured it was coming, something bad was coming."

## Moving to the Other Side of the Levees

Two people whom President Rodriguez implored to leave, because they were outside the levee protection area around midnight, were Chuck Thurman and Frankie Asevado.

Thurman has a raised home off of Florissant Highway on the way to Yscloskey, while Asevado lived about a block and a half down on Eagle Street, off the two-lane highway. Thurman had already sent his wife, Sandy, and their two children, Chuck, Jr. and Destiny, out of town because he worked at the Dynegy gas plant until Saturday night. Both men spent all day Sunday moving everything they wanted to save to Mr. Ray Nehlig's home in Kenilworth that sits inside the levees. Nehlig is the grandfather of Asevado's girlfriend, Vivian Nunnery, but they call her B.B. They moved vehicles and tools, and Thurman also moved his commercial fishing boat to safe harbor.

However, Sunday night, the two thirty-seven-year-old men were still in their homes, keeping in constant touch with each other. The power had gone out much sooner than in the upper end of St. Bernard, and the winds were building speed. Thurman could feel his wooden framed home swaying, which he says is fourteen feet above sea level.

"The wind was so bad it was just deteriorating my house," said Thurman. "My house was only six years old but decking off the roof was flying off. My backdoor—I had some chairs propped against them; I had French doors to the north, and the wind was trying to open them. Roof panels blew off and it was like [a] force on my back door; I couldn't keep it closed no more; I had to get out."

He called Asevado.

"Dude we got to get from down here; it's getting too bad."

Thurman and Asevado got in their trucks, and with Thurman leading the way, they met up on Florissant Highway going toward Kenilworth. The streetlights were out, making it easy to drive off the raised highway into a tree or the ditches that lined the road.

"Stuff blowing by, branches, trees, running over stuff and tree limbs," said Thurman. "It looked like it was fifty to sixty miles an hour flying by you. The truck feeling like it wants to flip."

The men made it safely to Mr. Nehlig's house, which sits right in front of Nehlig's Trailer Park. Mr. Nehlig's brick house is raised about four feet above the ground. Riding out Katrina were Thurman; Asevado; his girlfriend, B.B.; her grandfather, Mr. Nehlig; two other men; and seven pit bulls, six of which belonged to Asevado. They put the seven dogs in the back garage. They had an eighteen-foot V-Hull boat parked outside and were ready for Katrina.

## CHAPTER FOUR

# Charlo Does the Wave

## Sunday, August 28 to Monday, August 29

### Day One to Day Two

BULLETIN
HURRICANE KATRINA INTERMEDIATE ADVISORY NUM-
BER 25B
NWS TPC/NATIONAL HURRICANE CENTER MIAMI FL
2 AM CDT MON AUG 29 2005

MAXIMUM SUSTAINED WINDS ARE NEAR 155 MPH WITH
HIGHER GUSTS
KATRINA IS NOW A STRONG CATEGORY FOUR HURRI-
CANE

While most had a nervous Sunday night and Monday morning, Charlo found out just what a category four storm felt like,
rolling right over him with no levee protection. While the rest of
St. Bernard lost power around four o'clock, Monday morning,
Charlo's electricity dropped at eight o'clock, Sunday night. With
his oyster boat tied down with knots of a seaman, Charlo
skipped riding out the storm in the cabin of his boat and instead
watched the increasing bands of Katrina from his home.

"I could feel the house shaking," said Charlo. "When the wind
comes from about 120 degrees southeast, it pushes the water in
and the coastal [land] floods, so the water started getting high
and up the steps of my house."

Charlo's house was a shotgun-style home on short pilings and railroad ties, maybe "four to five feet off the ground," and he says that's because it was built before they made laws on how high you had to build down there. He has lived there for ten years, and states that the home survived "the rest of the hurricanes" over the past four decades; however, he didn't know exactly how old his house was. Charlo said his neighbor told him that he could stay at her home next door; it was much higher on pilings; and that it was hurricane proof.

"Well they lied!" Charlo laughed with a hearty bellow.

He wondered whether he would head higher to his neighbor's house or just jump on his boat. The sky was black as coal, and the wind and rain were steadily picking up; the water had risen so high that Charlo would have to swim across the flooded road to get to his boat. He had seen water over the road many times before, but this was different; it was "higher than normal. It spooked me."

Grasping an orange life jacket in one hand, Charlo wasn't quite sure if he needed to bring the orange life ring with Capt. John J printed on its side as well. He mindlessly slung the life ring over his shoulder, disregarding the boat, and sloshed through the water past the two palm trees and up the steps of his neighbor's house. While Reggio, Kenilworth, Poydras, Violet, Meraux, Chalmette, and Arabi wondered how bad Katrina would be, Charlo was ready for the battle inside the ring.

"The house starts breaking apart, I couldn't see my house next door no more," Charlo remembered. "No lights, no stars in the sky, so you can't see no moon, nothing, you can't see five feet in front of your face, just black."

The timeline gets very foggy when you're in a house that's shaking like an earthquake that lasts for hours, not minutes. But after feeling like a man who's sat on a dryer for an eternity and having thoughts of his life being cut short, Charlo said sometime about "two or three" early Monday morning he decided if the good Lord was going to take him, he wouldn't do it unidentified.

"I was getting kinda nervous, so I duct-taped a driver's license to one leg and an expired Sam's card to the other leg; in case I drown or lose a leg or something, they could find me, so my wife could collect a little insurance. It was getting dangerous, life threatening."

His mind was embracing morbid thoughts; the wind blew stronger and the sound grew louder.

"I can see the water was high, but I couldn't tell how high the water was, so I took the stairs and pulled them down to the attic. The siding and lumber is nailed with arm nails not a nail gun. I went to the top of the stairs and from the ceiling to the roof it's some kind of rafter holding the roof up. I was holding on one of them, but I didn't want to go in the attic and get hurt in the attic."

A Christian, Charlo said he liked to keep it simple. He was baptized a Catholic; however, he lives his life by following the Ten Commandments.

"I was saying a Hail Mary, and the board came off in my hand."

The roof began separating from the house's frame, and Charlo hustled down the stairs away from the crumbling attic overhead.

"The only thing I could think of next was to go in the wind, to the way the wind's blowing. Don't go hide behind a wall."

An hour or so before dawn, Charlo said the sideboards were separating from the nails, as the structure splintered in every corner and crevice. With the deafening roar of destruction stinging his ears, the rugged fifty-nine-year-old mariner wasn't sure if he would live to see sixty. He wondered if a life lived on the water would be claimed by the water.

He remembers growing up in Port Sulphur and Empire, and his mother and father's divorce when he was twelve. He thought of his grandfather who was an old trapper and what he learned about the water growing up in Plaquemines Parish, and when his mother emancipated him as a teenager to become a seaman. He thought of his days fishing in what he calls the best "fishing village on the Gulf Coast," the shrimping and dredging of oysters. He even owns a shark-fishing license, having been grandfathered in by the state after they stopped issuing them. But most of all he thought that he might never see his daughter, Charity, or his wife, Terry, again.

He put his old school survival skills to the ultimate test. As he was fighting for his life, he knew he had to outsmart the growing force of Katrina. The roof blew completely off, and the rain soaked Charlo and the inside of the house. He fumbled around the house searching for a piling to tie himself to.

"The house is tearing apart, so I went to the front of the house. The side next to my house and that's the way the wind was blowing, southeast. There were some pilings that went through the ceiling and I was going to tie a rope around. I cut the rope on the life ring down to about twelve to fifteen feet. I was gonna tie that to the pilings and hold on. The wall started breaking loose. I'm wrapping the rope around the ring to wrap around the piling, that's when a wave hit! I don't know how tall it is or how big it was, how deep the water was. It blew the house away and me too!"

Charlo was swept across Hopedale Highway and across Bayou La Loutre with the life ring in his arm, his boot was ripped off and he quickly kicked off the other boot, as he became a part of a wave of water rushing through the dark chaotic morning.

"I knew I had to struggle, so I spit my teeth out so I can breathe. I didn't know how long I was in the water, but it wasn't very long in the one hundred something mile an hour winds, and I don't know how fast the water was moving and how big the wave was, but I know I was traveling."

Miraculously, none of the falling debris from the destroyed building hit Charlo fatally.

"God protects the dumb and the innocent, and I know I ain't innocent." He recalled with a repentant chuckle.

"I didn't fall, the wave just picked me up and threw me like in the surf or something, white capping on the waves. I didn't actually go very far, but I didn't know this, I lost track of everything."

He was alive sloshing anywhere from five hundred to a thousand feet across Bayou La Loutre toward Yscloskey. Charlo said after Hurricane Betsy, they dug through Bayou La Loutre and made a hill where some trees grew. With no light to give him any idea where he was, he found himself near those huge oak and hackberry trees between the bayou and the open marsh.

"I knew to grab a hackberry tree, don't get in an oak tree because an oak tree will float up and go away, but a hackberry tree got longer roots, so I stuck with getting in a hackberry tree."

Tying the rope from the life ring around the flat, gray bark tree with the small leaves, Charlo tried to get inside the ring but kept flipping upside down, refusing to let go of the life ring. He doesn't know why he didn't drown in that instance, but he was able to grab a hold of and tie himself to a tree, while Hurricane Katrina was pounding at him with her triple digit gusts and pellet gun strength rains.

"The rain hurt the worst, but you don't think of that; you don't feel it, but you know it hurts."

He held on to the tree with one arm and the life ring with the other. He still had his glasses on and realizing the utter miracle that was; he stuffed them inside of his shirt.

"I was holding on that [ring] for dear life. I was very uncomfortable; I guess I was fighting a hurricane."

Without his rain soaked spectacles, Charlo kept his eyes peeled for debris or anything that could potentially be launched at him by the forceful wind. He positioned himself behind the tree with the wind blowing around him, but he was still getting hit, and the water rushing below him churned and pushed like whitewater rapids.

"I knew to look at what's coming whether it was another house, pilings, ropes, twigs, whatever. You gotta look because you don't hide. You hide and you're gonna die."

It was at this moment that Charlo fell back on his modest Christian beliefs, and he asked God to help him out.

"I started saying a few more prayers and I realized, god damn, I'm gonna make it! I ain't giving up; I'm gonna make it!"

Even though he was tied to a hackberry tree with branches ripping his skin, reduced to a human target by the rain, and brushed up against by only God knows what, Charlo calmed down long enough to reflect on his survival.

"I knew that people was gonna die; I knew a lot of things was gonna be destroyed, and I prayed for the people. I'm a make it, and I know I'm gonna make it. That's what I put in my head. I lost track of complete time by then."

The sun rose and revealed a leveled Hopedale. Homes were now nothing more than pilings, and the boat docks were under water. Tired, rattled, and determined, Charlo got the break he so desperately needed; he was in the eye of Katrina.

"It was the eeriest, strangest thing I ever felt in my life. It was so peaceful, so calm, birds that made it around. Animals, no poisonous snakes, but snakes, everything that made it all around you on drift, debris floating, and I don't know how deep the water is, but I knew the other half was coming, I don't know if the animals and the birds and all that knew the other half was coming."

He untied the rope from the life ring and pulled himself around to the other side of the tree, so he would have some protection when round two began. The winds were blowing in a northeast direction this time. Wanting to know how deep the water was in case the tree gave way or the rope to his life ring popped, Charlo grabbed a ten-foot two-by-four that was floating by and shoved it down as far as he could. He didn't touch anything.

Charlo was moving out of the eye; the wind began blowing

again, and Katrina began pushing the water toward the Gulf of Mexico. Left with no levee to hold the water back, Charlo began another savage beating.

"I had several hundred cuts and bruises all over me, my hands, my elbows, my knees, my chest, and the bottom of my feet. I was disoriented; I wasn't sure how far I went in the water, and I didn't know where I was."

## CHAPTER FIVE

# Dodged a Bullet?

## Monday, August 29

### Day Two

*"The eye kind of skirted us in Chalmette; we didn't realize that the eye had passed until the wind shifted direction; then we knew we were on the back side of the hurricane, cause we were thinking when the eye comes out we're gonna go out and take a quick assessment; that never happened in Chalmette. When the wind shifted direction, I said, Oh, we made it."*
— Thomas Stone, St. Bernard fire chief,
Govt. Complex, 8201 W. Judge Perez Dr., Chalmette

*"I thought we had lived through the storm. I think most people had that same feeling. The wind had come; it was really bad, but we could tell it had subsided enough; now it wasn't the monster hurricane."*
— Wayne Warner, Chalmette High principal,
1100 E. Judge Perez Dr., Chalmette

*"At 8:30 A.M., my wife calls up and asks, 'how you made out?' The only thing we lost was the fence; the fence blew down; I got it beat."*
— Alan Clomburg,
3108 Gallo Dr., Chalmette

*Lebeau: "I think a little after 10:00 [A.M.] closer to 10:30."*
*Ourso: "The wind was still blowing."*
*Lebeau: "Of course the debris still flying, we was trying to keep every-body in the hallways away from windows, so we was making comments*

*like man if this is a category five bring it on again, cause we're ready; we fared out fairly well down in this area."*
— Rodney Ourso & Michael Lebeau, St. Bernard firefighters, St. Bernard High School, Poydras

*"We had the generator and the television, and the storm is going toward Slidell; it kind of passed us, the bad part I see. I believe we got it, looks like the storm kind of passed us, never had no water, everything was dry. All of a sudden I was kinda feelin' a little relieved."*
— Gene Alonzo, St. Rita's, 1422 E. La Hwy. 46, St. Bernard

NATIONAL WEATHER SERVICE BULLETIN

BULLETIN — EAS ACTIVATION REQUESTED
FLASH FLOOD WARNING
NATIONAL WEATHER SERVICE NEW ORLEANS LA
814 AM CDT MON AUG 29 2005

THE NATIONAL WEATHER SERVICE IN NEW ORLEANS HAS ISSUED A FLASH FLOOD WARNING FOR . . .
ORLEANS PARISH IN SOUTHEAST LOUISIANA THIS INCLUDES THE CITIES OF . . . NEW ORLEANS
ST. BERNARD PARISH IN SOUTHEAST LOUISIANA THIS INCLUDES THE CITY OF CHALMETTE
UNTIL 215 PM CDT

 A LEVEE BREACH OCCURRED ALONG THE INDUSTRIAL CANAL AT TENNESSEE STREET. 3 TO 8 FEET OF WATER IS EXPECTED DUE TO THE BREACH.

LOCATIONS IN THE WARNING INCLUDE BUT ARE NOT LIMITED TO ARABI AND 9TH WARD OF NEW ORLEANS.

DO NOT DRIVE YOUR VEHICLE INTO AREAS WHERE THE WATER COVERS THE ROADWAY. THE WATER DEPTH MAY BE TOO GREAT TO ALLOW YOUR CAR TO CROSS SAFELY. VEHICLES CAUGHT IN RISING WATER SHOULD BE ABANDONED QUICKLY. MOVE TO HIGHER GROUND.
A FLASH FLOOD WARNING MEANS THAT FLOODING IS IMMINENT OR OCCURRING. IF YOU ARE IN THE WARNING AREA MOVE TO HIGHER GROUND IMMEDIATELY. RESIDENTS LIVING ALONG STREAMS AND CREEKS

*Officers are looking out of the front doors of the detective bureau at the parish boundary. Photograph by Al Clavin*

SHOULD TAKE IMMEDIATE PRECAUTIONS TO PROTECT LIFE AND PROPERTY. DO NOT ATTEMPT TO CROSS SWIFTLY FLOWING WATERS OR WATERS OF UNKNOWN DEPTH BY FOOT OR BY AUTOMOBILE.

One of the deputies ran to the back of the Sheriff's Detective Bureau to get the head of the department, Major John Doran. Water was rushing up St. Claude Avenue toward the bureau, which sits right on the parish border. The two-story bureau is on the St. Bernard Parish side at 6501 St. Bernard Highway, while The National Guard's Jackson Barracks sits on the New Orleans side of the boundary line.

A number of the eleven deputies sheltered at the substation ran to the tinted, double glass, front doors to see what was happening. Within minutes water rolled past the green "Enter St. Bernard Parish" sign planted in the median and flowed into the building, forcing the detectives to hustle through water nearly knee deep. Major Doran radioed Sheriff Stephens.

"Y'all getting water in that building?" said Stephens with more than a little concern in his voice.

"Yea we're getting floodwaters here," said Doran.

"How much water you guys have?"

"About two to three feet right now."

Anyone tuned to that radio frequency heard the unnerving call. They heard it at the government complex, Chalmette High, the civic center, just about every deputy and firefighter heard it along with anyone in earshot of the radio system. With the look of urgency clearly on his face, Stephens turned to his deputies to figure out a way to get his detectives out of that bureau.

The water consumed Jackson Barracks, and like an endless row of dominos, surrounding buildings began filling up with the brown, murky water, such as Al Leto's plumbing and paint supply, Café Ole, Carnival Mart, and every building lining St. Bernard Highway. It was a most unwelcome visitor as the water flowed underneath the dulled, sun-beaten, blue-and-white "Welcome to St. Bernard Parish" sign.

Doran and the others made a mad dash upstairs gripping the metal railing along the way and trying to get whatever they could salvage to the second floor. A blue, armless, desk chair started floating around the room along with a wooden desk. A lot of their sensitive information stored on the first floor would be destroyed if they didn't move fast. They grabbed computers, records, food, and mattresses.

Some of the deputies spotted a man swimming for his life on St. Claude Avenue, trying to fight the current to make his way to the bureau. The man was struggling but making headway in the flowing water. Doran watched as several detectives made a human chain, locking hands in the rising rapids rushing down the avenue. They pulled him from the current, and the man is a National Guardsman. His "deuce and a half" had been swept away in the floodwaters. Doran radioed Sheriff Stephens again; this time to let him know they had just pulled a guardsman out of the water that was now more than five feet. The water was rising and white caps were forming. Then the waters smashed through the glass on the front door.

"This huge wall of water came tearing into the building," recounted Doran. "We realized we were in serious trouble at that point, because the water was just coming up. From that point on, [the] water just came up so fast; we barely had time to get ourselves up to the second floor. The bottom floor was completely engulfed in water, pouring in through the windows and the doors, filled up the bottom floor and started to come up to the top of the stairwell."

*Floodwater covers the first floor of the detective bureau. Photograph by Al Clavin*

The sheriff and some of the detectives feared the building might not stand up to the flooding and pounding. Stephens said the two-story building was built in the 1920s, and before the department acquired it, more than a decade ago, it was an old bank and once a beauty college. The wind peeled off part of the modern roof that was built on top the old flat roof. Metal beams and sheet metal were torn away from the building and propelled across Old Arabi. The guys could see the dark, swirling clouds of Katrina through the old roof that was never fully repaired. Then windows in the building began to shatter.

"You could see black sky at that point and as the sun started to come up every now and then you could see something fly over the hole," said Doran. "Like a freight train coming through."

The sheriff wanted to know if they had a plan.

"We'll get on the roof if we have to; we have a boat here, but we're not ready to bail out," Doran said.

"Y'all think you can hold on?"

"I think we'll be all right once this wind dies down."

However, Stephens believed otherwise.

"I could sense from my last communication with them that they thought it was gonna fail," Stephens said.

Some of the older guys who lived through Hurricane Betsy tried to provide a voice of reason for the unreasonable. Betsy was the worst storm this area has experienced for more than fifty years. With Betsy setting the precedent, the veterans who lived through her, couldn't foresee it being any worse.

"How high do you think this water can get?" asked Doran.

"During Betsy it will crest out over by the Center Street train tracks [about six blocks down] and then it's gonna go down and go to the river," one of the men answered.

From the second floor the men watched Lieutenant Al Clavin's boat fill up and sink. They saw cars being tossed around like Hot Wheels®, including Doran's Dodge Intrepid in the parking lot. He watched as the floodwaters, "picked it up, spun it around, the trunk popped open, the lights started going off, and it sank, and I never saw it again, disappeared, that's how strong the water was."

As the men watched the water rise to unimaginable heights, creeping ever so higher in the bureau, the men who lived through Betsy thought, "This is no Betsy, something else is going on here."

*Lt. Al Clavin's boat fills up with water. Photograph by Al Clavin*

## St. Bernard Port

Two miles from the Detective Bureau on St. Bernard Highway is the St. Bernard Port in Chalmette, which sits between the highway and the Mississippi River. Eric Acosta, the facility security officer, did his own analysis, calculating the worst-case-scenario as being a twenty-foot plus storm surge, and "the levees being 17.5 at the highest point in the parish that we're gonna have overcappage. The big question, Betsy had a twenty-foot storm surge but only lasted half an hour. We was looking at four to six hours [of] overcappage of the levees, do the math."

Around "sixty-five to seventy" tenants, employees, and family members sought shelter in various businesses on the site, because the facility was an evacuation site for Hurricane Betsy where they housed "thousands" of people when it was the Kaiser Aluminum plant. Acosta retired from Kaiser in 1988 about five years after they closed the plant, so he was very familiar with all the buildings and had an idea of where everyone was on the one hundred acre facility. It's a number of corrugated aluminum buildings that house businesses doing commerce at St. Bernard's small but active port.

While the port facility had reportedly never seen water, Acosta had a plan to move people to Foster Awnings, building number 301 if the floodwater threatened. Sometime after 9:00 A.M., Acosta along with several of his security personnel found out whether Katrina's overcappage would surpass Betsy's. Sitting in the small office, behind their black, metal desks, they watched the monitors overlooking the facility and something near the train tracks caught their eye.

"When that water started coming over the tracks we noticed it with our surveillance system," said Acosta. "I saw the force of it coming; I knew it was coming and coming up quick. I just started banging on doors, pulling everybody out. It [the water] was climbing up like a bug crawling up on ya."

"Let me get this," pleaded one tenant.

"We don't have time to get anything."

If they didn't have it in their hands, then it stayed behind. As the floodwater rushed up and whipped around their feet, everyone moved as quickly as they could to higher ground. Before they could get to the back of the facility to Foster Awnings, the water had reached waist high.

"We pretty well ran to each place, made everybody get out," said Acosta. "Kind of like an assembly line to the back of the facility. The water came up about four-and-a-half to five feet in less than a minute and a half."

They had everyone from elderly folks to an infant. With the stronger men in the front and rear, they locked everyone together, so the strong current wouldn't break anyone free from the pack. Acosta said panic did not set in.

"They were just doing whatever we told them, pretty quiet, working together."

They marched the crew up the stairs at Foster Awnings, and everyone Acosta could reach was safe from the rising waters.

"One group we couldn't get to that was all the way in front of the plant, cause the water came up so fast," said Acosta. "But it's a two-story area and it was one of the old Kaiser buildings they built like bomb shelters, so the second floor, provided they made it there, was a safe haven. We went and circled it with a boat, and the wind was real fierce, and the boat was giving us trouble, so we circled it a few times. We could see they had the door open

*Evacuees staying at the port hustle to Foster Awnings for safety. Photograph by Mikel Schaefer*

and brought a boat over there. We knew they were safe, but they couldn't hear, cause there's no windows on the building."

As the port's security officer, the forty-seven-year-old lifelong resident of St. Bernard had undergone terrorist training as a condition of his position. While he was somewhat prepared, he applied what he had learned about a terrorist strike to the devastation of Hurricane Katrina. Acosta and a few of the other men went to get supplies, like ice chests, bedding, and barbeque pits to bring to the second floor of Foster Awnings. The bottom floor was under around three feet of water. They wouldn't move for the rest of that day and night. Acosta thought about his house on Old Hickory Avenue in Chalmette; he knew it had to be under water and all of his extended family had to be flooded as well. If the water came up that high at the port everybody in the parish had to be flooded.

## Government Complex

At the government complex in Chalmette, the wind shook the building and rattled the windows. Tony Guerra walked hurriedly past the huge painted swamp scene mural in the main lobby toward the glass entrance, so he could see what was happening outside the front of the building toward Judge Perez Drive. The painting depicts the iconic images of the parish, the marsh with a pelican sitting on a cypress tree stump, the Chalmette Monument, designed like a mini Washington Monument, on the grounds of the famous battle of New Orleans in 1815, along with an antebellum home and the old paddlewheel riverboat, *Natchez*, rolling down the Mississippi River. With the crash of one of the windows, many people moved quickly away from the shards of glass scattered on the floor.

They were well aware of the detective's plight at the bureau, but they had yet to find out what was happening at the maintenance yard on Paris Road that was smacked up against the 40 Arpent Canal levee in the north central part of the parish. An arpent is a French measurement equal to 191 feet. So they measured forty arpents from the Mississippi River to the canal, thus the name 40 Arpent Canal. To the northeast are Lake Borgne and the Mississippi River Gulf Outlet (MR-GO), while the Mississippi River snakes along the southwestern edge of the parish.

Martin Onidas and fourteen men assigned to take care of the

parish maintenance yard that houses equipment like dump trucks and bulldozers set to go out after the storm to clear the roads of debris, found themselves running for their lives. They walked down a flight of stairs to open the door that faced the back of the facility, dozens of feet from the levee.

"We happen to see some water and the water was coming in so fast we grabbed a lot of our rain gear, boots, and stuff," said Onidas.

The rising water forced them to leave almost everything else behind. As they exited the back of the three-story, aluminum siding building, the floodwaters spilled violently over the 40 Arpent levee. They shoved their backs to the wall and slithered against the side of the building until they made it around to the front, and from there they saw the water coming from the Lake Borgne and MR-GO area as well.

They were hit from all angles, and they fought the force of the current and ran up the metal staircase to a more secure second floor section of the building. This section was once an old incinerator, and the concrete is "three feet deep all the way around." The men ran into a room where the walls were partially ripped off and the siding on the back wall facing the levee was peeling as well. They could clearly see the endless supply of water pouring over the levee. They didn't feel safe inside a room where they could see Katrina stripping the building surrounding them.

"We wasn't sure how bad this was going to be, so we had a couple of guys up in age was kinda trapped down there," said Onidas.

Onidas said he along with his boss, parish road superintendent Stanley Everhardt, and Louis Pomes ran back down the stairs into the water that was now waist deep to rescue the other men stranded in the tool room, the room next to the office he and the guys had just escaped from.

"I was worried cause it got dark in the building we were in. I didn't get no response for a few moments," Onidas said. "Finally one of the guys came out and asked where the other one was. He was way in the back, so us three got together [and] held on each other."

After rescuing those men and getting them back to the other side of the building and upstairs, they crammed into what amounted to a five-foot by twelve-foot concrete cinderblock bunker. However, round three of wading through the floodwater awaited Onidas because his boss wanted to save some of the chainsaws; they would need them in order to chop trees that had fallen on the roads after the storm. So again Onidas, Everhardt, and Pomes plunged back into the water.

"By then I had water up to my chest," said Onidas.

The fast moving water made Onidas question the plan.

"Man, y'all get out of there; get out of there; c'mon let's go; don't worry about the chainsaws, we gotta get out of here!" Onidas screamed.

Nevertheless, they hung on long enough to grab the chainsaws; the water was now to the men's necks; they hugged the side of the building to give them leverage against the strength of the current pushed by the storm surge and gusting winds. The strong 240-pound Onidas felt he was in trouble as the current pushed against his entire body, while he held the chainsaw over his head and above the water.

"I guess if I didn't have that weight and by me leaning next to this building, the current was trying to take me, and we kind of held each other just to get around the building. After that, all we seen is doors ripping off all my bigger tractors, tires ripping out of the shop doors, debris flying everywhere. We were asking the Lord when this gonna stop, it had us going."

This is the bunker where maintenance workers huddled together to get out of Katrina. Photograph by Mikel Schaefer

Soaking from head to foot, Onidas tried to make a cell phone call to the government complex to let them know they needed to be rescued. Onidas, luckily, got a line to President Rodriguez who wanted to know where the water was coming from.

"It's coming over the levee and we stranded back here," Onidas said.

With the sides of the aluminum building strewn into the flood-waters below, the fifteen wet and cold men gathered in their windowless concrete bunker and huddled up to stay warm. Soon the entire maintenance yard was under water and all the vehicles and equipment submerged. The men could no longer see the levee, and it looked as if they were stranded in the middle of a lake. Now they wondered when the water would stop rising and who was coming to get them.

"They said they were on the second floor, and I went, we are so screwed. I knew it was coming," said Chief Stone.

Then all communication was lost between them. At that time phone calls were pouring into the Parish Office of Emergency Preparedness. Bob Turner, the head of the Lake Borgne Levee District, heard the desperation in the voices of the callers.

"Calls from people around Veronica Street, Laplace Street, and they were frantic calls. 'Please come help me; I have my children on the roof,' the same lady called three to four times. All we could tell the people were we'll try to get to you as soon as we can. We would mark down the areas where they were. I knew some of the people who were calling, and everybody in the room knew some of the people who were calling. I was really concerned we were gonna have a lot of people who were gonna die in this storm."

Brenda Ingargiola kept getting calls from that woman who said she couldn't get to the buses on Sunday, and each call was more frantic than the one before. As Katrina grew worse, the woman asked for someone to come and get them.

"We can't risk our lives in 150 mile per hour winds to come and get you when I told you to leave the last time," said Brenda.

Then she called saying water was coming in and she was in the attic and to please come get 'em.

"Finally, she didn't call anymore," said Brenda, unsure what happened to the woman and her two children.

Those at the government complex realized the water that swamped the detectives and made its way into homes across St. Bernard was now gunning for them. Five firemen went to secure several boats they had outside the complex, in order to keep them from floating up and getting stuck underneath the overhang.

"As we were out there doing that, the winds were blowing us around, and we could see the water coming across the Wal-Mart parking lot," said fire captain Steve Gallodoro. "We could see a couple of inches of water, and when you looked back you could see about six inches of water coming across the parking lot. It wasn't no big wall of water but we continued trying to secure the boats. In a matter of a few minutes we were knee deep in water, and then we saw the ice machine in front of Wal-Mart float across the grass lawn of the complex, and then we were in about waist high water, still trying to secure these boats."

Councilwoman Judy Hoffmeister heard the warning.

"Someone said the water's coming under the door. Still thinking it's wind driving that rain water underneath the door, so I look down thinking boy this is sure a lot of water for rain and all of a sudden I told my husband, I don't think this is out the door. I looked, and when we went into the other part of the building, you could see the water was just coming up, so we grabbed what we could [first and foremost the kennel with their boxer, Caramel, inside] out of those first floor offices."

Meantime, the mad rush was on. People were running around with their arms full and with one thought on their minds, get to the second floor, up the concrete stairs in the dark stairwell. Hoffmeister made a second dash downstairs to get more things out of her office, and the water had already risen to her knees.

"We were able to just grab our bags at this point, what clothes we had and went up to the second floor and the water just kept rising and rising and rising."

Councilman Kenny Henderson ran to the north side of the complex and looked out over Torres Park; he could hardly fathom what he saw, the water flowing from that direction was merging with the water coming from the Industrial Canal area down Judge Perez. Now they were getting the water that sent the guys from the detective bureau and the maintenance yard employees running for their lives.

"I ran to my office, tried to get some of my pictures and stuff and bring it to the second floor," Henderson said. "I made one trip up to the second floor, went back down, and the water was chest high, and I said that's it"

Accustomed to floodwaters coming over the roads during

high tide and any threatening storms living down in Hopedale, Guerra and his son Troy left their cots and whatever else they had and ran upstairs. But one thing Guerra did take notice of was the storm protection bolted over the windows outside. If the water doesn't stop, then how would they get out?

"We gonna be trapped; how we gonna get out," said Guerra. "Sure enough we had to go find the ax to go cut out the storm windows, so we could have access out the building in case something would happen, fire, anything, we gotta have a way to get out."

Someone called Larry Ingargiola, who was in the middle of calls from freaked out residents, and told him to move his car that the floodwater was coming into the parking lot.

"Before I could get downstairs, there's two and a half feet in the stairwell; that's how fast it was coming up. I come back upstairs; well I guess I lost another vehicle."

Outside Captain Galladoro and the men managed to tie two of the five boats together, and then the other three were tied together as the water floated the boats up.

"When the water got to where we were hanging on the boats, not being able to touch the ground, we had to abandon that and take refuge back in the building," said Gallodoro. "The last guy in had to go underwater to get into the door. All five of those boats were inoperable after the water went ten-foot high; the boats got hooked under the overhang and sunk."

Chief Stone had parked some of his vehicles up against the building, earlier, and was walking around the outside of the complex when he saw local affiliate WDSU-TV's SUV floating by and resorted to some gallows humor.

"I laughed at 'em," said Stone. "Not two minutes later here comes two fire department units floating right behind them, and they turned and laughed back."

At that point, it was either laugh or cry; emotions were running high and the adrenaline pumping so fast that some forgot to worry.

"The wind's still going at this point; we had protection on the windows, but the windows was still popping out," said Hoffmeister. "But it's strange because I never ever once thought I was gonna die."

One of the young workers from public works walked over to Hoffmeister and asked her that very question.

"Mrs. Judy, you think we're gonna die?"

"Oh no."

And she thought maybe she should be thinking about dying because the water showed no sign of stopping. Many would stop by the atrium in the center of the complex and look over the concrete railing at the water accumulating below.

"We were all in the atrium looking down and that water kept rising, and they had already told us that the water would rise for six hours," said Hoffmeister. "The storm surge would be six hours. I'm looking at my watch and every hour was looking, cause it was rising quickly."

"Some people were putting on life preservers and we realize that we're stuck here," said Stone. "There's no way to get us; we know we've got maintenance workers on the roof of the mainte-nance garage; we've got people at Chalmette High School, people at St Bernard [High], people next door at the auditorium [civic center], people at the sugar refinery."

## St. Bernard Civic Center

Before the water slammed the civic center, which is next door to the government complex, Katrina teased a number of fire-fighters, police, and pump station operators with what they should get ready for. The majority of the front part of the civic center is made of huge panes of glass and it's not some place you want to stand next to when gusts are blowing one hundred miles per hour plus. The glass doors were only going to hold the water back for so long. Levee district employee Jaurell Aisola found himself standing next to one of the giant windows when his coworker warned him that wasn't such a good idea.

"Jaurell get away from them windows right now cause you don't know when that windows gonna go."

At that moment Aisola started to move away; he felt as if someone had pointed a ship canon at him and fired. Aisola's reflexes threw him into a defensive position and glass spewed, spraying his body but luckily not cutting him.

"The next minute I know they was just popping out like crazy," said Aisola.

When the floodwaters came, they watched as the neutral ground (median) went under; then the water made a beeline toward the civic center. Some of the firefighters yelled for every-one to run up the winding, dual staircases to the second flood.

Meantime, through the glass doors and windows, they saw the water swallowing the land outside of the ground floor.

"Lord, just help us here today cause there's some water coming out of New Orleans," Aisola said.

"They had double door entrances on the side of the building, and they were starting to bow," said firefighter Brian Mule. "You could see the water was coming in, almost like a movie. Everybody's hustling to get whatever water and food we had and can goods up to the next level. We just about got everything up and then the doors busted open and the water started pouring in, and we all got our fire gear and went to the second level, and then that's when the water really started getting high. Before you know it the bus stop was covered and the wind was blowing. We didn't know when it was going to end."

"I thought the place was gonna come down, we were just running," said Aisola.

The men moved out of the breezeway, through the double doors, and into the auditorium. It has multi-level seating and a stage. The auditorium is where they held high school graduations, concerts, and dances. If old enough, the men may remember the Junk Yard Dog and Andre the Giant body slamming their opponents long before the pyrotechnic spectacle of today's world wrestling extravaganzas. Legendary, rock band Queen even played not one but two concerts in this place before they made it big in the 70s, and now it's sitting under water.

At the government complex, they were no longer thinking of the second floor as a safe haven; if the water did not stop, they were going up and out.

"The next step was the roof, and it's almost surreal when you think of it cause I really still didn't get a little nervous until someone said we need to open the door to the roof," said Hoffmeister. "I'm thinking to myself now we're going to the roof? Now I better get concerned."

Bob Turner was haunted by the calls coming into the Emergency Operations Center. He found himself wondering if the guys at the maintenance yard were going to make it out alive, and after losing the boats they had stored at the complex, they quickly needed to figure out how they were going to reach those that were stranded.

"The wind was still too strong and we've got to get some boats," said Turner. "We've got to get out of this government complex, because I'm doing nobody any good sitting in here."

While they were scrambling at the government complex, the courthouse and sheriff's department received a double dose of bad news.

"Someone said the water's coming down Jackson [Boulevard] from the 40 Arpent [Canal]," said Colonel Forrest Bethay. "Everybody get to your vehicles and park them in front the courthouse on the lawn!"

It was common knowledge at the government complex that the men at the Detective Bureau on St. Bernard Highway were going through a harrowing experience and that water was flowing southeast from the Industrial Canal. If the water was coming down Jackson, then that meant it was running in a southwest direction, indicating that it most likely would be coming over the MR-GO levees. The water was rolling on both sides of the court- house toward St. Bernard Highway, ascending onto the steps of the courthouse.

"Water was coming like rapids down St. Bernard Highway, and it just met [at St. Bernard Highway and Jackson] and kept ris- ing and rising and rising, and that's when people started freaking

*Floodwater rolls into the courthouse. Photograph by Errol Schultz*

out and hollering 'oh my God,' said Bethay. "I just told them they all had to be quiet, everything was going to be fine, the water's not gonna get up to the second floor. Go back into the main court-room, sit down, and everything's gonna be alright."

Then Bethay turned to one of the deputies.

"Go find the escape hatch to the roof."

"You're kidding, Colonel?"

"No, I'm not, just in case."

Bethay looked at the dirty water; he had a bad feeling the river may have breached and people in the parish were drowning. He just wanted that water to stop. The sheriff was in the annex next door, and he would have to make some really tough choices if the water did not stop rising.

"Who goes up to the roof? It's not gonna hold three hundred people and it's a rickety old ladder to get up there," said Bethay. "An older person couldn't even climb up the ladder."

The next moment revealed that his prayers would not be answered—water flowed into the courthouse.

"It was like one step, two steps, three steps, now it's coming in, going up the steps to the second floor," said Bethay. "We know we were in trouble; we looking out and we see the railroad cars blowing down the railroad tracks; we thought somebody was pulling them or pushing them, and we're looking for the engine, but there is no engine, this is the wind blowing those things!"

Major James Pohlmann, a twenty-year veteran of the sheriff's department, believed the situation was about to get real ugly.

"We have employees we're responsible for, initially it was their safety," said Pohlmann. "We had everybody on the second level, and we made sure we had an escape hatch open to the roof of the courthouse had the water gotten that high. In the back of my mind I said it really can't get that high because it would go over the river levee, first, but I really didn't know what level the flood was on the river, maybe the river was toppling the levees and then what?"

All anyone could do was watch and wait.

"The water at one point leveled off, my guess three feet in the lobby of the courthouse," said Pohlmann. "Once the hurri-cane got past us, we had some commanders trying to develop a grid system where we can go start searching in areas and put crews out to do rescues. We probably had eighteen sheriff's employees and court personnel that stayed."

Worried the water wouldn't stop rising, Martin Onidas at the maintenance yard on Paris Road finally caught his breath.

"It stopped right under the beam by the second floor. It seemed that you really didn't know what's gonna happen," said Onidas. "You don't know when it was gonna stop it was coming in so fast. Wind was blowing, roof and debris was flying everywhere, it something you never want to be into. We didn't know if they were coming or nothing when it did die down."

When the water stopped rising some six hours or so later, some at the government complex went up to the roof to see their homes, businesses, and way of life, deep underwater.

"It was unbelievable, next door [at] the auditorium [civic center] the second floor had water in it and all you could see when you looked over the homes [of] the Buccaneer Villa [Subdivision], you couldn't even see the tops of the homes. It looked like you would look at the marsh cause all our cars had already floated away," said Hoffmeister.

"You look for the trucks, you couldn't see them no more everything completely underwater, like Sav-a-Center, everything

*Residents boat into the courthouse to escape the rising water. Photograph by Errol Schultz*

under, all you could see was water, wind, and trees coming toward you," said Aisola at the civic center.

President Rodriguez took it the best he knew how.

"I wasn't scared, jittery might be a better word for it, but you don't have to be too scared when you're seventy."

Larry Ingargiola broke down the situation like this, "My mobile command center, by the time water finished rising I had roughly six feet of water over the top of the bus, so I had a good eighteen feet of water out here. When you look across the top of the building in the back, the small part of the building [civic center], the only thing you could see was the air conditioners. Water came all the way up to the bottom of this floor; we lost communications about 12:30, one o'clock Monday afternoon. We lost our eight hundred radios with state police, we lost all our parish radios, our telephones went down, and all our cell phones went down. We had no communication; we were alone, by ourselves."

At the courthouse, Bethay said, "When that water stopped, I was like thank God I can handle anything else."

## CHAPTER SIX

# Arabi Falls

## Monday, August 29

### Day Two

### 232 Angela Street, Old Arabi

Never in his family's history had Kevin Reichert's home flood-ed. For generations the house that sits on pier and beams in Old Arabi has been in Reichert's family. His not so funny saying after Hurricane Betsy was "everybody's gutting their houses, and we're cutting the grass at my house." This history kept Reichert from evacuating his home that sat just houses away from the Mississippi River levee, thinking they would be safe from flood-ing no matter what. However, the intensity and size of Katrina sent Kevin, his wife, Jennifer, and seven others to Kevin's father's place of employment, the Domino Sugar Refinery, which sits adjacent to the levee and several blocks from their home.

They felt safe on the ground floor of the thirteen-story, brick, administration building. Reichert's father, the district controller at the refinery, had a big office, which they settled comfortably into. Sunday night and Monday morning were rough, but they were still dry.

"My wife got a call from a friend of hers that's in the military and said the levee had been breached [at the Industrial Canal] and the water was coming."

The nine of them grabbed what they had off of the floor. The problem was that the administration building did not have

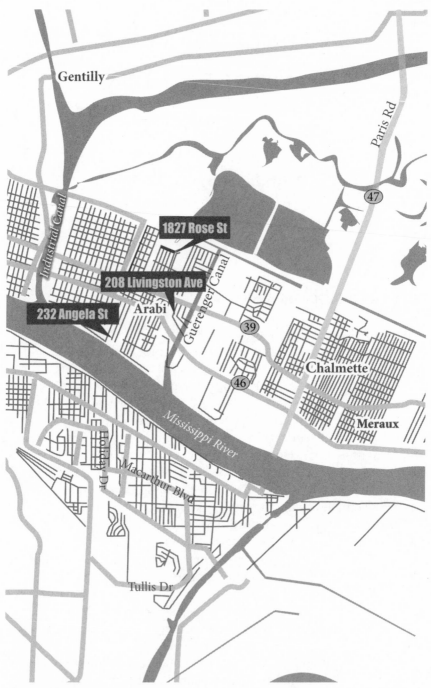

1827 Rose St

208 Livingston Ave

232 Angela St

Gentilly

Paris Rd

Industrial Canal

Guerenger Canal

Arabi

47

39

46

Chalmette

Meraux

Mississippi River

Holiday Dr

Macarthur Blvd

Tullis Dr

*Courtesy Mariella Pariente*

access to the upper floors. There were others staying at the United States largest sugarcane refinery, but they were tucked away in a part of the building that had access to higher floors.

"We were the only ones that were silly enough to think we could stay on the ground floor," said Reichert.

Since this area is one of the highest in the parish, it was hard for him to grasp what was happening. The thirty-three year old thought of his family's history in Old Arabi; he could not believe the water outside had made it all the way to the river levee. Reichert drove a truck onto the grassy levee that was tilted on an angle next to a concrete I-wall structure to Angela Street to check on his home.

"When I got to my street from the river I could see the water; there are no words to describe the feeling of just knowing that you're about to enter into your home that has water in it, cause you're walking through it in the street and you can see the water level, knowing it's in your house."

Reichert waded through the waist-high water. He opened the storm door, then the front door. The water had yet to reach inside the home, but it was lapping at the wood floors below. Another four inches and the water would completely invade the house. The water outside was rising; he grabbed necessities and put them on anything that was above the floor—the refrigerator, the kitchen table, anything elevated. He had a generator and a well-stocked house; he fully expected to return home once Katrina had passed.

"It wasn't ten minutes later, the way the water came in my house was actually bubbling up though the hardwood floors," said Reichert. "It didn't come in through the front door or back door or seeping through the weep holes. It literally bubbled up within the home itself and just started accumulating more and more, and then finally through the threshold from the front door and came in with quite a bit of force."

Reichert measured his material possessions against his life. He threw some things in an ice chest and bolted out of the house toward the river levee. He knew the ice chest would float in the nearly chest-high water. By the time he got back to the river, the water was almost inside the truck.

"We had got back in just enough time to save the vehicle, so we could drive on the levee, sideways on the levee a good half mile to the refinery where the rest of the family and other evac-uees had accumulated by this time."

Reichert went into somewhat of a panic. He couldn't find Jennifer or the others. They had decided to go back into the administration building and that's when the three-foot high water pushed against the closed doors. The pressure of the floodwater trapped them inside the well-sealed unit. They were becoming increasingly nervous as the water built-up outside.

"Their faces are pale white and they feel trapped inside of this building that they can't get out cause they physically couldn't get the door open," said Reichert. "The door would swing out into the water and the pressure of the water was keeping the door where they couldn't open it up. There was five of them in there, my mother-in-law, wife, father-in-law, two younger cousins, all in there. Not that they didn't try to push it open they figured they were safer in there at the moment, because the water was low and coming in slowly and out there was a very, very rough looking environment. The water was coming in with force."

The water rippled and looked like a fast moving tide. The mission was to get them outside of the doors, so they would not drown. No one knew when the water was going to stop rising; their fear intensified. Reichert pulled as they pushed. They forced the door open just wide enough for the water to rush around the inside of the door. As water poured into the room, they escaped and pushed the door shut, sealing it once again. The group walked to the only unflooded area for miles, the Mississippi River levee.

Reichert had his two Labrador retrievers, Jasmine and Maya, their instinctive swimming skills were going to be tested. The older of the two, Jasmine, had arthritis and it looked as if she wasn't going to be able to swim her way to safety against the current. Knowing it was the only way for the dogs to survive, Reichert took their leashes off and coaxed them to swim along. While the smaller and younger Maya had no problems keeping up, Jasmine was having trouble. Jennifer tried to help Jasmine, but there was only so much she could do without putting herself in danger.

"She couldn't bear feeling the weight if the dog didn't make it, so she allowed the dog to swim by herself," said Reichert. "She did it, swam like she never swam before and kept up and made it to land up on the levee and everyone was then physically safe."

With everyone together they now had to brave the torrential wind.

"You could barely stand up when you were in the water, it

was easier to walk than when you're out the water cause the winds were, I wouldn't even want to guess how many miles per hour, it was hard to just stand up. Debris blowing everywhere, roof shingles, there's a lot of slate roofs [in the area] so there was danger in the air."

They found a place on the levee and were surrounded by water. The Mississippi River on one side and what looked like Lake Pontchartrain on the other. They knew this was going to be home base for a while, so they crouched up against the concrete wall in an effort to protect themselves. Reichert, his father, and father-in-law went back to the administration building to get the supplies they were unable to carry out before.

Back in the building, they found themselves in the same situation as before with the water outside higher than inside. They pried the door open, went inside, and hastily closed it behind them. They wanted to allow themselves as much time as possible to collect water and canned goods. They stuffed what they could into an ice chest that would float. They also put supplies on an air mattress and were going to float that out. The water was about knee-high inside and four feet outside.

"You could see it look[ed] like an aquarium, at that moment; what do we do now? It was unbelievable; the adrenaline that you had didn't allow you to have a lot of fear; it just had you doing what you had to do in survival mode, cause you knew these moments were the moments that were gonna make or break you. What you got now was the only thing you were gonna have for who knows how long. The power's out, no water, the good thing it's during the day so you could see."

They busted out and fought their way to a shed on top of the levee. The shed was nothing more than a sugar shack. It was made to store raw sugar, not people.

"It's the most awful accommodations even if there weren't a hurricane that just come through. We bunkered down in there and with that we start seeing other people finally making it to higher ground, and they're coming from all directions. From homeowners to people from the refinery itself starting to make it up."

Within the timeframe of three to four hours, "fifty to one hundred" people had gathered inside this sugar shack. The level of the water outside began to settle down, but the wind was still bad, and the river was so high it threatened to flow over the levee. On the land side the levee is made up of mud and clay, but on the river side there's concrete armoring and huge boulders that's topped with a concrete I-wall sitting in the middle of the levee.

"We've been here all our lives; I've never seen the river so high and so angry looking; the waves had to be four to five feet high in the river. That's ocean type stuff; gulf type stuff in the river, and the water was flowing in the wrong direction, it was flowing up river because of the surge. That was probably the scariest point because now you were finished doing what you could do and you were just bunkered in, hopefully safe, very uncomfortable, and wondering how long am I gonna be here. How many people know I'm here? How we're gonna get out of here? Are we gonna stay? What about people who aren't so fortunate? Are they on rooftops like the pictures you saw of Hurricane Betsy? All these images start coming in your mind, and you feel now almost lucky that you are here even though it's as bad as it is. You still have the people around you and possessions immediately became obsolete; we didn't care about anything else."

### 1827 Rose St., Arabi

Glenn Sanchez spent an entire weekend saving whatever he could. He took down all of the pictures in his trailer in Hopedale, near where he worked as co-owner of the Breton Sound Marina. Afterwards, he ventured down to Arabi and boarded up his mother's quaint, cream-colored, vinyl siding-covered home with brown trim. The home, on concrete pillars, was raised about two feet off the ground. He covered the front twelve-paned window and its adjoining four-paned windows with plywood. He hooked up the generator, read a book, and was settled down by five o'clock Sunday evening when the news smacked him.

"Oh my God, it [Katrina] wasn't that big Saturday!"

He stayed up all alone at his mother's home, the one he was born in fifty years ago; his girlfriend had long since evacuated. Around 4:30 Monday morning, he got a call from his brother wanting to know how bad it really was. He held the phone outside in the wind.

"It's blowing about eighty."

"Are you scared?"

"I'm petrified!"

Little did he know he had every reason to be petrified.

"I was standing in the door when I saw the water come, started to come through and it was only about an eight-inch wave, but it was dirty."

Sanchez ran to the back of the house to grab his mother's safe; he laid it on top of the refrigerator. By the time he got back to the front door, water was already inside. He wasn't going to ride it out inside the house. He responded, as would a man who has spent thirty-five years fishing, by jumping into his boat. He had bought the Avenger, a custom-built, twenty-two-foot Bay boat with a 200 Yamaha motor, a jack plate, three bait wells, and "everything you could ever want," less than six months before, as part of his new charter fishing business.

He threw water and chips into the boat, thinking, all along, he was going to help in some kind of search and rescue mission. He ran out into the blinding wind and rain, unhooked the boat from the wench, and jumped in.

"My battery switch isn't even turned on cause I don't even expect this to happen," Sanchez said. "As I'm putting a life jacket on, the front of the boat goes underneath a carport and gets wedged. I watched the lampposts fall like dominos; I saw a house float past me. I saw stuff flying in the air as if it was the *Wizard of Oz*. It was just crazy."

Nevertheless, the Avenger getting stuck turned into an unexpected blessing. Being wedged kept him in one position as the floodwaters floated his dreamboat skyward. Sanchez was ten when Hurricane Betsy hit, and he clearly remembers the four feet of water that flooded his mother's house. He thought with the improvements in the levee system over the last forty years that he would be safe.

"I just assumed the water was gonna take the path of least resistance and go north. What a fool."

He tried to protect his head by ducking below the walls of the boat.

"I'm laying down in the back of my boat behind my seat with a life jacket around me buttoned up and one over my head, so nothing hits me in the head and praying and praying and praying."

The ride was rough because the boat absorbed a constant beating from the squalls. He needed to have a brief talk with a higher power.

"It just felt like a bad dream, but you knew it wasn't," Sanchez said. "God I have to make some life threatening decisions here in a few minutes; I've got to keep my composure, not screw up. If you screw up you're dead."

After spending about an hour with the bow of the boat in the wedged position, the rest of the boat went vertical as the water rushed up; it was time to jump out. Sanchez had to swim somewhere, anywhere, as long as it was to higher ground.

"I swam to a two-story garage about 150 feet away and they end up having some people in there, two guys, a wife and three little kids," Sanchez recalls. "I looked around in this garage and all the rafters were bolted together and plates were bolted; I thought at least I picked the right garage to get in."

Then they saw a teenage boy swimming frantically, trying to make it to the same garage Sanchez had just swam to. He had a life jacket on, but the winds and current were so strong that he had a tough time making any headway.

"He ended up getting blown across Patricia Park playground and he came up and worked his way along the homes. The winds probably forty to fifty miles per hour blowing in his face; I don't know how he made it. He was pretty exhausted, and he couldn't quite get to the house, but he got in a tree. He's holding on to a tree, and we got a big piece of molding out of this two-story garage and fished it out to him and pulled him in with that, and he came inside."

Sanchez and his group of neighbors had a radio to listen to and tried to process what they were in the middle of.

"We stayed in there for a couple of hours and we listened to the radio and they said it looked like New Orleans had dodged another bullet. The French Quarter was fine, Metairie, and I'm on the second floor with thirty-three inches of water we're standing in, and I can't believe nobody knows this is going on."

Around one o'clock Monday afternoon a boat filled with some of their neighbors came along and picked up the entire group. As they cruised out of the area heading toward Chalmette, they could see that everything was underwater. Many houses were no longer on their foundations with some perched in the middle of the street, especially on Benjamin and Alexander Streets. The streets were like minefields of power poles and power lines. The damage in this area of Arabi between Judge Perez Drive and the 40 Arpent Canal was catastrophic.

Sanchez was one of the first to end up at the makeshift shelter the sheriff's department had created at the Region's Bank on

*Two men stand on top of the Region's Bank after it became a makeshift shelter.*
*Photograph by Errol Schultz*

Jean Lafitte Parkway right across the street from the civic center. It's a three-story mostly reflective glass building that sits on the corner of Judge Perez Drive.

"We got out of one boat into another boat and just stepped right in the second floor of the Regions Bank," said Sanchez. "The first boat was a flat boat and they put us in a big Grady-White. We put everybody up in the bank."

## 208 Livingston Avenue, Arabi

Wayne Whitfield, his younger brother, Chris, and Danny Nelson, who lived right across the street in Carolyn Park, had a plan like many men in this boat-infused parish. The ladies leave and the men stay behind, and they had their boat "ready to roll just in case."

Especially fond of fishing down in Delacroix, Whitfield didn't think he was going to have to use his boat to save himself. His brother, Chris, took a disturbing phone call early Monday morning as Katrina raged on.

"One of Wayne's friends called me on the phone and told me

one of his workers was on the roof in the Ninth Ward," said Chris. "I told my brother Wayne."

"They're just messing with you," Whitfield said.

After five or ten minutes Chris began to watch the water.

"Let me know when it gets to my tires," said Whitfield.

On the phone with his wife, Diana, who evacuated to Arkansas with their three children, the thirty-eight-year old heard the anxiety in Chris's voice when he ran into the house to tell him water was rolling up the street.

"It's probably just flooding, rainwater," said Whitfield.

"No, no I think it's bad; I think it's the water," said Chris.

Whitfield ran outside of the tan-bricked, ranch-style home he's owned for the past four years; the water was up to the center of the tires on his Ford F-150 truck.

"I've got to go!" Whitfield hung up the phone and ran inside to grab his cat, Belle, and his pug, Dante. He didn't have much time. Whitfield handed Dante to Chris who put him in a carrying cage and ran outside to place him in the boat.

"I'm wondering where the hell he's at, he's still in the house looking for the cat," said Chris. "He goes to grab the cat and the cat attacks him. He gets the cat, we go to the front door, we had boarded up the front door. I'm trying to get them [the water is] already up to his chest and he gets out. We put the cat in the cage and took the dog out."

"At first ankle deep, waist deep, chest deep," said Whitfield. "The water wasn't a surge, it was a steady flow like a river; it actually carried you away a little bit if you stood still long enough; at that point, when it got chest deep, we said it's now or never, we're getting in the boat."

Whitfield and Chris grabbed a five-gallon and a one-gallon container of gas, threw it into the sixteen-foot Cape Craft fiberglass boat with a Mercury 75 motor, and hopped aboard. They had about half a tank of gas already, so they had plenty of fuel. They wondered where Danny was. If he waited any longer, he would have to swim for it. Danny was also home alone; he had made his wife leave early because she was nine months pregnant.

"Danny came running out of his house in chest-deep water and barely made it across the street into the boat," said Whitfield.

The men unhooked the boat from the trailer, and they had nothing to tie or hold onto. The water floated the boat high enough to where they could grab hold of the roof. This was a tough task due to the force of the current rushing around them.

"In twenty minutes, the water was three shingles up the roof," said Whitfield.

"We got onside of his neighbor's boat this big, old, shrimp boat or something," Chris recalled. "We held on to the big, shrimp boat, for a while; the boat picked up off its trailer and just took off. We was right there by the guy's house about a house down from my brother's house and we had a little peak of the roof by the front door by the porch area, just enough to put our head right there."

The guys were able to grab on to the shingled roof with their hands. Whitfield's truck was now submerged, and the sky was filled with projectiles. The men tried to watch each other's backs because shingles were coming off the roof behind them, hitting the boat. Anything that wasn't of significant weight went zinging through the air; even the small things thrown around by hurricane-force winds could hurt.

"Little leaves flying off of trees feel like rocks hitting you," said Whitfield. "The rain was coming on an angle where you couldn't look up and it would hit you in the eyes and it stung, everything stung. The leaves hurt; the wind, if you stood up in the boat, would flip you backwards."

The wind grew in intensity and with each gust the trees around became more vulnerable; eventually, it wasn't just the leaves joining the aerial assault.

"We were at the mercy of nature; and when we saw the tree limbs start cracking and flying through the air, we thought at one point we could possibly die by getting hit with something."

What helped, somewhat, was the wind blowing from the northeast as they hid behind a house, but that still made it difficult to get a good hold on the roof. It took all the strength and muscle of the three men to stay in that one spot, which was preventing the boat from floating uncontrollably in the current.

"We had to sit down so long because of the wind that our legs started locking up, and every now and then you had to stand up and stretch," Whitfield explained. "We were getting blue in the lips, it was cold. I don't know if it was hypothermia or what but you were locking up."

Beating constantly on their entire bodies, the forceful wind made them lose their grip. The guys then grabbed another roof, holding on for dear life, for another couple of hours. Whitfield said the eye of the storm never passed, and they never received the break they so desperately wanted and needed.

"It was strange, I was born after Betsy, so I never witnessed anything like this before. We stayed on the left corner of that eye wall the whole time, six straight hours. I stayed for Cindy. I thought that was bad. I think I learned my lesson for staying for storms."

In the fight to save his life, Whitfield, a resident of St. Bernard since 1972, thought about how close his family came to waiting out the storm at home and what he would be doing now if they wouldn't have made that decision to leave.

"Luckily they left, cause I have a one year old and what we went through on that roof with that boat, I honestly don't think he would have made it. It was too rough, too much rain, too cold, too much wind, too much debris, and it would have been too many people to worry about. We had hard enough time worrying about the three of us."

## CHAPTER SEVEN

# Water Flows into Chalmette

## Monday, August 29

### Day Two

**8432 Colonel Drive, Chalmette**

The wind pounded the front of Bubby Bodden's house as it blew in from the northeast. Like many who still had phone service, Bubby was on the phone with his sister when he heard his brother-in-law say that the water was coming from the Ninth Ward of Orleans Parish from the Industrial Canal.

"I'm just thinking the waters just gradually coming up from the rain, not really registering the levee had broke," Bubby said.

At that moment a shingle exploded through his bedroom window and he ran toward the sound.

"I've got to go; I got a problem," and Bubby hung up the phone without telling his sister what had just happened. Bubby ran outside to grab a piece of wood and water was coming through the front door.

"Oh this is not too good."

He quickly hammered the wood into the windowsill to block the horizontal rain from coming into the house. He ran back outside to get another piece of wood, and water was seeping in through the backdoor. Bubby sprinted back into his bedroom to finish covering the window; he looked down and noticed he was standing in a foot and a half of water.

"Something's wrong!"

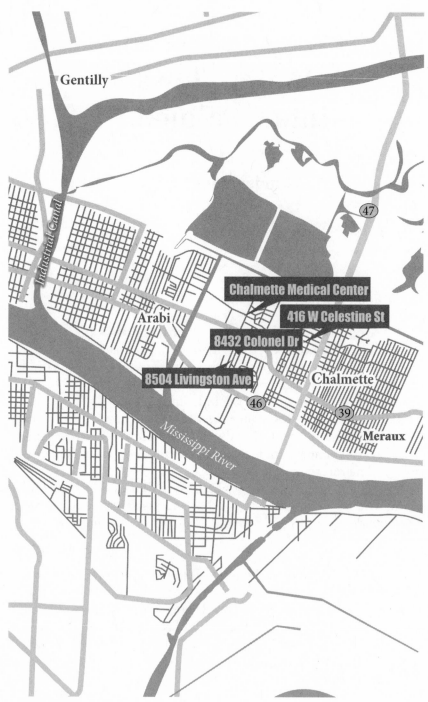

*Courtesy Mariella Pariente*

He immediately went for his cat, Neo, and opened the pet carrier.

"It was incredible; he jumped about six feet into my carrier. I put him upstairs [in the attic], came down the stairs, I had about three feet to three and a half feet of water in my house. I looked out the window through the front; it looked like a washer machine the way the water was going crazy, and it was coming up quick."

Bubby grabbed a few things and went back up into the attic. He went back downstairs, and the water was up to his waist. When he tried to return to the attic, he found the stairs floating. All of this water arrived within "thirty to thirty-five minutes."

"I got in the attic, and my foot happened to go through the sheetrock, which was good, cause I was looking at my kitchen, so I could monitor the water."

Less then half an hour later, the water plunged its way through the hole in the ceiling and poured into the attic.

"That's kinda when my adrenaline really kicked in, cause I knew I needed to make a hole. Luckily, I had all the tools necessary."

He had put a battery operated reciprocating saw in the attic, and now it was time to cut a hole through the roof and get out of the house. He raised the saw, placed it on the plywood, and turned it on; the sawdust and shingle shavings floated into his face and down into the water, wrapping around the two-by-fours that made up the ceiling. He opened a hole large enough for him and Neo to jump out of and onto the roof. The spot he chose to cut placed him on the part of the roof the wind was blowing over. This allowed him to settle in a nook that was protected from the wind.

"The water kept rising to probably about two feet in my attic; I had to get out, so I took a couple of things with me out. Put the cat on the roof and sat up there."

Every time he looked over the peak of the roof into the wind, he ducked to miss the flying debris, and every time it missed, he knew his life could end on the top of his roof.

"It was very horrific, a very harrowing position to be in. You don't know how long its gonna be; you're worried about the wind pounding you; you're worried about the temperature going down to where you catch hypothermia cause of the wind. Also the water's rising, you don't know how much more the water's gonna rise, so you also have to pick off your next situation and the next place you want to be in case the water does get higher."

*The hole Bubby Bodden cut into his roof to escape the rising water. Photograph by Mikel Schaefer*

Bubby, lying down on his back in a groove in the hip of the black-shingled roof, pulled his body in, situating his feet and head just below the peak of the roof. He put Neo down below him, and the roof guided the wind in such a way that he did not have to hold on to the carrier. Nevertheless, when there was a gust of wind, he would grab it and would sometimes throw his left leg over it just in case.

Watching and thinking, he was constantly surveying the situation. Behind his house was an empty lot, and he could barely see any of his neighbors' homes on South Jean Lafitte Parkway through the driving rain. On a clear day the former Kaiser smoke stack looked as if it was adjoined to the roof of Andrew Jackson High, while to his right, in the distance, the Domino Sugar Refinery rose above everything else. Bubby saw his backyard shed floating like driftwood, and then he eyed his neighbor's two-story home. Feeling confident he could save his cat, he was forced to call an audible.

"Right then the wind comes and I feel my roof jump and jump back down and I'm thinking, wait a minute if my roof flies off I'm gonna go with it. Another act of God, my next door neighbor had a boat on a trailer, the wind came up, blew his carport off, and up pops his boat, and the first thing in my mind was jump in that boat, so I grabbed the cat, grabbed my little back pack with me, I had two of them, jumped in the boat."

With the boat still hooked to the trailer, it was submerged below the water line. Bubby's neighbor was a Cajun man, a fisherman, and in the boat he had trawl board; Bubby threw it out to lighten the load. He grabbed a life jacket from the boat and put it on over a rain jacket and his short pants.

"I was getting very cold and looking around in his boat he had an awesome pair of rain pants, which probably saved me from getting hypothermia."

Secure and lying in the boat, Bubby wasn't entirely still. He had to make sure the boat didn't sink.

"It would get full of water and I'd have to bail it out, so I felt as long as I kept moving a little bit, I'd be O.K."

While he protected himself from the dropping temperatures and from being hit by the moving destruction, the relentless wind took its toll mentally and physically.

"The noise, the constant pounding of the wind, the pelting of the rain just wears you down, and it wears you way down. It brought me to a point of I didn't know if I was gonna pass out or fall asleep, but something came and said don't go to sleep, get up, and it made my eyes open up. I guess it's not time for me to go; I still got things to do. I really feared for my life."

While his mind was racing, Bubby's side of the family was in Gonzales and Baton Rouge, Louisiana, so he felt they would be safe from Katrina. However, his wife, Connie, and her family evacuated to Moss Point, Mississippi, just north of Pascagoula, about one hundred miles east of Chalmette, and he knew they would also get a good beating by Katrina.

"Everything's going through your head; everything you could ever imagine is going through your head, your survival, what you're gonna do next. But I think that's what kept me going; what's my next step."

For three hours he lay in the boat. Then the eye of the hurricane opened the sky. With the wind almost non-existent, Bubby could hear the birds, a sure sign things had calmed down. He jumped onto his roof to see what had happened in his area and toward the front of his house he could see the water on West Judge Perez Drive.

"It was just incredible looking across the field to the new Wal-Mart where the water was up to the Wal-Mart sign, a good twelve to fifteen feet. Seeing the [government] complex, seeing the people on top the Regions Bank, and the only other person I saw was maybe a quarter-mile on top of his two-story house, and that was it. I was totally desolated, by myself, very eerie feeling, nobody knew I was there other than my family."

Bubby estimated that round two began about twenty minutes later, and he jumped back into the boat with Neo. After a few hours, he heard the birds chirping again. Bubby had survived.

"The sun, wasn't like it was bright, bright, bright, it was still very, very overcast and still a little windy. I was pretty much trying to figure out how I was gonna get this boat unattached from the trailer cause the chain's on it. I started it up, going back and forth, and just freaking me out why it wasn't doing it, so I just quit that."

Then he heard what he hoped he would, a Coast Guard helicopter passing by. He grabbed a fluorescent yellow, life jacket and waived them down. They circled him; then they flew toward the government complex, and ten minutes later, two boats arrived and rescued him and another man, who was a few blocks away. He did not know his rescuer, but he was a civilian on a rescue mission and had a special friend, man's best friend.

"Believe it or not he had a freaking yellow lab in his boat. Incredible, I have no answer for it."

Bubby did not know if it was the same yellow Labrador that had paid him a visit the day before, but the oddity of it made him wonder if it was part of a bigger plan. After seeing Neo, the man told Bubby they weren't accepting animals at the courthouse.

"I gotta bring this animal," Bubby said.

"You can bring it to A.J., Andrew Jackson."

"Yea, bring me, just get me outta here."

### 8504 Livingston Avenue, Chalmette

Eric Colopy was outside of his modest, red brick home with white columns, a few blocks away from Andrew Jackson High School, when the shed behind him disintegrated and blew away as he was filming the spectacle. He knew it was going to make for some good footage of the storm. He went inside to take another sip of his breakfast-of-champions and listened to the radio. He was drinking a beer, sitting in shorts and a T-shirt, with no shoes or socks on, when he felt water touch his feet.

"What the hell, I looked around, and they had water coming through the cracks of the doors; I didn't think about looking through the window to see if the water was high," recounted Colopy. "I opened up the door and the water was already up to the door handle of the house and it was like swoosh, it threw me back. I put my two feet on the wall and two hands on the door with my shoulder. I got the door shut and once I got the door shut, I said shit, man."

He quickly threw whatever he could into the laundry room toward the back of the house, so he could get out of the back door or the window. He busted out and made his way to his neighbor's boat. The day before, Colopy's neighbor told him to take the boat if there was any trouble and gave him a set of keys, and he needed them big time. His first priority was the five dogs he and his wife owned, four poodles and a Pomeranian. Then the front door blew in.

"The furniture started lifting up, the refrigerator started flipping, sofa started going, the computer cabinet started flipping. I'm climbing over furniture trying to find all the little dogs in the house."

The way the water was playing 52 Pickup with the contents of Colopy's house, he knew there was a possibility that he might lose some of the dogs, if he didn't recover them quickly.

"I was just grabbing 'em by the hair and throwing 'em in the laundry room, cause I had to go find the other dogs in the house. The Pomeranian was all the way in the back of the house in my daughter's bedroom, behind the computer cabinet, swimming, and he was trapped in there, so when I finally climbed over the beds and sofas and all that to get to her room, I heard him splashing back there; I just reached underneath there and I grabbed him by his leg, pulled him under water, and threw him on a bed that was floating."

After doing a quick check of his daughter's room he found a Ziploc™ bag. In it he stuffed two packs of cigarettes, a wallet, and keys to his now flooded truck. Unfortunately, his video camera was gone along with his cell phone. He managed to place all five dogs in the laundry room, but now he had to get them out of the house and into the boat along with his ice chest.

"I just had enough time to get the dogs out and my ice chest.

I looked back and the water's up to the gutters of the house, so after that I said I'm not even going to attempt it, to go in the house, and I got them in the boat."

Then he saw his next door neighbor standing in his doorway with water almost up to his neck.

"Mr. Billy, get your ass in the boat!" screamed Colopy.

"I'm gonna go in the attic."

"You ain't going in that attic; you getting in this boat one way or the other."

"I can't get in."

"I'll get you in."

An older, heavyset man, Mr. Billy (Colopy doesn't know his last name) was more than Colopy could lift on his own. Therefore, he told Mr. Billy to stand on the motor and hold on.

"I'll lift up the power tilt, and it will lift you up and you'll go right into the boat."

So Mr. Billy, who lived at 8508 Livingston, waded through the water, climbed onto the fin of the motor, and held on with one hand.

"When I hit the power tilt up, it got him into the boat. Once I got him in the boat, he just had a grin on his face."

The smile did not hold for long, because they had to fight the intense elements.

*Mr. Billy in the breezeway at Andrew Jackson High School. Photograph by Eric Colopy*

"I was behind the console by the boat, Mr. Billy was sitting on the floor of the boat in the front," said Colopy. "The only thing we found floating was a tarp so he had that blowing over him so the wind wasn't hitting him."

Much like Wayne Whitfield's crew in Arabi, the men tried to hold the boat steady and positioned it so the wind would blow over them.

"We got behind this one house, the peak on the roof and porch coming out so we was holding on to the gutters of the roof, but as the water came up we couldn't hang on to nothing else."

Colopy turned to Mr. Billy and said over the din of the conditions, "We got to find a taller building or house."

He thought about Andrew Jackson High School, and turned his boat in that direction. It wasn't the smoothest ride, but Colopy said the weather did not push the boat anymore than you would expect. The doors at the high school were blown open and a number of windows shattered, but it gave them a place to get out of the wind and driving rain.

"We pulled right up to the railing, stepped off over the railing, got out of the wind, [and] tied up to the railing. We was there about a half an hour, and we got a little break where it stopped raining but the wind was still blowing."

Right after the men unloaded the boat at the high school, someone sent them a Mayday signal.

"They had one guy shooting a shotgun in the water trying to get my attention, cause we couldn't hear him with the wind blowing."

### Chalmette Medical Center, 9000 Patricia Street, Chalmette

The parking lot began to fill up, and some inside the medical center had bad feelings—it wasn't raining hard enough to produce the lake that was growing around the facility. Looking through the emergency department glass windows, Dr. Lee Domangue did not think the rain was flooding the parking lot. "There had to be additional sources."

"About 9:30 or so I was looking out the window as I was talking with patients and you could see the water coming in," said Dr. Bryan Bertucci. "It wasn't coming up. It wasn't a wave."

Most of the patients were already on the second floor, but a few remained on floor number one and the staff was trying to get them upstairs.

"Not only were all patients and personnel moved but supplies were taken to the second floor by pharmacy as well as dietary and other areas within the hospital," said Dr. Domangue. "Moving things that would be a necessity to maintain some measure of normal function."

"I had left my suitcase and my supplies in the doctor's lounge, which were on the first floor," said Dr. Bertucci. "I ran down the hallway to downstairs. By the time I got down to the first floor, there was a foot and a half of water in the hospital and three and a half feet outside the door. I had to go through an electrical door, so I kind of opened it up and just grabbed my suitcase and left everything else in there, including my cell phone."

Nurses, doctors, and everyone else moved as fast as possible, carrying pills, food, and oxygen. It did not take long for the water to rise to the canopy of the emergency department; the hospital was going under water.

"It was very rapid, and there wasn't much time to dally. Much of our record keeping and computers, and even I happened to be in scrubs, and my clothes and my keys and wallet were all left down in the emergency department," said Dr. Domangue.

As nurse Barbara Warren looked out across the parking lot, she was glad she had someone drop her off at the hospital, because she had left her car at home in Slidell.

"My concern was how high the water would get and would we have to carry the patients to the roof," said Warren. "Dr. Domangue kept assuring me the water would not come any higher. I was concerned it going past thirteen to fourteen feet, coming up to the second floor, physicians assured me this was as high as it was gonna get."

The hospital's two generators kicked on when the parish lost power. In the organized chaos for higher ground, the rising waters soon submerged the generators. Suddenly the lights and all critical equipment for patients went off; it became tough to see and maneuver inside the hospital.

"Everybody knew the water had gotten to the generators, which were on the ground floor, and we weren't gonna get power back," said Warren.

The goal was now to give the best care they could to the people trapped inside the hospital with the staff they had remaining. The lights had gone off and it was dark in the hospital. It did not take long for a sealed facility without cool air circulating to become warm, hot, and then steaming. The critical situation was clearly evident to Dr. Domangue especially when the bathrooms began backing up.

"It's a huge problem for any facility, particularly one that's entrusted with taking care of patients, when you have no power," said Dr. Domangue. "Because of the water and the damage done to multiple utilities there was no sewerage as well. It complicated the situation, especially with the stench related to not having adequate sewerage and capacity to take care of refuse."

The four doctors and more than seventy nurses and assistants split up the care of the patients and made rounds providing "whatever orders for those patients needs, based on what the hospital could do for the patients at the time."

"You just watched the water," said Dr. Bertucci. "We kind of marked things. You could see it go up a foot an hour to thirteen feet."

Stuck on the second floor, everyone was looking out of the windows. The hospital quickly became an island in the middle of a flooded parish.

"There was no easy access or movement away from the facility unless you had a boat," said Dr. Domangue.

And then the people flocked to the island, escaping their flooded homes by swimming and by boat, and they came by the hundreds. The boats were unloading people onto the second floor balcony. Hospital staff gathered sheets and lowered them down as a makeshift hoist to the boats in order to lift the people into the hospital.

"Some of these people were actually injured or in medical need. Many of which were diabetics, seizure patients, people who had compromised renal function, [and] didn't have their normal medication," Dr. Domangue stated. "Not all arrived were merely citizens who could stand up, many became patients; I would suspect five to ten ultimately became patients of the hospital."

One person who came to the hospital after fighting Katrina's force was one of their own, nurse Albert Schell. The thirty-four-year-old, Chalmette Medical Center employee wasn't expected back to the hospital until Wednesday, so he sent his wife, Theresa, and their two daughters, four-year-old Alyssa and one-year-old Alayna, out of town.

He was on the phone with a friend who told him the levee had broken. Schell was not sure what to think, because he hadn't seen any water building up in front of his half of a one-story, rented double at 3322 Shangri La Drive, just a few blocks away from the medical center.

"I started to kind of monitor that and within about fifteen to twenty minutes the water was already into my driveway, already at the brick line," said Schell. "The next time I looked out the door it was coming over the front door step; the next time, it was starting to run through the door; next thing I remember my carpet getting wet thinking, this is pretty bad."

After throwing important documents such as his marriage papers, an ice chest, bread, and bologna in his attic, he saw the power vent on his roof flapping.

"I noticed it was starting to flap cause the wind was coming out the back of the house, and it was catching on one of the vents," said Schell. "I had some metal straps up there and started strapping the thing through the motor and strapping it down, nailing it to the rafter cause it seemed like the wind was gonna take this thing off if I didn't do something."

He went outside and found his boat and trailer floating. Therefore, he decided to skip going up for going out into the elements. He took his dachshund, Oscar, and climbed into his boat and unstrapped it from the trailer that was parked under a carport in his driveway, but he didn't have his keys.

"I went inside; I didn't want to open the door anymore because when you'd open the door the water would come in faster," said Schell. "I was climbing in and out my little girl's window thinking I was trying to keep some of the water from coming in the house, but I did leave the main door of the house open and left the glass door closed. I could see the water level on the glass door was so much higher than what it was on the house."

He grabbed his keys, wallet, and cell phone and decided to head for the hospital because he knew they didn't evacuate. He put a dog life preserver on Oscar that had a handle on the back of it.

"Me and the dog are in the boat and we're sitting under the carport, the wind was blowing so bad," remembered Schell. "I got the boat started, I decided to sit in the boat under the carport and wait for the center console of the boat to start to hit on the carport cover. We sat under the carport fifteen to twenty minutes before I realized the console had started to hit, that's when I pushed out."

He gunned the motor, moving the trailer from underneath the

carport to the driveway, which dips toward the street. The boat pushed off of the trailer when the wheel hit the street, and the water level gave the boat enough separation to do so. The propeller crunched against the metal trailer and pulled one of the boards off as he idled into the lot across the street.

"I looked back at things and noticed the car of the neighbor was floating, the back end was floating up in the air and the lights were on like the brake lights were lit up as though the car was started. I parked my truck a couple of doors down because the other people had evacuated so by parking my car in the neighbor's driveway it was further tucked under between the houses, to prevent things from flying into it."

That no longer mattered as it was covered now. Schell had a tough time seeing where he was going through his glasses; he had no way of keeping them dry. He saw a shed floating down the street, and took a left through a building construction site.

"It was hard to control the boat because of the wind; it was blowing me all around. When I went through the construction site, I remember, distinctly, I hit their temporary fence put around it; when I ran over it, it was under water; the water had to be six feet; I couldn't see that. All I know is they had those pilings out there that I did not want to go in the middle of it, so I was trying to stay along the fence line to these houses, cause I knew the pilings weren't up in that area, but I forgot about his temporary fence."

He turned right, crossed Patricia Street, and maneuvered his boat as close to the power poll as he could. He glided between the poll and the droop in the power line and entered the hospital parking lot.

"Every once in a while you would hit cars in the parking lot, I was trying to go down the area where I knew it was the drive part but every once in a while you'd hit stuff."

Once he reached the back of the hospital, Schell drove his boat to a new wing of the facility that had a balcony.

"I pull up out there and nobody was on the balcony and the wind blew me into one of the big light poles. I started seeing people looking out the window and people ran out on the balcony realized that it was me. This guy, Anthony, came outside and grabbed one of my ropes and that's when we hoisted the dog up on the balcony and then I tied it around my hand and I just walked up the building with him putting tension, I was able to walk up the side of the building and climb onto the balcony."

After doing his Batman impression up the stucco-covered wall, he tied his boat to the iron balcony railing. However, Schell was so shell-shocked he left his boat running and wouldn't realize this for another couple of hours.

"I was scared to death to go back down there. Some people made some comments about the boat hitting the side of the building, they was worried about the damage the boat was doing to the side of the building," Schell laughs at the absurdity of the statement.

Once inside, one of his coworkers provided him with a change of clothing. He was safe but had unfinished business. He would have to find the courage to eventually get back in his boat and venture out to look for his mother and father, who he imagined were on top of their roof on 407 East Celestine Street in Chalmette. It was about a mile or so east of the hospital and after seeing just the tips of the roofs sticking out of the water in the homes in Buccaneer Villa, which was across the drainage canal from the hospital, he figured they were in deep trouble.

"I was worried about getting them as well but I was also scared to leave the hospital. I felt comfort being around other people but eventually I built up the courage. Two other guys decided to take a ride with me, so we ventured out. They had phone lines hanging down, which are lower than power lines, so every once in a while we snagged a telephone line in which case sometimes it would pop, sometimes it would hang up on the back the lower unit and we'd have to trim the motor up and one of the guys would pull the wire out."

Patricia Street turns into Genie Street as you move deeper into Chalmette; the men guided the boat around polls and debris. But like many boaters found out, you could not go far without hearing a call for help.

"You would hear people when they would see the boat just yelling, 'over here, come help us, we got two young kids over here on the balcony,' people just crying for help basically. I told them, I need to go help my mom and dad and I'll try to help everyone else on the way back."

They eventually crossed Paris Road until they came to East Celestine Street.

"As we pulled up in the neighborhood, everything looked so different from this viewpoint. I didn't see them on the roof and I realized the water wasn't quite as high as I predicted it to be."

While that may have been somewhat of a relief for Schell, the water was high enough to have reached the attics of the homes. Then he saw someone on a roof.

"The lady over there looked like my mom, so I went around to that house and that wasn't my mom and dad but that was three other people a lady and two gentlemen and before I can even say anything now they climb in the boat."

Schell told them who he was looking for and they told him they saw some people looking out of a vent every once in a while.

"We looked over there and someone was waving to us, it was my mom. The two younger guys that had come with me, one of them jumped out and swam to a roof top and then swam over to my mom and dad's roof and helped pull my mom through the vent and my dad through the vent. My dad took the spinning part, the top part off, which left a hole in the roof they could actually get through. I idled back around and went to the front of their house, they came walking along the roof and got in the boat."

Although quiet, it was a happy reunion.

"Everybody was just so scared, I think I began crying and my mom has never ridden in my boat since I've had it four years, but she didn't say a word about riding in the boat that day. Everybody had a look of disbelief, scared."

Schell brought his parents back to the hospital. Every tired and wet person added to the list of people at the hospital, took a terrible toll on the water and food supply meant for the patients. They arrived with barely any of the essentials. The hospital would ultimately have to provide for everyone. Due to the heat and stench of the inoperable sewage system, the decision was made to open a few windows; the staff didn't want anyone to become dehydrated.

"It was just keeping everybody calm and concerned about the patients, [with] no ventilation, the heat was horrible, stifling hot, we tried to break several windows with fire extinguishers and oxygen tanks," said Warren. "Most of the windows were hurricane proof, the ones that weren't were very difficult to break. The ones that did open in the older section opened about six to eight inches, the maximum amount they opened, and that's because we had a jumper years back, so they put screws in all the windows to prevent people from getting out, so they couldn't jump."

Even though there was some natural light shining through the darkened facility, the nurses gathered up all the flashlights they could find. Working by flashlight and with limited supplies, the nurses made constant rounds. There was a lack of some medications and IV fluids due to the flooding on the first floor; however, Warren calmed their fears and told them to use common sense in taking care of the patients.

"They couldn't do the care they normally did and these were younger nurses used to following strict routines," Warren stated. "I just kept telling the nurses all you need to do is make sure the patient is comfortable and do the best you can. If they're soiled you change them, if they're dehydrated, try to rehydrate them the best you can, and if you're not able to get their medications on time, it's not that big of a deal."

As the hours ticked off the clock, the hospital swelled to an extra three to four hundred more people according to Dr. Domangue. They were wet from the rain, floodwater, and the sweat that just poured out of them.

"They're hungry, dehydrated, grumpy, lining the floors of the halls," said Warren. "The nurses were kind of fighting over flashlights so that they can care for their patients [and] make their way around into the rooms; we had very limited flashlights."

With a hospital now occupied by doctors, nurses, family members of the staff, patients, and neighborhood people, the conditions went from bad to worse. Without the assistance of electricity, an elderly woman, who was terminal, struggled to stay alive.

"She was full of fluid, kind of gurgling in the bed; we didn't have any suction capability," recounted Warren. "She had fluid building up from aspirating into her lungs, and there was no way to get that out of her lungs, she was drowning. The young nurse that had her was just very distraught, she couldn't suction her and stuff so I got a physician in there to make her as comfortable as possible, so she wouldn't suffer and that was just so hard. The son was there and he knew we couldn't suction her."

He told Warren, "Just make her comfortable, that's all I'm asking, just make her comfortable."

"I think we gave her a little morphine to relax her a little bit and make her a little bit more peaceful, and she hung on for awhile before she passed. The son was just grateful she was more comfortable," said Warren.

It was a low time and there were more people to care for, but more importantly, they too had to survive. It became evident they would stay in survival mode longer than anyone would have dreamed.

"It just seemed like time just drug on and nothing was getting better, you kind of lost hope that things were gonna get better because we weren't hearing anything from the outside," said Warren. "We didn't know when they would rescue us; we had refugees coming in by the hundreds and no word from the outside. Didn't see helicopters flying outside assessing the area, I was counting on all that and it was very disappointing that was not happening."

### 416 West Celestine Street, Chalmette

David Griffin was watching TV when he remembered someone say, "We hope that this message is going out to nobody." Griffin, his son, Frank, and seventy-nine-year-old mother, Miriam, did not think it was such a bad idea to stay. Like the thousands who rode out Hurricane Betsy, they survived the storm and did not expect Katrina to be any worse. Griffin's twenty-one-year-old son had already gone to a friend's house and his mother was in her home, two doors down on West Celestine Street. A self professed, "crazy kind of guy," Katrina tamed the wild man.

"I was afraid to go out. I'm a nut, when they had Tropical Storm Bill I was in Mississippi," said Griffin. "I ran out on the beach but when I seen this I'm afraid to open the door; It was unbelievable; it was howling shuuusussusuus almost like a tornado. Everything rattling, doors, shhuuuuush buzzing sound. I was afraid to go get my pig; she was standing outside. I said 'you better come in!' I was afraid to get out there to get her and I'm never afraid to do that. I was really deathly afraid."

Then there was a loud crash.

"I heard something tremendous hit my roof, and I thought it was just a giant branch, and water started leaking through the light fixtures, and I have a sixteen-foot ceiling, and water started pouring in."

Not having anyone but himself to worry about, the forty-eight-year–old, social studies and science teacher from Our Lady of Prompt Succor in Chalmette grabbed his chow-Labrador mixed puppy, Moses, and ran out of the door. There was a huge tree blocking the walkway; he ducked under the tree and walked to his mother's house.

"Her house was still O.K. She had gas, so she cooked some eggs, and we had coffee. We're eating eggs and drinking coffee and the storms blowing through and all of sudden water started coming through the back door," said Griffin.

"Just put some newspaper, that's just the rain," she told him.

"Mother, that's not just the rain!"

The water poured in through the door. Griffin quickly grabbed his mother and dragged her into the upstairs attic.

"It's still coming!" said Griffin.

"We gonna be O.K.," she calmly replied.

"I don't think we're gonna make it!"

Griffin thought about dying and surviving, and if he couldn't save his mother, he was prepared to go with her.

"I thought it was going to be the end; at least, I thought my mother was gonna die cause I knew I could swim," said Griffin. "But I wasn't gonna leave my mother, so that's why I was there. There was no way I was gonna leave her cause I could have got out long time ago."

One thing he knew for sure was that he had lost his pig. He could not get her inside during the storm, and when the water came up as fast as it did, he was unable to do anything to get to her. In the rush to get upstairs, Griffin realized his mother's medicine was in the water below.

"She's got stuff for blood thinner, high blood pressure, all kinds of stuff, she needed it."

Without hesitating he dove into the brown, murky water.

"I was on a boogie board and I was pushing myself off the ceiling. I went under water, dived in the muck."

He found the medicine and brought it upstairs. Soaking wet in a hot, August, Louisiana attic, Griffin had no other clothes up there. He remembered the cardinal rule— store an ax in the attic, in case you need to chop a hole through the roof—but he did not think about a change of clothes. He rummaged around until he found something more than unique to the area.

"I found Mardi Gras costumes."

He changed into one of the bright and shiny costumes, maybe not ideal for surviving a hurricane, but it did have that New Orleans' flavor, and at least he was dry. The wild man had a fitting get-up for his persona. When Griffin's son returned home on a boat after the wind had died down, they kicked in a side wall, so they could reach the carport and then the roof. In grand Carnival spirit they threw a party, somewhat.

"I was on the rooftop; I looked like Michael Jackson doing the moonwalk. I was waving at the helicopters; we were lounging; it was nice, and we had water-front property," Griffin said tongue-in-cheek.

Griffin's son and some of his friends went to the Winn-Dixie grocery store near the house because the store's windows had been destroyed. They scavenged what they could out of the water, scooping out chips and bags of nuts.

"That's how we were getting food and all kinds of food was all over the place."

It may be the first unofficial post-Katrina party.

"It was like a picnic at first; they would park the boat right behind my van, and they were drinking cokes and eating chips and hanging on. It was cool for the first day, it was kind of fun. It was sunny; we brought the mattress out, and we were having a good time."

Despite the Krewe of Katrina hanging out in a sea of madness, there was not much else that could be done.

*The inside of a Winn-Dixie grocery store. Photograph by Errol Schultz*

"There was helicopters flying by; we were waving at them, thinking somebody's gonna help, no help," said Griffin. "Some people in boats, we were yelling at people from rooftop-to-rooftop like prehistoric days, communicating that way. They had this one lady, she had one leg and a heart condition, and she couldn't get in the boat and had to wait for a helicopter, and we had to go over there and bring her food and water. I don't know what happened to her."

Amidst the devastation, Griffin found his five-year-old, pot-bellied pig, Piglet, alive.

"She swam to the neighbors. I didn't know where she was. I didn't know pigs could swim; she swam."

Listening to the only link to the outside world, an old battery-powered radio, Griffin knew Katrina had wiped out the area but there was one thing that really worried him.

"We were hearing about all the other parishes, but we weren't hearing about St. Bernard."

# CHAPTER EIGHT

# Chalmette above Paris Road

## Monday, August 29

### Day Two

### 2809 Golden Drive, Chalmette

Barry Uhle received a couple of phone calls from his next-door neighbor Monday morning. His neighbor was at Memorial Medical Center in Uptown New Orleans. He had contacts within St. Bernard Parish and the National Guard, and he told Uhle the Industrial Canal had breached at Tennessee Street.

"Are you sure you're not seeing any water?"

"Man look there's no water," Uhle said looking out past three pine trees towards the canal that runs parallel with his street.

Uhle, who manages the maintenance and facility department for Textron Marine & Land in New Orleans East, had every intention of leaving his two-story home with the Spanish-style archways and windows on Golden Drive in Chalmette. His family left for Destin, Florida, while he worked Saturday to secure the shipyard; then on Sunday he boarded up his house. As did many others who saw the traffic on TV, Uhle changed his mind and stayed. He had never evacuated for a storm and vividly remembers sitting on the roof of his flooded Arabi home after Hurricane Betsy when he was eleven years old, so riding out Katrina was not a scary thought.

Uhle understood what his friend was trying to warn him about when the water made it outside his door. He had already

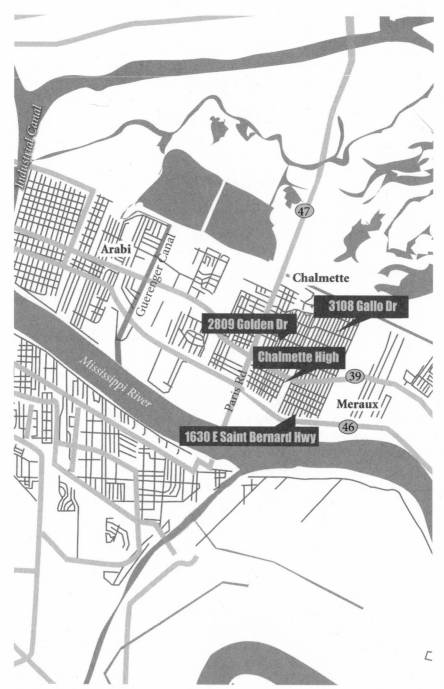

Industrial Canal

47

Arabi

Guerenger Canal

Chalmette

3108 Gallo Dr

2809 Golden Dr

Mississippi River

Chalmette High

Paris Rd

39

Meraux

46

1630 E Saint Bernard Hwy

*Courtesy Mariella Pariente*

raised a number of items three feet above the floor. He brought a wedding album, valuables, and other keepsakes upstairs. With the water outside his door and planning to invade his home, he plotted a new plan.

"What stuff did I [have] down here now that's up three feet, that I want to get upstairs cause I know I'm probably gonna lose that too," Uhle said. "I got everything upstairs of value and stuff I thought I would need like butane, a barbeque pit, a generator, a compressor, my nail guns, everything I thought I would need to get the house straight before my wife got home the next day."

The water started coming into Uhle's house and he went up on his stairwell and watched as his oval-shaped glass front door tried to hold back five and a half feet of water.

"I was looking at a muddy water aquarium sitting on my stairwell, looking at my front door," said Uhle. "It was surreal I couldn't think of what was gonna happen next. I didn't have a thought to think, damn, look at this. And I'm wondering at what point is all that water gonna come in my house. You'd think the water being six feet outside would kind of like be five feet inside because it never rushed in."

While the glass front door was successfully holding back the water, he heard something break; looking underneath his legs through his arching doorway, he watched as the doorframe of his back door was crushed under the weight.

"Six feet of water came into my house in thirty seconds," said Uhle. "Water was coming in my den; it's not like anything you've ever seen. If you ever open up a washing machine, my furniture was going around in a circle, it was jamming up in the doorways, keeping the water in my den, not letting it get into my kitchen, and not letting it get into my front room. It was five feet in one room, three feet in another and a foot in the front and it was coming through the house. I've never seen a movie depict a flood like this."

Uhle's sense of calm didn't leave him until that water touched the ceiling and he could no longer see anything but the dark, corroded water resting on his stairwell.

"I never really felt afraid or trapped with the water until the water came up to the ceiling of the first floor cause then I'm standing on the stairwell and I'm looking down. There's a certain scene in the *Poseidon Adventure* when they're on a stairwell looking at that pool of water, I remember thinking, it's not clear. You look at any flood they show on TV you can see in the water, lights in the water like a lighted pool. This was just river, black water in your home up to the first floor. As soon as the water hit that ceiling of the first floor I realized my whole first floor was under water. I'm looking at a four by eight-foot pool with the stairs going down into the water."

Knowing he was just about the only person who had stayed on his block, Uhle realized there would be no more riding this storm out in his house. He thought about the people he knew who had also stayed behind.

"I knew my neighbor across the street and my friend was home, that's all I was worried about. I knew they were able-bodied; they were physical. One of them had a little boy in a wheelchair, a paraplegic, and I knew they were there and I was worried about them."

He looked out of his second story window and saw his neighbors across the street getting into a rescue boat. Soon after that he saw another one of his friends cruising down the waterway in a boat. He could also hear the family with the paraplegic child telling a rescuer to pick up Uhle's other friend. Feeling confident all of the people he knew were getting out of their homes, Uhle planned his getaway. It wasn't what the former Holy Cross High tiger expected. He had a barbeque pit, butane, and food; he was prepared to live in his second story, but he wasn't prepared for a catastrophe.

"I took two shoulder bags, put six pairs of clothes in it, a couple of pairs of shoes, had my boots on, I had a parka on with a rain jacket covering my head. I took another bag with water and stuff to eat, some fruit, some dry goods, and some can goods, threw them in the bag. I opened the window; I had a baseball hat; I waved my hat to a guy coming by; I took one step out of the second story window and into his boat."

There was a teenage girl, wet, with her pajamas on, sitting in the rain. As Uhle scanned the boat, he wondered why more of the people weren't like him, dressed for the occasion.

"I'm not even wet, I unzipped my jacket standing over her, thinking how unprepared can people be. I started looking around in the boat and saying some of these people shouldn't have stayed here, kids and dogs."

**Chalmette High School, 1100 E. Judge Perez Drive**

The Chalmette High cafeteria was filled with the smell of

breakfast; the head of the cafeteria Kathy Barbier and others made grits and little sausages with hotcakes wrapped around them. Believing the school was the highest point of the parish, with no sign of significant water in the street and diminishing winds, people allowed themselves to think the worst may have been over and it was time to eat. They lined up thinking about the warm food that would finally fill their stomachs and hoping that in just a few more hours, when the storm cleared, they could go home.

The mood changed drastically when word filtered through the school that there was water in Arabi and that it could reach Chalmette within the next forty-five minutes to an hour. It was time to get everyone upstairs. The heads up was probably a lifesaver for the special needs patients they had at the school.

"The fireman said 'we're gonna probably get some water, let's start moving 'em up.' Thank God they had communication cause we had no communication at all," said Principal Wayne Warner. "They started to take a little bit of food out of the cafeteria and put it upstairs and that was very important to us, because what happened was very quickly the water started coming up and you could see the water building up outside within a matter of minutes. We had a lot of infirmed people, a lot of elderly people who had to be helped upstairs, so the firemen being there was really a godsend."

Whoever was unable to walk the firemen carried, including people needing oxygen, the bed-ridden elderly, and the two fragile, young men on ventilators.

"We didn't have no stretchers, no baskets, no nothing, so we took the salad bar in the cafeteria and put them on the salad bar and carried them upstairs," said Fire Captain Eddie Appel. "We were worried to death, the guy said the battery only last four hours and we had to go hustle and find some gas. One of our firefighters brought his generator from home and that's all we had was that."

The room they put the men in was near a stairwell in order to separate them from the generator; this would keep them safe from the carbon monoxide fumes the lifesaving generator cranked out.

"These kids if they blink their eye it's a big thing. If they watch a program and blink their eye it's like they're responding," said Warner.

The move upstairs was challenging for many because Chalmette High was not equipped for this.

"Probably twenty special needs people that probably shouldn't have been there because we didn't have the facilities for them, but we couldn't turn them away," said fireman Charles Liccardi, Jr. "We had people in wheelchairs, we're doing the best we can with them."

The idea was to put those who were really sick in the presentation room, which is more like a college classroom. Used for school plays and other functions, the room has eight ascending rows of steps and gray carpeting.

"The problem with that was there was no ventilation, and so we broke the windows out in there to try to provide ventilation," said Warner. "It helped a little bit but that was an issue it was so hot, we were in a closed building and it was dark. Every time we'd go, even in the daytime, we had to use a flashlight to walk around back there. We were always worried like the guys who needed dialysis."

Liccardi then went into the school gym. The gym can be entered through two separate hallways from inside of the school. The first hallway in the front takes you up a ramp into the gym lobby, then into the gym; in the back you can enter by walking up eight steps. There are twenty large sections of pale, rectangle-cut, wind panes that move in an upward direction. They are in the front of the gym, stretching from its center, rising to the peak of the gym, and outward to its ends. The wind peeled off a part of the front edge of the gym's roof and the window was blown inward.

"Myself and a couple of the other guys were in the gym looking around, they had a couple of teachers there, we were talking to them when the roof was flying off so when we got a chance, we got back into the school," said Liccardi.

There are eight sections of wooden chair back seats grouped in rows of six in the gym. A beautiful throw back facility that returns you to the 1960s, it is the reason Walt Disney Pictures decided to film part of the basketball-themed movie *Glory Road* there. It is a place thirty-two-year-old Liccardi is very familiar with; he attended the school, and his wife teaches there.

The two-story school has classrooms that face the main drag, East Judge Perez Drive. The inhabitants of the school finally saw the water they were warned about building up in the street and creeping toward the school. Within minutes it had covered the front parking lot. Now there was very limited time to grab the food they would need to feed the hundreds of people in the school.

"You realize all your food is downstairs, all your cooking utensils are downstairs, everything is downstairs," said Warner. "So Mrs. Barbier started to gather stuff to bring upstairs and some of the firemen had made one trip."

One thing they did manage to bring upstairs was Kellogg's Fruit Loops®, plenty of Fruit Loops® cereal. The terrazzo floors were extremely slick from the water, and Mrs. Barbier's husband slipped and cracked his head on the floor, suffering a concussion and cutting a significant wedge into his head.

"We all had to stop and take care of him at that moment because we wanted to make sure he was O.K. We got very distracted with that; he was bleeding," said Carole Mundt. "That was a stop and start kind of thing, and you lost your momentum for what you were doing because you had to attend to an injury at that moment."

The water was seeping through the doors; the bottom floor was now ankle deep. The firemen hurriedly sloshed through the water, carrying the last of the needy patients to the second floor. Warner knew they would need more food than they had managed to salvage and some attempted to go back down to the cafeteria to get more. The floodwater pushing on the doors of the school finally won the battle. The only thing they could do was run for the stairs, leaving the food behind. Liccardi was standing in the hall and watched as the doors exploded open.

"To see the doors blow open, we started running and we got upstairs," said Liccardi. "Within thirty to forty-five minutes we went from no water to over your head water downstairs."

"It was just like whew, all of sudden the water was there!" said Mundt.

"It was quick, you never realize that much water can come in so quickly it just rose," said Warner.

Not only did the food in the cafeteria go under water but so did an entire truck filled with federal provided commodities. School board member David Fernandez had driven the truck filled with canned goods and boxes of food to the school to be used for the shelter. It was parked in the back of the school and submerged under the floodwaters. Meantime, the teacher instincts in Mundt rose like the waters in the school and she said to Fernandez, "I've got to try to save some records."

The two waded through the rushing water to the front office, opened the glass door, grabbed what paperwork they could, and placed them on file cabinets in the conference room next to the principal's office. It was no longer safe to try to save any more inanimate objects.

"We did manage to save a little bit but not nearly enough," said Mundt.

A fireman instructed her to get up the stairs, but she walked to a window facing the football and baseball fields in the back of the school facility.

"I watched the rest of the water come in from the window across our football field; that was incredible."

The people upstairs were noticeably shaken up and very agitated. The situation was made worse when the water shorted the battery for the alarm system. The extremely loud, unnerving, shrieking sounds and the flashing lights of the alarm almost made a tense crowd come unglued.

"You could see in their eyes please, please make it stop," said Mundt. "You feel bad for the people that didn't understand all that was happening."

There was only one way that alarm was going to stop, and Mr. Warner decided he would get back in the dirty, chest-high water.

"I went down to the office, I had to walk through it and it was

*Chalmette High football field under water. Photograph by Wayne Warner*

*Chalmette High Principal Wayne Warner walks through the muddy water. Photograph by Debbie Gaudet*

very oily, not the Murphy Oil type of thing," said Warner. "I don't know if it picked up the oil from the cars or it was just a slick that came in from the MR-GO, wherever it came from the water definitely had a gasoline smell. It was thicker than just plain water and it had a lot of mud underneath and it was pitch black. Right when I got to the office one of my custodians Walter Barcelona was there. We go into the office and everything's turned over, topsy turvy the whole thing and we had to push things aside to get to the fire alarm box and we couldn't see it, couldn't see what we were doing. I just opened the door and started pulling the wires, he [Barcelona] pulled another battery off of it so that stopped that noise and lights."

Soaking wet, Warner made his way back to the second floor. Looking out of the windows out across the streets and into the neighborhoods, he could see people emerging from their flood-swollen homes.

"From the stairwell you could see people on the roofs," said Mundt.

"We could hear them yelling, saying we need help," said Warner.

Then some of those people began leaving their flooded

homes, frantically making their way to the school in the driving winds and rain of Katrina.

"People walked in, swam in, there was one gentleman who tried to go to Judge Perez but it kept getting deeper, so he went back to cross the street and waded into Chalmette," said Warner.

The paraplegic young men, who needed the generator to keep their ventilators running, became a top priority; someone was going to have to get fuel. There was no electricity, no water, and it was hot; they no longer had any bathrooms. The floodwater caused the plumbing to back up; there was no flushing anything down, it was only coming up. The filth and stench bubbling up out of the toilets added another layer of misery for the storm battered people.

"What we did was create a system where they went downstairs, they got the flood water, brought it up in buckets, and they would flush. They would use a disinfectant that we had. The paper waste became a problem, so we put buckets in the bathrooms, hoping people would throw the paper in the buckets," said Warner.

The school would soon be overrun with people trying to save their own lives and the lives of others.

### 3108 Gallo Drive, Chalmette

Not far from Chalmette High is Alan Clomburg's home. Clomburg is another Louisianan who has never left for a storm and was not going to leave this time. His parents Mickey and Elva Clomburg, who are in their eighties, asked if they could stay with him and he told them to come over.

After telling his wife, Jan, he thought he had the storm licked because of the minimal amount of damage to their home, he walked outside to check on his daughter's car; the water was touching the bottom of the tires on her car. He was glad his wife and three children were not at home with him.

"I walked twenty steps to my front door, to my kitchen counter grabbed her keys, walked twenty steps back, and in that amount of time the water was half way up the tires, and I turned around and went back in there and told my parents saddle up I think we got problems," said Clomburg.

By that time he had walked up to the front door again; he saw the water inching up and went back inside, but his warning was much more urgent this time and his parents could hear the tone change in his voice.

"Hey y'all hurry up and do what y'all got to do, get what you got to get; we gotta get outta here; we gotta make a move."

Clomburg ran into his garage to get his boat motor; the water was coming into the garage. He went around his house to the side door; he tried to get out through the front door but could not; the water pressure was too great. The water was now coming into the house. He went into his son's room, opened a window, and jumped outside. He had the motor and put it on. Clomburg retrieved his gas can and yelled to his parents.

"Hurry up, come on, we in trouble!"

His dad, Mickey, was dragging an ice chest filled with supplies through the water.

"What are you doing grabbing an ice chest?"

"We got water in case," his father responded.

"Man let that thing go."

Clomburg made his mother and father put on life jackets. He pulled his mother through the window, but his dad couldn't get through without help.

"Dump the ice chest, fill it up with water, and use it as a step. You gotta hurry up! Clomburg said.

Unfortunately, no matter how hard Mickey tried, that ice chest just floated and there was no way to make it a step up to the window to get out. So Clomburg and his mother grabbed him and yanked him out of the window into the waist-deep water.

"If something did happen, at least they'd float and catch on a tree."

Clomburg helped Elva and Mickey into the boat. He went back inside for a knife to cut the boat from the trailer but got sidetracked looking for his three-year-old, yellow Labrador retriever, Maggie, and his parents' golden retriever, Ba Ba (Ba-bay).

"By this time it was up past my waist, and you could see all the furniture floating around, stuff tipping over and walking on carpets like walking on a sponge cause it just bellies up," said Clomburg. "I went in the garage and hollered for the dogs. Went in the den, bathrooms, went in my sons' rooms, went in my daughter's room. So I said they've got to be in my bedroom. By this time the water's up to my chest, so I kicked the door in somehow, I guess it was just cheap doors thank God, hollered the dogs' names. Mine come to me and I grabbed her by the collar and by the time we got to the window, the water was coming in the window. I had to push her underneath the water and through the window, and I dove under the water and through the window and just pulled myself along the bricks because the current was coming pretty good. I got around the side there and put her in the boat, cut the ropes off the boat and stood between the two houses for I don't know how long."

Clomburg could not rescue Ba Ba, and as he watched a large set of trees near his home bend and sway violently, the forty-nine-year-old, lifelong resident of St. Bernard worried that if they fell toward him, he and his parents were goners. He guided the boat around to the front of the brown, brick, ranch-style home and tied the boat onto the clip of the gutter cans.

"As the water come up and got to the gutter cans, I got out the flat boat and just held the boat. I stood on the roof and I was on the least side of the wind by then. I was using the roof as a shield. I was just worried about a shingle coming across and hitting one of them in the head. A shingle come off there it was like a saw blade, just keep on going till it was out of eyesight."

The horizontal sheets of rain and searing wind made the superhuman effort of standing on a tilted roof while holding a boat in place with two elderly parents inside a monumental feat of stinging proportions.

"Every once in a while it would just catch me and just pull the boat off, and I'd just pull the boat back on but if you can imagine going uphill for eight hours, just leaning forward going uphill, you had a constant pressure against you the whole time. My daddy had a bucket, bailing the boat out from the rain; he put that on his head, so the rain wouldn't sting him."

A hardworking, blue-collar man, the gritty Clomburg, with gray hair and gray goatee, put every muscle into the effort; he felt it down to his bones.

"I was tense the whole time holding that boat, it was like vice grips, I couldn't let it go. That's the first time I ever wore a life jacket for being scared, not for drowning, for being swept away with the water."

All they were able to do was sit and ride out the storm in the driving rain; then the temperature dropped.

"After three to four hours that rain got cold and I could see my parents; they were shaking from the cold water hitting and then my mama said, 'You must be tired, you alright?'"

"I do this all day long."

The hours drifted away like a mind tripping time warp and they saw the strangest events unfold right in front of their eyes.

"I seen a duck flying over he was trying to head east but he was going south, the wind just took him and blowed him. I seen the roof blow off the house around the corner. I seen a van bobbing up and down with the windshield wipers and the lights on, and I'm thinking I sure hope some pour soul's not in there cause they're gonna drown. Seen debris, nutrias, and snakes were coming up on the roof, the turtles, I saw a mink."

Down the street he saw three elderly ladies and two guys on the corner; the wind made it impossible to communicate with them. Around four that afternoon a boat coming up Missouri Street stopped to pick up the ladies and they went off. Twenty minutes later the same rescuer came back; Clomburg called over.

"Where can we go where it's dry?"

"Nowhere in St. Bernard Parish."

"Arabi's flooded?"

"Arabi was the first to get it; they got ten feet of water."

### 1630 E. St Bernard Highway, Chalmette

The namesake of Clomburg's Gallo Street home are the ancestors of Glenn Gallo, whose house sits on property his family has owned for generations. The house sits between the Mississippi River levee and East St. Bernard Highway between Corinne Street and Charles Drive. Corinne and Charles were Gallo's great-grandmother and great-grandfather; they once owned a big swath of land that stretched from the river to the 40 Arpent Canal. Gallo's grandfather built the home in 1893 and never in its 112 years had water flooded the home; therefore, he felt no urgency to abandon his house.

"I treated it like Betsy, like Flossy in '57, and Camille in '69. I knew it was going to be a bad hurricane, I went and got some food and water and stayed home," said Gallo. "Even the hurricane in 1915 or the hurricane in 1947 didn't put water here."

Watching the big pine trees whipping in the wind, some time around 9:30 Monday morning, Gallo went out to survey the situation.

"I walked around the house to see what kind of damage I had; well, I had no structural damage at all cause the house is real,

real, real super strong, and the only thing I had was a little fascia pulled off on the front and a little fascia pulled off the side."

Stepping away from the house far enough to get a view of his roof, he surmised that looked fine as well. He was back up on his porch when he saw water pouring down Corinne and Charles Drive, heading toward St. Bernard Highway.

"It was like two rivers; it was just rolling up the street and pouring into everybody's yard. Next thing I know the water's about three feet deep across the street. The water came across the highway, when it hit the railroad track, I said oh, oh we're gonna get water over here."

The water quickly covered the train tracks that sit on the south side of St. Bernard Highway and rushed toward the Mississippi River levee sitting directly behind Gallo's house. Gallo had told his ex-wife, Susan, who was staying with him, that she would not see any water, but when it started flowing around his home, she started freaking out.

"If it gets too high we just gonna go up on the roof," Gallo said.

He quickly pulled down the ladder to his attic stairs and climbed into the attic. The fact that this house had never had water did not mean Gallo wasn't ready in case it ever did. He had built a door that locks from the inside and leads from the attic onto the flat part of his roof. He unlocked the door and opened it; he did not want to have to hack his way through his roof like so many were doing at that moment across the parish.

"There's no time for that when the water comes up. It comes up very, very quickly and that's how people drown, they get in the attic and the water keeps rising and rising, by the time they cut a hole through the roof they drown. I had thought of that years and years ago."

From the time he saw the water until it flowed past his house was as quick as "ten minutes." He thought either the water was overtopping the levees or the levees had broken. Instead of being worried about he and his ex-wife's safety, Gallo thought about the legacy of his house. His home was built on top of pillars and constructed of cypress beams, and with the exception of some vinyl siding added throughout the years, all the woodwork was original. The porch was also wooden until they replaced it with concrete, about forty years ago.

"I wasn't scared, I was getting angry cause you know this water's gonna come in my house and ruin my house, and that's what I was thinking. I had no idea whether it was gonna be waist deep inside my house or neck deep or whether I was gonna have to get on the roof."

Gallo's father used to tell him stories about the big floods that never touched his house and as the water walked up the steps he thought of all the ones before; Katrina would be the worst.

"My daddy used to tell me in 1915 when the hurricane passed before they had the levees and they had water up the highway and they had water right there in the back and this was like a little crest sticking out of the water and they didn't get no water here at all. In 1947, it was the exact same thing again. He used to tell me all the time, if you ever see water here, the rest of the parish is gone, it's under the water, so I knew that; when the water came up to my porch, I knew that everybody else in the parish was under water. That's the advantage of living in one place for years."

Just when the floodwater was an inch away from coming into the house, "it stopped. I managed to escape that water."

Most of Gallo's family lives in St. Bernard and all of their homes were flooded except his cousin, who also lives between the levee and St. Bernard Highway. The question now: would one of the oldest homes in the parish be one of the only homes not destroyed by Katrina?

## CHAPTER NINE

# Meraux, Violet, & Poydras

## Monday, August 29

### Day One

**2305 Bartolo Drive, Meraux**

It was not such a good time for David Defranza; he had been sick, having seizures, and was on medication. The forty-five year old first heard about the mandatory evacuation about twelve hours before Katrina was to hit. David's seventy-six-year-old mother, Emma, could not sleep, and they had to go out to his truck to hear any news about the storm. This went on all morning and Defranza was not about to go to sleep like his brother, Mike. Defranza was sitting on the sofa illuminated by the haunting glow of the candles when a number of transformers blew out.

"Oh God, ma, you wait right here; I'm going out in the front; I think there might be a tornado," said Defranza.

Outside in the lightning-filled sky and driving rain, Defranza hears the telltale noise.

"I can hear something like a train and my heart was pumping; I started crying and some more transformers starting going off and when they went off, I can see something like twirling."

Defranza didn't know if it hit anything or not, but it was real close and the trauma of Katrina had struck her first blow. A pine tree outside of his house snapped with a loud crack; Mike, twelve years younger than Defranza, told him at least it missed

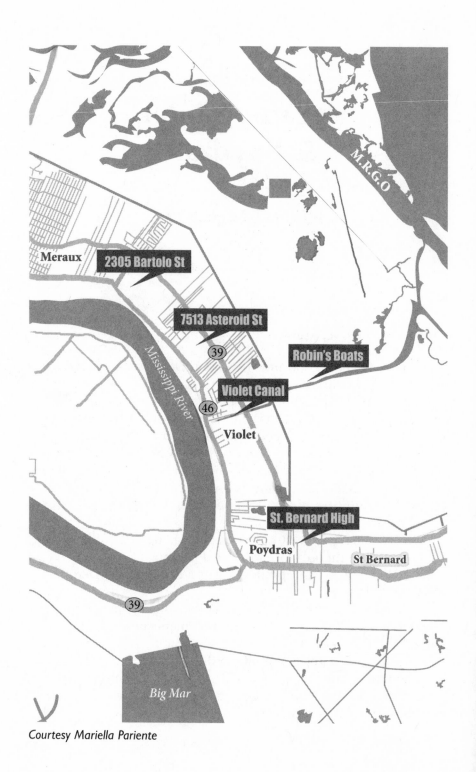

Meraux

2305 Bartolo St

7513 Asteroid St

Robin's Boats

(39)

Violet Canal

(46)

Violet

Mississippi River

M.R.G.O

St. Bernard High

Poydras

St Bernard

(39)

Big Mar

*Courtesy Mariella Pariente*

his truck. When sunlight appeared, Defranza and his mother made another walk out to his truck.

"I turned my truck radio on; then they said they had a sixty-five-foot wave 150 miles out in the Gulf; then my mama starting getting nervous, so I made 'em all put life jackets on," said Defranza. "When they all put life jackets on, I told my mama I was going outside in my truck to listen to the weather."

Emma insisted on accompanying him to the truck because she felt more comfortable being with him.

"The next thing I know, I guess God told me to open up my door, my mama was sleeping in my truck, and I look down and the water was up to my knee," said Defranza. "When I looked up the street going towards Judge Perez and the water was just rushing down the street. I started crying and I grabbed my mama out and when I grabbed her out I told her to get up in the attic."

They beat the rushing water inside their home and closed the storm door, locking it behind them. Defranza's mother was crying and screaming for her younger son.

"Wake up, Mike; wake up, Mike!"

"Ma, get in the attic, I'll get Mike," yelled Defranza.

They caught a glimpse of the water; it had risen to about three quarters of the way up the storm door; they barely had any water on the inside. Reminiscent of a bad horror flick, water was oozing through every accessible crevice in the house, from the creases in the door to the cracks of the windows.

"I just couldn't believe my eyes, it was like looking in a fish aquarium and the next thing I know the door getting higher and higher."

Defranza woke up his brother Mike and rushed him and his girlfriend, Lynn Beckwith, into the attic along with his mother; but before he could get into the attic, Defranza was caught.

"That's when the glass and windows and everything blew out and it sucked me out the front window," said Defranza. "Thank God the pine tree broke cause I grabbed on it."

Holding on for dear life in the current that tried to swallow him back into the water, he experienced what few could only imagine.

"I started feeling something biting me, I start looking at my arms and I was all full of ants cause the ants make like a little pile and they just float on top the water, and it was all over the trees. I said heck on it; I'm still alive; the ants didn't even bother me."

Defranza's brother Mike had hacked his way out of the attic

with a pry bar they had put up there before the storm hit. He climbed onto the roof. Knowing Defranza was sucked out of the house, through the shouts and the tears, they saw him holding on to the pine tree that had broken earlier.

"Hold on, hold on, Dave! Swim to the roof," Mike screamed.

"I can't swim to the roof in this current."

The current was too strong; Defranza knew it. He would have to bear the ant bites long enough for the water to settle down; he planted himself on the tree and watched as everything was devoured by the brown water. Once the current had slowed down enough, Defranza climbed from the tree to the roof and from there he saw someone in trouble.

"There was a colored man on the other street, and I could see he was hanging on; he didn't know how to swim or nothing," said Defranza.

A young girl swam from Walker's Lane to Defranza's house.

"I pointed at the guy in the tree and I said do me a favor; I was nervous and upset; I didn't want to drown; plus they had a little current and all kind of debris."

"You see that guy over there?" Defranza asked.

"Where?"

"On that tree."

"Oh my God, he don't know how to swim."

A devoted fisherman, Defranza was well stocked with life jackets; he pulled one out and gave it to the girl. She was going to try to take it to the man in the tree.

"The wind started kicking up again, so she swam over there and she got him on the roof on the next-door neighbor's house across the street and he wind up swimming after the current stopped, and they all came up on my mama's roof, and we just hung out until somebody came and got us."

### 7513 Asteroid Street, Violet

The violent weather shot something off of Paul Borden, Jr.'s roof in the Frances Place subdivision around 7:00 A.M. He opened the door to his attic and saw that the attic fan had blown away, leaving his house exposed to the pouring rain. He tried to clog up the hole, but he couldn't get anything to stick. Thirty minutes later something crashed through the picture glass window on his back door and the rain blew in that way as well. Two holes, two places for rain to come in and he wouldn't get a chance to fix either one for another hour and a half because Katrina was raging.

At home with his sixty-four-year-old mother, Gloria, and fifteen-year-old nephew, Colby, he figured around nine o'clock there was a break in the storm, which allowed him time to patch up the hole in the attic and to cover the broken window. He glanced toward his backyard patio and figured he only had six inches of water.

"When I fixed the glass on the back door, I walked back inside and took my rain suit off and my boots off," said Borden. "I was drying myself, listening to the radio. I wasn't sitting down five minutes when my mother said, 'Come look the water's coming in!'"

He thought she was talking about rainwater.

"No, you gotta come see," she said in a moment of utter bewilderment.

"When I walked in the back, I could see through the sliding glass door, the one that was still good. They must have had three foot of water in the backyard. I went to the front of the house, and I looked through the picture glass window, and I could see the trucks and garbage cans coming down the street, and I grabbed my mother and my nephew and put them up in the attic."

The forty-one-year old went downstairs; looking out of the window, he watched the water rise until it was higher than him.

"Man this is bad," Borden said to himself as he grabbed his battery-powered radio and climbed up into his attic. That's when the pressure from the water outside blew the door off its hinges, pretending Borden's house was an indoor swimming pool.

"The house started filling in," said Borden. "Within fifteen minutes I had ten and a half foot of water in my house."

Caught between the roof and accumulating water, Borden grabbed his battery-powered Ryobi Saw, along with the four batteries he had charged up over the weekend, and began sawing away at the hole in the attic, preparing for the possibility he may have to pull his mother and nephew through the expanded vent onto the roof. The attic vent was toward the peak of the house, knowing his mother would not be able to step up that high to climb out, Borden cut downward toward the base of the roof. He sawed until the hole was, hopefully, big enough to get his mother through in case the water came up any higher.

"I peaked my head out the hole," said Borden. "The water got only three inches above my sheetrock, and I said, there ain't no use in getting on the roof with all that wind blowing and the rain and my mother, I didn't want her to fall off."

Thankful they did not have to make the move to the roof, Borden, his mother, and nephew sat in the attic in disbelief, for the next eight hours. They looked out at the neighborhood, gazing at the water-covered rooftops, waiting for someone to come by in a boat. They were finally rescued when Borden's uncle found out from a neighbor that they were stuck in the attic.

"At 5:30 [P.M.] my Uncle Earl, which I never knew he was staying, and he never knew we was staying, was riding around with some friends in some boat, and the guy that lives on the corner from me seen me earlier and I'told him let somebody know. When he told them [Uncle Earl] said, 'that's my nephew,' and they came over."

Watching the boat approach the house, Borden did not even realize it was his uncle until he pulled up. They were surprised and relieved to see Uncle Earl. He was surprised to hear from his neighbor that his sister-in-law was in the attic.

"Yea, Mom's with me," said Borden.

The first thing Uncle Earl and his friend realized was that the hole Borden had made was not big enough for Borden's mother to get through.

"We had to make it a little bigger to get my mother out; she's kind of a big lady," said Borden. "They started pulling it and prying it with pry bars."

Borden grabbed some buckets, so his mother could step up and out of the hole. The three men grabbed her underneath her arms until they maneuvered her out of the hole; they sat her down on the slippery-shingled roof.

"They slid her across the roof to where the flat boat was, and they put the flat boat in gear and it was hitting the roof till where they got her right there. A total of six of us had to pick her up and put her in the boat to make sure she didn't slip off and fall."

Uncle Earl was building a two-story home a few blocks away on Landry Court. They motored over to his house and made their way to the second floor.

"I didn't think it was gonna be this bad. I stood back for hurricanes and luckily they all turned when they came through they were shoo shoos. This one came in with force."

The time on the clock in Borden's house was stuck at 9:27 A.M.

## Oyster Boats, Violet Canal, Violet

The fleet of oyster boats Doogie Robin and the other fisher-men had tied together behind the 40 Arpent levee under the high-rise Violet Bridge, near Walter Cure's place in the Violet Canal, were rocking and rolling early Monday morning. Riding out the storm with Doogie in the seventy-foot oyster boat was the "Judge," Guy Costanza. The awnings of the boats were being torn apart as Doogie was listening to reports of winds up to 160 mph and with gusts up to 200 on the radio.

"Jesus, God, Lord, they're banging; that wind is blowing; you can't put your head out the door."

Doogie did not sleep at all that night; he spent it mostly watching Katrina.

"I'm in the cabin of the boat, behind the glass, watching everything going on. Most of the night [was spent] sitting in the captain's chair, looking through the glass and up and down you know."

Of Doogie's three sons who stayed in St. Bernard to ride out Katrina, the only one he could communicate with was Don. He could not reach Pete or Chris. After he lost power, around four o'clock in the morning, he called Don to see how he was doing; he was doing fine. Just when Doogie had finally let his guard down, thinking he may have beaten Katrina, he saw a wall of water about four to five feet high coming his way.

"Jesus, God, the levee broke! Judge the levee broke!"

"The levee broke?" the Judge answered without even getting up from his bunk.

"The levee broke!"

So Doogie, who had parked his Ford F-150 truck on the levee about one hundred feet away, jumped off the boat and ran for the truck. Trying to save his truck, he got in and drove it to the top of the levee.

"When I got out the truck I was in water up to here already [chest high], so I went for the boat and I made a pass at the boat," said Doogie. "The first pass I kind of missed it; the second time I grabbed it; I got myself up on the boat. When I got on the deck of the boat I looked back for my truck. There was no more truck, my truck was gone."

The boats sat about five feet below the levee, but in nearly a blink of an eye the surge had devoured the levee.

"By the time I got on the boat, they musta had four to five feet over that levee already, I'm talking seconds. And all the boats went on the land cause the way the wind was blowing it blew all the boats on top the levee and this was nothing but concrete and that's where it was resting. If we wouldn't been in the boats, we'd a lost them all."

Doogie immediately called his son Don whose house is a little farther east from the Violet Canal on St. Bernard Highway.

"How ya doing honey?"

"Daddy, looks like everything is over," Don said.

"You got water over there?"

"I don't have any water here."

"You've got a boat over there huh?"

"Yea, I have a boat, but I'm O.K. over here."

"Don, run for the boat, run for the outboard motors, cause the levee broke, it's gonna be minutes and you gonna be flooded."

"It broke? Dad, stay on that boat, don't get off the boat, just make sure you stay on that boat."

"If you can get a hold a Pete, tell him run for the party barge."

Don called Pete, who lived off of Judge Perez in the Magnolia Plantation Subdivision farther east, and told him what his father had said about the levee.

"What are you doing, playing a joke on me?" asked Pete.

"You have a boat?"

"Yea I have a boat, but I have an attic; I'll get in the attic."

"Daddy says run for the party barge, cause he says the levee broke and there's gonna be water."

"Daddy ain't drinking huh?"

"Look Daddy ain't fooling around!"

"You don't have any water there yet?"

"I'm getting some rain under the doors."

Doogie said that around this time Pete remembered looking at his front door and there was already four to five feet of water against his door window. The door broke; the water rushed in and floated him up to the ceiling where he grabbed on to the attic ladder and climbed inside.

Don called his other brother Chris who had stayed at his home in Southlake Estates in Violet. He told Don that the water was starting to rise on his street and that he had received a call from Walter Cure who was in the Violet Canal with their father Doogie.

Chris said, "Mr. Walter said something's wrong. I'll call you in a little bit."

Someone else was calling Chris to tell him about the chaos in the canal.

The ride was like nothing else Doogie had ever experienced, even Betsy was no match for Katrina's power and fury. The seventy-foot *Donna Ann* survived the storm surge and everyone in the boats made it out alive. Doogie knew he had played a dangerous hand, but that was one game he was more than willing to play.

Don's cousin Stacy Geraci called and said he was going to come to Don's house in an effort to escape the water that was coming his way. Don and his brother, Brad, who had evacuated, own side-by-side A-frame homes on St. Bernard Highway in Poydras. They were told they had the highest place in St. Bernard, and Don said that this was probably why it took a while for the water to make it to their homes.

"It wasn't until about ten o'clock that morning when the water did get here," said Don. "It didn't come in rushing, when I watched it come up on the trailer park road next to my house it was like walking speed, maybe, and it was just coming in, not a big rush of water and that's when we got our water here."

Don said the arrival of the water coincided with the eye of Katrina passing over his house. When the wind shifted and it started getting nasty again, they jumped in a boat and headed out to Violet.

"It was probably three- to four-foot seas riding down St. Bernard Highway. When we got up there, it was like a war zone with water," said Don. "Houses in the streets, electric lines hanging down, gas lines just shooting off, we finally made it to the boats, and then we started checking to make sure everybody was O.K. I didn't go on the boat my dad was on, I went on another one of our boats, and then I could see my dad where he was; it was storming, and I seen that he was O.K. Then I started thinking about Chris and Pete."

A few minutes later Chris maneuvered down the canal joined by a couple he had picked up. The woman was seriously injured. A window inside of her house had fallen on her, badly cutting her arm and leg. Geraci's wife, who was studying to be a nurse, was taking care of the cuts. They called the Coast Guard for an emergency rescue.

"We had to have her airlifted out of there," recalled Don. "That's when Coast Guard started moving around and taking emergency cases out. The hurricane was still going on."

Don paired up with his cousin, Geraci, while his brother, Chris, and another man headed for Pete's house.

"The wind was blowing hard, seas five feet and we really didn't know if he was gonna be O.K. or what to expect," said Don. "When we finally got to where we could see his home from the highway the first thing I spotted was the window on his attic. He's got these windows on the roof and the window was broke, and when I seen that window broke I knew that he was O.K."

The water was nearly up to the eaves of Pete's house; he emerged once they were close to the house.

"He was in the attic of his house with just a pair of short pants on and that's all he had, no shirt cause he couldn't get anything. We got him off the roof of his house, and that's when we picked up his little party barge."

Since traveling down Judge Perez would have meant riding against the wind and seas, they decided to take St. Bernard Highway instead.

"As soon as we turned on the highway there was probably five or six people on the roof of a home right there, and we picked them up and put them on Pete's party barge. Then we all started coming up St. Bernard Highway to where my home is. Pete went and brought them people to St. Bernard High School."

### St. Bernard High School, 2601 Torres Dr., St. Bernard

Very few, especially St. Bernard Sheriff's Sergeant Greg Hauck and firefighters Rodney Ourso and Michael Lebeau, were able to sleep at St. Bernard High Monday morning. When the sun came up, they watched Katrina in action. Lebeau looked through the double doors and watched as a tree next to the building was pushed so hard by the wind that its leaves brushed the dirt and its roots started popping out of the ground. They had heard the reports of the officers trapped in Arabi, but they weren't sure how bad it really was. Mitch McDaniel was at the shelter working for Shari Baiamonte, the head of human resources for St. Bernard; she was in charge of the shelter. McDaniel said the wind outside was whipping around so fiercely he wondered if the building was going to hold up.

"It was harrowing, I've never seen wind that devastating," said McDaniel. "You could feel it, even on the second floor, you kept waiting for the roof to get blown off, it felt like jet engines all around you."

Lake Borgne Levee District foreman Troy Douglas, Sr. said he and one of his operators, Joseph Douglas, were outside trying to start up the generator, so he could charge the battery on his cell phone.

Residents from the lower end of the parish began arriving at the school; they informed Sergeant Hauck that something unnatural was happening.

"I started getting reports from my fishermen friends, people from the lower end saying, man that water's coming up," said Hauck. "When someone from Delacroix's telling you the water's high, you know it's high."

Listening to a small transistor radio, Lebeau remembers hearing a weather report stating that the eye wall had passed, but St. Bernard and Plaquemines were not yet out of the danger and that residents should expect the largest storm surge between the hours of ten and noon. Wondering if this was the last bit of dry land they would see for a while, the firefighters gave the smokers a final call to go outside and have their last cigarette; they were kept together in one spot for safety reasons. McDaniel assumed the eye was over the school because of the calmness of the wind. Suddenly Lebeau heard someone scream.

"When I turned and looked we saw this water rushing up the road along side the school, and that's when we started scattering everybody upstairs," said Lebeau.

"We could see the water coming down, it was about six to seven feet of water and we're still on the first floor," remembered McDaniel.

The water was flowing north to south, from East Judge Perez Drive toward St. Bernard Highway; rushing alongside the baseball and football fields, it finally reached the eastern side of the school by the office.

"It looked like somebody diverted the entire river, and the river was now taking a new course and was heading right down that street," said McDaniel.

Hauck was on the phone with his wife, telling her about the quickly rising water. People were still pulling up in their vehicles; many stalled before they could even reach the school.

People were running toward the school and Hauck began yelling for them to get inside.

"I was having to go out there and go as far as I could and pull them in," said Hauck. "I was pulling people in by the hair, by their shirts, I had people fighting me trying to stop me cause they were trying to retrieve stuff from their vehicles."

Pump operator Joseph Douglas looked around the building and saw the wall of water.

"Holy shit, look Troy!"

"Good God a-mighty!" Douglas, Sr. shouted.

The men, who were about to get tackled by the water, ran for their bulldozer and Douglas, Sr. thought, "If I can get my bull-dozer, throw my guys in the back, haul it up to the Mississippi River levee, maybe we can get to our other guys or maybe even get to the [levee district] building, because I can pretty much swim from the levee to this building, no go. Water rose so fast we got stuck out."

Inside the school the floodwaters touched off a frenetic rush. McDaniel, Ourso, Lebeau, and others yelled, "Get up to the second floor!"

Hauck made sure he got everyone he saw inside the building. The firemen sealed off the doors and windows; they had only minutes to save their gear and supplies, grabbing hats, clothing, protective gear, ice chests, food, and medical equipment. While the water seeped into the first floor, it began to rise on the outside and rose over the windows.

"Those windows outside are about seven to eight feet tall," said Lebeau. "I felt like I was in a submarine; the water was rising real fast, we had a concern, what happens if this thing takes over the second floor; where are we gonna put everybody. We can't put them on the roof; we don't know if we're gonna get tornadoes."

The two Douglas's were sitting on the bulldozer when the floodwater submerged the heavy-duty equipment.

"But as long as you hold that accelerator down that diesel engine won't kill," Douglas, Sr. explained.

With the doors shut and both men outside, Douglas, Sr. did what any sensible person with a flooded bulldozer would do.

"We bust through the building; we raised the blade as high as we can, I jumped to the top and pulled my operator up with me to get inside the building, and that's where all chaos was at."

The destroyed concrete and cinder block wall lie splattered all around the bulldozer as Douglas, Sr. and Joe thought of what they should do now that the water was rushing in through the collapsed wall.

"Once we bust through the school I'm looking down there cause we gonna jump in and run to the hallway," said Douglas, Sr. "I graduated from that school, so I pretty much know it cause I be down there everyday."

The current was strong and Joe yelled, "Do not jump, do not jump."

"Pick me up to the roof as far as you can, I can jump there and that's when I jumped and pull him up," said Douglas, Sr.

Everyone was scrambling to get to the three highest places left at St. Bernard High, the second floor, the roof, and the gym.

Hauck was leading dozens of people into the rushing water toward the gym as McDaniel was arriving with a second wave of people.

"We got as many as we could, we had to go downstairs back through the floodwaters, walk down the corridor till we reached the gym," said McDaniel.

They, ironically, waded past a painting hanging on the wall depicting an underwater scene with an octopus, shark, and dolphins. Also attached to the wall above them were book ends to the trophy case; the photograph and jersey of number twelve, legendary Eagles quarterback Duke Robin, a four-year starter from 1958-61; and the jersey of all-State basketball star Lonnie Banks from 1981-82.

The water was so strong it shoved a refrigerator through the hall. "It knocked me clear across to the stairwell," said Hauck. "We made a human chain held arm-to-arm; across the hallway people were being flushed right through us. Water was just going up the school; we were able to just pass them on to somebody else until it got too deep."

Standing in the stairwell with the water threatening to swamp them, they attempted to climb into the gym above. Crammed onto the stairwell, a sturdy six-foot-one Hauck pulled once on the solid wood door inside of a steel frame; it was locked, deadbolted on the other side. Another officer was in the stairwell on the other side leading up into the gym; he was going to shoot his way through, but the others told him to wait. Hauck could feel the panic around him, so he placed his hand around the door handle, secured an intensely firm grip, and put all of his 225 pounds into a violent jerk; the door exploded open.

"I was able to rip it off. The bottom hinge came undone," said Hauck. "There was like a stampede from there, there was probably fifty people or sixty people on the stairway just piling up."

Half of that second group ran up the stairs and into the gym, which was higher than the second floor. The other half of the group ran back to the steps leading to the second floor.

"About halfway through to the gym from there that's when the pressure from the water on the outside the building busted into the windows, and the doorways and kind of looked like the *Poseidon Adventure*," said Lebeau.

An elderly man couldn't make it out of the raging floodwater, drowning inside the school, in the frantic rush upstairs. Meantime, the crowd knocked Hauck down, stepping on him and kicking him as the people fearing for their life ran in away from the rushing water below. Brushing himself off and escaping the stomping feet, Hauck gathered the people up.

"I had asked people how many people believe in God, a majority of the people raised their hands. I told them you need to believe the Lord was working through me, and we're gonna make it out of here; we're gonna survive. I gave everybody a little speech, said some prayers just to calm people down."

The gym was now off limits. The residents at the school were now separated into two groups; one group on the second floor of the main building and the other in the gym. With barely enough time to save themselves they tried to think of what provisions they had.

"A big issue was the lack of supplies for the people. A lot of the supplies were cafeteria food supplies, things that were in cans that were in the cafeteria under water," said Lebeau. "We did bring some of that upstairs prior to when the wind started kicking up, we had a little but no where near the amount [for the] people that we had."

The second floor had started to become a human cesspool; the toilets were backing up and there was no more water.

"We told people to find paper bags, plastic bags to go in, tie it up, and get rid of it. We had half the people actually starting to clean up cause they had dogs up there," said McDaniel. "Dogs were messing all over the place, bathrooms were overflowing, so people joined in [and] started to clean up. We found a few bottles of bleach and started disinfecting everything; that's what helped."

The residents had settled in the halls and classrooms of the steamy school. The cream-colored, ceramic-tiled walls only accentuated the heat.

"A can of sardines, everybody just cramped together," said McDaniel. "You might have had two to three feet from someone else laying down, so it was just having to bare it. You couldn't complain there was nothing you could do about it."

Once Douglas, Sr. and Joe returned to where the rest of the Lake Borgne Levee District crew were staying at the school, they found out that some of the guys had already had run-ins with some of those who had evacuated to the shelter, creating a real tense scene.

"My guys was being threatened that we blew the levee, so they was afraid. They got on the roof," said Douglas, Sr.

Therefore, Douglas, Sr. confronted the crowd.

"I come through there; I said who's doing it! I'm angry, you know, nobody wouldn't open their mouth."

Being stuck on the roof, braving Katrina, was not the best of scenarios for the men with the levee district.

"On the second floor it was sucking the windows out, and as you look out the windows, the roof of the cafeteria passed," said Douglas, Sr.

He looked at his men.

"Holy shit, time to get out of here now. Look I'm gonna go get the boat and I'll be back to get y'all as soon as possible."

In the gym and in the school people were grabbing cardboard boxes and making pallets to lie on. To separate themselves from the water on the floor, they grabbed just about anything they could get their hands on to use as bedding, piling on the stage and in the seats.

"Some old clothing in the gym, blankets, that's mainly it, nothing soft. A little uncomfortable but bearable for that type of emergency," McDaniel said.

Hauck had broken into a cage that had balls in it and played basketball. He also found dry clothes from the athletic department; he passed them out to women and children, so they could take off their wet clothing. Once they had overcome the initial shock of the flood, the first responders and other concerned citizens in the school knew they would have to venture back into the floodwater to rescue those stranded in the neighborhoods.

## CHAPTER TEN

# The Horror in St. Bernard & the Hope in Hopedale

## Monday, August 29
### Day Two

### St. Rita's Nursing Home, 1422 E. La. Hwy. 46, St. Bernard

Along with daylight came alarming sounds of broken glass. The raging wind outside pushed the windows inward at St. Rita's Nursing Home. Peering out of the unbroken windows, Gene Alonzo watched the trees that surrounded the nearly isolated nursing home twist and bend with unnerving ease. When Katrina's gusts blew over the nursing home Alonzo could feel the room compress.

"It would suck the acoustic up, you could see it was making some kind of vacuum pressure or something, the acoustic ceiling, "said Alonzo. "Lord, man, I hope this roof don't start flying off with all these people." Alonzo made a sucking noise to mimic what it sounded like, "I'm thinking like an airplane wing; when that wind passes over one side, it's making that vacuum on the other side; I thought the roof was gonna start letting go."

One of Alonzo's daughters had called to check on him and Carlos.

"I was telling them we alright, I didn't want to let on that it was scary, it was bad, cause I knew they was gonna be worried more."

St. Rita's was being powered by a generator and life inside was abnormally normal with the lights and televisions on, breakfast being served, and everyone eating. Between the hours of nine

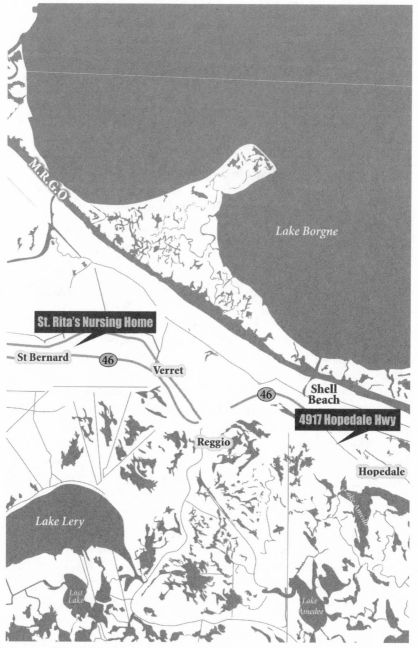

Courtesy Mariella Pariente

and ten it appeared the worst might have passed them by.

Alonzo received another call from his daughter.

"The levee broke on the industrial canal," she said.

"They ain't got no water here, it's all dry here."

Soon after the call Alonzo heard one of the young nursing home workers screaming.

"The water's coming, the water's coming!"

The terror in the young man's voice startled Alonzo.

"What the hell this guys hollering about, then the nurses start hollering," said Alonzo.

"Put everybody in the beds on their mattresses!" echoed the frantic shouts.

Alonzo had walked out into the hall from his brother's room to see what was throwing everyone into such frenzy.

"I looked, it was unbelievable; I stood stunned, the water was coming so fast, must have been like a tsunami," recounted Alonzo. "It was half way up the door; they was glass doors; they was shut, and they never had no water in this building hardly, just a little bit on the floor, and I could see the water half way up the door. I was dumbfounded just looking, all of a sudden the doors bust open, that water came through, like you were in a boat that was sinking fast."

The force of the water consumed all in its way.

"I seen a guy going with the wheelchair and that water was shoving him with the wheelchair going down the hall that current just going. They just had so many people. I was trying to save somebody and you were just going down the hall. The workers were running around this way and that way, most of them they had on their mattresses; they had a girl across the hall there she drowned. It was like whatever window broke or door that's where the water was really coming in through; it came so fast."

The pleas for help were deafening.

"They was hollering for God. One started hollering for God to help 'em and they all started. All them people was screaming for God. I ran back to Carlos's room, through the water, and boy it was still coming and I got in his room, put him on the mattress."

Carlos was having trouble processing the danger, and he and Harold Kurz, Carlos's roommate, stood up on their mattresses as the water rushed around the beds.

"Y'all stay on y'all mattress man!" Alonzo warned them.

Alonzo thought the water would soon stop, but it did not level off.

"The mattresses start floating up. The mattress starting to move, so he [Carlos] jumps off and he's really scared then, he's jumping up and down. The other guy Harold, he's staying on his mattress but he's hollering. So I'm trying to get my brother back on the mattress; I can't do it; the water's coming all the time, higher and higher first thing you know it's up to my chest. The man's floating on his mattress; I can't get Carlos on his."

The water picked up a large cedar chest and flipped it over, jamming it against the door.

"We gonna die, we ain't gonna get outta here," Alonzo thought. "We're in the room and I can't get the door open. I'm trying to hold my brother, he really don't know what's going on, he's jumping up and down, and I'm trying to hold his head above the water, I'm trying to hold him up cause he gets seizures."

Alonzo's own health problems began to surface. He had to have stints put in after an open-heart operation; now he was starting to have burning chest pains.

"My heart's trying to race up I know what it is, it's trying to speed up."

Alonzo, being the strong man that he is, firmly planted his legs, braced his body, and pulled the cedar chest away from the door.

"I'm thinking maybe we get in the attic by that time; I'm trying to get him on top of the cedar robe; I got that laying down, but he didn't want to climb up; he's just jumping."

Climbing on top of the cedar chest, Alonzo pulled the acoustic ceiling tile down; he was hoping there was an attic, but there was no such thing.

"I go back to the door and I get the door open, he's [Carlos] still jumping in the water. I see old Harold; he's floating pretty high; I don't know if he knew what was going on; he was almost to the ceiling floating way up. I couldn't take the two of 'em. I was thinking I might come back and get him, but that was stupid to even think that cause I ain't had no place to go. I was just trying to get out of there; it was all fast, you couldn't even think too much. The current's coming through this place down the hall, it was coming from the lake, by then everybody done quit hollering."

The workers had tried to bring some of the people in the kitchen; they also tried to put them on tables, but Alonzo said that didn't work.

"It [the water] was too fast, if it would have been slow, but you couldn't take them outside, there was nothing to put them on except the roof; you got the wind blowing one hundred miles an hour. Plenty of them done drowned, cause if they didn't have somebody with them, people was trying to save them but they ain't have many to save 'em."

The water was almost above Alonzo's head; he grabbed Carlos and pulled him out of the room, without a definite plan in place. He had to improvise and hope he was making the right calls to save himself and his brother. With a vice grip lock on Carlos, Alonzo pulled him out into the current in the cavernous hallway. The current was flowing north to south through St. Rita's.

"With no attic, in my mind, I'm saying my God what's this water's gonna do? We got out and I seen another man, he helped put my brother on a mattress. He was trying to get other people."

Alonzo grabbed the railing that lines the walls of the nursing home, which are used to help the elderly walk down the hall. Pulling the mattress and keeping himself above the floodwaters, he headed for the entrance hall that would lead outside. He was trying to find a way out of the raging current that had already drowned a number of residents. The current was also pushing objects out of the backdoor. Dodging the floating debris, he swung the mattress around the wall into the hall corridor and out of the current.

"I got outside, and I was behind the porch hanging on with a little rail, but I couldn't touch, I was hanging on to a window ledge or something, trying to hold my brother on a mattress."

In the fight to keep himself and his brother alive, Alonzo could not get Mr. Kurz out of his mind.

"I knew I had to get out the building. I was thinking if I had some way to go back and get the man. I hated to leave him; I couldn't go with two people."

Alonzo held on to Carlos's mattress; the floodwater was getting deeper, and with nothing surrounding St. Rita's complex except open fields and trees, whitecaps had begun to form. Carlos's waterlogged mattress was sinking and would probably not hold him much longer.

"We're just hanging there, then I'm really blanked out, I don't know what to do. I'm just hanging there trying to hold on to him on the mattress; he's huddled up, scared."

Then Alonzo spotted Sal Mangano, Jr., the owner's son; he had pulled a boat up to the edge of the roof.

"I don't know where he came from, he come with a boat, a couple of 'em. He seen me there."

"Put him in the boat, and we'll put him on the roof," Alonzo recalled Mangano, Jr. saying.

"They had some guys; they was trying to get people out too."

Alonzo climbed on top of the nearby railing and helped get Carlos into the boat. He managed to do this without slipping into the current below.

"I put him on the roof of the building, probably would have drowned if he [Mangano, Jr.] wouldn't have come with that boat."

Mangano, Jr. told Alonzo to get on the roof, so he could pass people up to him. Then a nurse climbed up to the metal roof, followed by others who had started to bring up rescued patients.

Alonzo was impressed with one of the young workers rescuing the patients; even though this young man did not know how to swim, he continued to jump back into the water to try to save whomever he could.

"He was a brave son of a gun cause when you don't know how to swim, jump in the water like that. He was getting people, good thing for him."

All along Alonzo's chest was pounding with pain.

"I'm spraying that nitro in me. It's a little spray bottle, in my mouth, kind of relieve me for a little while."

Several of those who had been saved were heavy; the helpers were having a difficult time getting them out of the boat and onto the roof, especially in Katrina's bruising precipitation.

"Some of them ladies weigh a couple of hundred pounds, and they ain't got no strength at all in them legs or arms," said Alonzo. "You don't know how to grab them and they're passing 'em to the roof up there to me and this nurse. We're laying 'em down on the roof and this rain's stinging, blowing."

The rescues were physically demanding and dangerous; the boats would dock against the roof and would bang against the building whenever Alonzo or the nurse would help someone to safety.

"I believe we broke one lady's ribs, trying to get her on the roof. The roof was on an angle; the wind was blowing; I was trying to pick up a lady cause you could hardly pick them up [on a sloped roof, leaning over]. They was hollering, 'aw, aw you killing me.' You [pulling them up and] they couldn't even crawl."

But there was one woman Alonzo knew was more able-bodied than she had claimed.

"If you want to live you better try and help here, try and shove yourself up man, cause I can't go no more here!"

She did not help, but they did get her up on that tin roof.

"Then they couldn't get no one else. We had eight or nine people, but they was getting some on the other end [of the building] too I couldn't see."

The people sitting on the roof were hysterical, yelling and crying. Alonzo would snag mattresses as they floated by, trying to keep the slicing rain from hurting the sickly and terrified elderly.

"You couldn't pick up the mattress cause they was getting waterlogged. I had a knife; me and the nurse cut the top off the mattress to cover them."

Alonzo was unsure of how much time had passed, but it was much longer than he wanted.

"We're gonna die on this roof if somebody don't come get us. Seemed like a good while there, the rain was stinging, cold, we're soaking wet. Plenty of them was half dead before without this hitting 'em."

### 4917 Hopedale Highway, Hopedale

Hanging on to a hackberry tree for all his life was worth, Charlo held that ten-foot two-by-four in one hand and the life ring in the other in case the tree snapped. He knew he had to be at least fifteen to twenty feet up in the tree, which stood anywhere from fifty to seventy-five feet tall. Cajuns in South Louisiana call the hackberry *bois connu*, which means known tree. With cuts and bruises on his hands, elbows, knees, chest, and the bottom of his feet, Charlo had become intimately familiar with his now favorite botanical friend. The tree had been helping him win the fight, but he had another round with Katrina coming; this time the winds would blow in a northeasterly direction. The wind had ramped up fast, and soon it was blowing so strong Charlo could not keep his eyes open.

"I started thinking I don't know how much water they did get [in Hopedale]. So when the winds switched the water was going down quick. Stronger wind was blowing, the water was going down, I couldn't watch it go down but it didn't take long, fifteen minutes, a half an hour. It went down very fast."

Charlo, out there in the marsh alone, was getting beat up for the second time, more debris slicing him, drawing blood as it mixed with the rain dripping down his body. He was numb from it all. He could not tell the wind from the debris from the rain, it all hurt. The water rushed back out to the Gulf as if some one had unplugged the world's largest garden tub.

"It blew all the water away from land. There ain't nothing to hold it back like the levee protecting people."

As the water receded, knowing he had had nothing to eat since Sunday, Charlo did not want to spend any more time than necessary in the tree. In that tree he knew there was absolutely no prospect of getting food or clean water. To make matters worse, he still had no idea where he was in relation to where the wave had thrown him into the marsh. Despite the dropping water line, there still was not enough exposed to make out the landscape.

"I couldn't tell where I was at, I was disoriented."

Once the water had dropped low enough, he shimmied his way down the hackberry tree until his feet finally touched the flooded earth. Hours upon hours he had sat in that rugged tree refuge like a snake or a monkey; now he could feel something below his feet.

"The water got down to my neck level and I moved around."

He started looking for anything recognizable; he finally saw something protruding from the water.

"I seen them palm trees [in his neighbor's yard], that's when I knew where I was. A palm tree in her front yard, it made me feel awful glad, sure ain't got too far to go and the water was still falling and getting close to dark, and I know I was taking a chance to swim across Bayou La Loutre to where those palm trees are. I didn't know what was over there, but I knew it was gonna be better than maybe where I was at."

Surprisingly, he saw something else that made his heart race with delight.

"Then I saw a red container in my yard, like a ship container. See the top of that, maybe a couple of inches out of the water. It's an eight-foot high by forty-foot long container. So I said I'm going for the container."

The container was Charlo's garage and work shed, where he

stored all of his fishing equipment like shrimp nets and poles. It had served him well, and had it been a regular old garage it would have been headed out to the Gulf of Mexico with everything else trapped in the current; all of his gear would have been lost.

Toothless, without a phone, shoes, or glasses, and battered like a whipping post holding a life ring, Charlo had to swim to the only remnants on Hopedale he would risk his life to reach.

"I got on top of the ring, and I started dog paddling with the life jacket on, and I got on top the ring, and I wasn't losing my ring," said Charlo. "I knew the way the tide was moving out the water, going out so fast I paddled on an angle into the current cause I didn't want it to bring me out with it. It was stronger than I can handle swimming; even if I was a young twenty-one-year old, I couldn't; it was too strong.

Swimming hundreds of feet, the current desperately tugged at him, and Charlo had to manipulate that current to carry him as well. It was a dangerous, delicate balancing act; one miscalculation and no one would ever know how much he had endured to survive to this point. With every stroke and kick the scarred Charlo moved closer and closer to his container. Once he was close enough to grab his red container, he pulled himself on top of the driest section. Breathing heavy sighs of relief, Charlo was home. The container was all that was left on his land, and this would have to be his safe haven.

There was not much for the battered and bleeding Charlo to do, except try to rest as best as he could on the steel container. He knew his brutal fight for survival would end prematurely if he did not find food or drink soon.

"I knew the whole night and whole day I didn't eat or drinking nothing. I put in my head I got to get outta here."

It was eerily quiet as dusk turned to night, and without light Charlo could barely see his hands in front of his face. He was too tired to worry about much; he could not even muster the strength to worry about snakes or any of the other varmints that might make their way on top of the dry portion of his container. He did think long about his wife, Terry, and daughter, Charity, who he hoped did not think he was dead. He fought like a mad man to right, admittedly, the worst decision he had ever made. Then a single sign of life flashed in the sky.

"The only thing I seen that night is a q-beam light, like a search light. Somebody was lighting it and I hollered and I blew a whistle. I had on the life jacket, a water whistle but I knew they couldn't hear me it was too far."

Maybe he was not all alone, but he figured no helicopters would be coming his way; it would be days before any boats or rescue workers would even think about going that far down in the parish. In the heart of flooded lower St. Bernard, Charlo understood that if he was going to be rescued, his container would be the beginning of a very long walk, and he needed to rest his badly swollen feet.

"I put in my head that when daylight comes no matter what I gotta walk out of Hopedale."

## CHAPTER ELEVEN

# Rescues Begin

## Monday, August 29

### Day Two

With floodwater creating a sea around the courthouse, home of the thirty-fourth Judicial District Court, and the sheriff's department, Sheriff Stephens and two other deputies attempted to launch a twenty-foot flat boat to rescue the detectives stuck inside the bureau in Arabi. They hopped into the boat, cranked up the one hundred-horsepower motor, and took off against the high wind and choppy brown floodwater. The sheriff couldn't get much farther than the towering oak trees in front of the facility and had to turn the boat around. Trying to figure out any way to get to his guys, Stephens thought of a special he had just watched on cable TV.

"The thing I watched on HBO® the week before, the guys that ride these giant waves and get towed out on a Sea-Doo®," said Stephens. "I thought the guys riding the Sea-Doos® were crazier than the guys surfing, but we had four brand new Sea-Doos® on the back lot. So I mobilized them and put four deputies on them."

He sent two men, specifically, to check on the detectives, Captain Chad Clark and Major Pete Tufaro. Clark had grabbed a life jacket and was snapping it on as the sheriff's cousin and Chief Deputy Tony Fernandez walked up.

"Son what are you doing?"

"The sheriff wants me to go up, get on a [Sea-Doo®], and go up to Arabi to check on the detectives."

"Are you losing your mind?" asked the usually calm Fernandez.

"That's what the sheriff wanted," responded Clark.

"Is he losing his mind!" said Fernandez adding curse words to the dialogue. "You ain't going."

"That's what the sheriff wanted."

In spite of the dangerous conditions, Clark and Tufaro jumped on their Sea-Doos®, hit the gas, and pulled away from the courthouse headed to Arabi.

"We never really knew how high the water was; we got on St. Bernard Highway from the courthouse and went straight down," said Clark. "The water was to the red lights in the street, you could sit there and touch 'em sitting on a [Sea-Doo®]. We didn't know if they [the detectives] had life jackets."

Clark's unfathomable ride took him past the port and the parish's dormant, iconic Kaiser Aluminum smokestack. By the time they made it to Meraux pasture, an open field right before the Palms Casino and Truck Stop, Clark felt more like he was riding out in the open waters of the Gulf of Mexico than half a dozen feet above an asphalt highway.

"I guarantee the waves were six foot rollers coming down St. Bernard Highway going toward the courthouse," said Clark. "We jumping the waves like we're playing but we're really try- ing to make headway to get up there to get to them. We was going against the wind in the waves, I said there's no way we can survive this we're gonna die."

Dodging downed power poles and power lines along the way, Clark came upon a lady in a two-story building holding an infant girl outside the window yelling at him for help.

"I'll be back; we're going to the sheriff's office substation; I promise you I'll come back and get ya."

Clark and Tufaro arrived at the detective bureau and met up with the men. The two stayed just long enough to relay the mes- sage that the sheriff was coming back to pick them up. Riding with the direction of the waves, as he headed back to the court- house, Clark had one thing on his mind, to get back to that woman and her baby girl. He pulled his Sea-Doo® alongside the building directly across from the Rite Aid drug store at the cor- ner of St. Bernard Highway and Lebeau St. The woman could hardly contain herself although she was not sure what to think of the rescue.

*Riding a Sea-Doo® through the storm, Major Pete Tufaro checks on men at the detective bureau. Photograph by Al Clavin*

"I never thought y'all was gonna come back," she said.

Clark grabbed the baby out of her mother's reluctant hands, loosened his life jacket, placed her snuggly between his chest and the jacket, and strapped her in as tight as he could. He handed the mother a life jacket; she got on and wrapped her arms tightly around Clark's waist, and they took off toward the sheriff's department.

"I'll never forget that baby's face and she's [the mother] like 'I don't know if we can make it,'" said Clark.

They fought the brutal conditions in the water above St. Bernard Highway, and Clark saved this woman and her infant child. Clark updated Stephens on the condition of the men and the building. Knowing his men were alive and ready to be rescued, Stephens took a second stab at launching the flat boat with one other deputy.

"It was bizarre running it," said Stephens. "The wind still blowing hurricane velocity and you had to duck under the red lights and it was sea conditions. I grew up on the water and it didn't bother me, but it was such an interesting twist to this whole thing."

The sheriff believes he experienced roughly four-foot seas on

*Captain Chad Clark at the courthouse the evening Katrina rolled through.*
*Photograph by Errol Schultz*

the highway and by Meraux's pasture he felt the chop grow to at least six feet just like Clark had warned him. Once the sheriff had made it to the substation, the detectives wasted no time getting out of the beaten building. The men stepped out of the window they had smashed open, grabbed onto the flagpole, and one by one climbed into the boat until there were fourteen men in the flatboat.

"Very heroic, it took a lot of guts for these guys. [They] came up on [Sea-Doos®] and scouted the area first," said Doran. "I think what his [Stephens] concern was, the building being compromised and coming apart and all of us drowning. He came himself."

When the boat carrying the rescue men pulled up to the courthouse, Stephens saw his wife and sons, thankful that their worst fears had not come true.

"They were hugging me and they said 'we'd never think we'd see y'all alive again," said Stephens. "It wasn't that bad."

Soon after his return, Stephens, standing in the lobby of the courthouse with water up to his knees, was surrounded by people; a moment of reckoning had arrived. The lobby was filled with judges, the district attorney, the assessor, court personnel, deputies, and their families. The courthouse had quieted to a murmur and Stephens's wife told him he had to say something.

"Everybody had this look of disbelief on their face, and you

*Sheriff Jack Stephens after picking up his men at the detective bureau.*
*Photograph by Al Clavin*

could see it, and I'm sure I must have had it too although I was busy; so, it wasn't like I was just sitting there stunned like this can't be happening to me."

Then Stephens gave a nearly thirty second speech.

"We're in the middle of the largest natural disaster in the history of the United States, and what we do over the next seventy-two hours will judge us, and it's how people will define us and how we will define ourselves for the rest of our lives, and there are people right now whose lives are in danger, and I know all of the deputies and everyone here knows what to do. We've been well trained; there's no reason to panic. We're gonna be heroes."

It was the last command Stephens said he gave for the next five days.

Knowing people were probably dying in their homes, Colonel Forrest Bethay, one of Stephens's rank, helped take the lead in getting people rescued. He approached one of his captains and a major.

"Y'all have to go out and start commandeering boats, go get food, water, get our guys started rescuing people," Bethay ordered. "Get water, medicine, go to Walgreens, go in and get the blood pressure medication, band aids, Mercurochrome, methialade, anything for cuts, bandages."

*Water reaches up to the sign leading into the Port of St. Bernard. Photograph by Al Clavin*

Bethay knew he could rely on his narcotics officers to select the right drugs for the people who needed their medication. He soon had officers locating supplies and running rescue missions. The courthouse was beginning to swell with the hundreds and hundreds of additional people.

"We knew a lot of people would stay in St. Bernard; they're not gonna leave their homes even though you tell them to leave," said Bethay. "We were worried about people dying!"

### Civilians to the Rescue

Fingers stiff, arms sore, cold, and wet Wayne Whitfield, his brother, Chris, and friend Danny survived Katrina and her fury in his small sixteen-foot fiberglass boat on Livingston Avenue in the Carolyn Park Subdivision. It was about 3:00 P.M. when he saw a guy paddling in a canoe pass his house.

"There's people all over the roofs."

It was their call to move. Minutes later, about a block from Whitfield's house, they made their first rescue. They came across a crippled, elderly lady, two young kids, and their mother. Because he had a small boat he could not take them all together.

"I've got to take your kids first," Whitfield told the mother.

*Deputies rescue a family out of their attic. Photograph by Errol Schultz*

She did not know these men and was very reluctant to send her children off with complete strangers.

"I promise I'll be back; I'm gonna bring them to a shelter; I will be back," Whitfield remembered.

Stressed and unsure of what was coming next, she gave in and put her boys, who Whitfield thinks were around eight and eleven years old, in the boat. Whitfield drove up to St. Bernard Highway and headed east toward the courthouse where he dropped the boys off. There were plenty of officers and officials taking care of the hundreds who had pulled up in their own boats, were rescued, walked, or swam there.

The front of the courthouse complex now looked more like the place Whitfield would launch his boat from, Delacroix, his favorite fishing hole; but the surrealism wasn't lost on the men. Roughly thirty minutes later they arrived back at the house to pick up the boys' mother and the crippled, elderly woman. The men had a tough time lifting the older woman into the boat, but the women were more than grateful.

No matter which direction they turned the men saw scores of people on their roofs, but with limited room they would have to make as many runs as they could with the daylight they had left. However, the runs were not without problems; many power lines had snapped and power poles were leaning, making riding the streets a real hazard, so there was no moving fast. After dropping off the women, they spotted a man in the water.

"There was a guy seventy-five years old, all I saw was his head sticking up. I thought he was dead. He was blue in the face and everything," said Whitfield.

But the man was not dead, and they pulled him out of the floodwater into the flatboat. The man was only capable of nodding his head. Whitfield, knowing this was potentially a life-or-death mission, moved as fast as the path ahead of him allowed.

"He needed medical attention."

Whitfield and crew made their third drop at the courthouse. The men went back and forth to their Arabi neighborhood. One time an elderly woman and her two sons were stranded about a block from Whitfield's house. They pulled her off the roof, brought her to the courthouse, returned, and did the same for the two men. One of the sons tried to hand Whitfield a hundred dollar bill for saving his mother.

"Keep your money; you're gonna need it," said Whitfield.

"No, you saved my mom."

"I don't want your money; this is something we have to do right now; I'm glad to do it. If I was in your situation I would hope you would do it."

"I'm gonna remember you."

"Do that."

There was massive destruction with mass confusion, and the men with the boats were the most relieving sight around. With every person the men rescued, the emotions of the people they had saved varied.

"They were excited, some of them were crying, some of them were just too cold to do anything," said Whitfield. "They knew at that point they were going to be rescued cause everybody that stayed went through a long ordeal. I'm sure it was just as scary for them as it was for me. It took a long time to get them all. I'm sure they were wanting to be out quicker, but I promised 'em I would come back and I did for everybody that I saw. I remembered what houses they were on. I made a promise that I wouldn't stop until I got the forty or so people I saw."

All of the people Whitfield and his crew had saved were from his immediate neighborhood. Unfortunately, they were running short on daylight.

"I felt good doing it; I felt bad that everybody lost everything; I knew they needed help, and I wasn't gonna leave them. I did see boats going up and down St. Bernard Highway, and I told them there were people back here and none of them came. I don't know who they were, but they were looking for dogs."

Whitfield shouted at some of them, "Man there's people back here!" Whitfield said his boat was the only one running in his square of about three to four hundred homes.

"We had a couple of people that were diabetics who needed medicine, so we got them first, brought everybody to the courthouse. The cops had very few boats to work with, so they were encouraging us to go out and look if we could. We had no weapons, so we were basically taking a chance."

However, the obligation weighed heavily on Whitfield, Chris, and Danny; they knew if they did not get to those stranded before darkness set in, people could lose their lives. Once nightfall hit anyone in a boat would have to park it, because there were no lights on anywhere. There would be only moonlight, if they were lucky, but even that would not be enough light to venture out on rescue missions.

"I was getting a little worried and we had to go find a couple of friends that we could stay by because everything here was under water."

Whitfield, who graduated from Chalmette High in 1986, underestimated Katrina and reflecting back he wonders what would have happened if people like him would not have been there to help those who could not help themselves.

"These people might not have made it, they would have died. A lot of them were elderly. I had a friend who lives in Chalmette, I saw him the same day and he was rescuing people in his area and he must have rescued maybe fifty to sixty, cause he just kept going, and I'm glad there was people like me, my friend, and other people. There was hundreds of boats saving people. These people had no boats; they were on top their roofs the whole time with 120 mph winds at least. We had a boat to duck and cover; these people had nothing; I mean they were just stuck out in the elements getting hit with whatever was being flung at them. I saw some of the stuff flying; I can only imagine being just stuck out on top of your roof what that must have felt like."

## Andrew Jackson: Unofficial Shelter

The wind made it difficult for Eric Colopy to hear anything at Andrew Jackson High School. He had saved Mr. Billy, was wet, and felt the pressure of the event unfolding upon him and in front of his eyes. Having been one of the first people to arrive at A.J., he knew there were others that needed his help. It was not long before someone who saw Colopy and Mr. Billy park their boat at the school wanted to get their attention. So, when Colopy saw the water splash he knew someone was shooting a gun; he realized this was not an aggressive act but a call for help. He did not know what kind of gun it was and nor did he care.

"I was looking around and I didn't see him, then I seen him waving his hand in the window," said Colopy. "He was in a two-story apartment."

Colopy told Mr. Billy to stay there while he went to get the man shooting that gun. He started up his boat and took off by himself; he pulled up to the apartment building, noticing the man was standing in water on the second floor.

"That's why he wanted to get out."

And just like any other rescue, one usually led to others. He guided his neighbor's seventeen-foot flat boat from apartments to houses.

"I wind up getting, like three apartments down from him, five or six people [were] there and we brought them to A.J."

For a man who loves to scuba dive and wind surf this was one outdoor adventure Colopy never thought he would ever take up, especially after moving to St. Bernard from Metairie nearly a decade ago. His wife, Debbie, is from St. Bernard. Colopy dropped off the boatload of people and headed out for more, carrying his ax in case he had to chop his way through any attics.

"I'm thinking get as many people out."

He did not have to travel far for another rescue; he closed his eyes and concentrated, listening for anyone who may be trapped.

"I'm hearing people hollering 'help;' they're banging on the roof; so I pull up to the house, alright I'm here, calm down. I'd hit the roof with the ax, and I'd climb up there and knock the vent off, talk to them, calm them down, give them water.

By this time another boater was bringing Bubby Bodden and his cat to Andrew Jackson High. Bubby was almost in shock after seeing his neighborhood under so much water. They coasted to a

*Evacuees on the breezeway at Andrew Jackson High School. Photograph by Eric Colopy*

covered breezeway between two buildings and Bubby and his freaked-out cat, Neo, climbed to the second floor walkway. He figured fifteen people had arrived before him. Most, if not all, were picked up by Colopy. Several people had their animals with them; they were outside on the breezeway because the heat made it unbearable to go inside.

Having made it through the storm and then to higher ground, Bubby, again, began thinking of his next step He methodically planned his every move, and like in a good game of chess, he studied and played patiently.

"My first thing I was looking for a place I could put my back pack, put my cat up and be in a safe area, and I was able to do that," said Bubby.

If anyone was going to get any rest it would have to be outside on the cement in the breezeway, no one wanted to go into the sweatbox inside. Since A.J. was a magnet school, Bubby knew they had a wrestling team and went looking for the mats they wrestle on inside the gym.

"Me and two other guys walked on the roof to the gymnasium and some of the windows were open and we were looking in and just seeing the water in the gym. The water was up to the bottom of the (basketball goal) net on a ten-foot rim. All the mats were floating so we knew we couldn't get those."

Although they missed out on something to sleep on, they stumbled on to something more important.

"We noticed that the window of the concession stand was open," said Bubby. "I got in a boat and me and another guy paddled over to it, and there was five cases of Kentwood water. We were able to grab four cases of water and some chips and stuff that were floating and brought that up to the people. You look at it as providers of a tribe."

Even though they had banded together, Bubby still kept an emotional distance.

"People you don't know, people don't know you. Kind of relax with it. Everybody went through a lot of stuff to get to where they are. No freaking out, it was a very good group of people, although you're kind of a little standoffish."

Colopy said he and Mr. Billy were the first people at A.J. and every person they picked up seemed to look to them as the leaders of the pack. Several people turned to Colopy to ask what they could do or if they could have some water.

"This is for everybody help yourself; if you're hungry get ya something; make yourself at home," said Colopy. "We had a couple of old ladies they were sweeping up and keeping everything clean and organizing everything."

At dusk, Colopy risked riding in blackness to get to the people he heard in their attics. He estimated that he brought about twenty-five people to A.J. that first afternoon and evening. There were a number of people trapped inside their homes without a way onto their roofs, and with time being so precious, Colopy wanted to help as many as he could out of their attics.

"I hit that [exhaust fan] one time and that came off and they have a small hole and people were trying to squeeze out. Whoa, whoa, whoa how many do you have in there? Look here's some water, back up we gonna make the hole bigger, so I chopped a few times, made the hole bigger and they come out."

When they climbed out into the darkness he gave them some extra waters and told them to stay put until he could come back.

"Just stay on the roofs I've got to get people out the attics first," said Colopy. "They was cool with that as long as they was out the attics. It was pitch dark; they were in water waist deep in the attics. It's like they couldn't sit down; they couldn't do nothing; they were panicking. Every third house they had people banging on the roofs that didn't have no way to get out. The people on the roofs already had axes and ways to get out."

Soon Colopy returned to the school and parked the boat for the night. He wondered who else was out there, but they would have to wait until the break of dawn. They had what they needed to survive the night, and people cordoned off space on the concrete breezeway to rest. It had been an exhausting day and most probably had not yet had the chance to process the full extent of the tragedy. Sizing up the situation, Bubby was content with playing the hand dealt so far, but that did not mean he was not thinking about what was next.

"Sleeping on cement was what it was, but it was better than sleeping in an attic or sleeping on the roof," said Bubby. "It was uncomfortable but it wasn't that bad. I was in a mode, give me two hours of sleep then I'm good. You kind of wanted to be aware of the situation that next step."

### Chalmette High Gets First Rescue Boat

Although the storm was still raging outside, the streets around Chalmette High had filled up with boats. The school custodian Walter Barcelona had parked his truck on the ramp of the gymnasium; it inadvertently became a makeshift boat dock and launch with the back of the truck about three feet in the water.

"The first boat came up and it was a gentleman who had a couple of people with him, and I believe he had an elderly mother, some of our guys saw him from our window," said fireman James Liccardi, Jr. "We pointed for him to go to the gym, some of our guys got to the gym."

In the boat, soaking wet, were Donald Colletti and his neighbors Jim Pitre and Pitre's mother, Joyce, and a handful of people they had rescued.

Colletti had stayed behind because he was worried about looters after the storm and wanted to protect his home at 2921 Plaza Drive in Chalmette and business, A-1 Outboard Motors in St. Bernard. The forty-seven year old sent his wife, Rita, twenty-two-year-old son, Donald, Jr., and twenty-seven-year-old daughter, Natasha, to Texas. He had convinced them to leave without him under the pretense he was going to grab a few precious family items and meet them in Texas.

"I went down the road to Hopedale and got my big boat,

which is called the *Big Fish*, filled it up with 140 gallons of gas, [and] put it on a trailer in front of my house hooked to my truck," said Colletti. "Don't ask me why I did it, but I did it. I put 110 gallons in the boat, and I had six, six-gallon jugs in the boat that I filled."

Some of his neighbors who had stayed saw the stocked boat.

"Are you staying?"

"Yes."

"If the water comes up I'm gonna be in my house, come get me."

"Quite a few neighbors told me this within the surrounding blocks," said Colletti. "Most of them were joking but I was not."

Family members continuously called, wanting to know when he was hitting the road; his answer was always, "I'm gonna be in Texas don't worry about me."

Then his younger brother, Brian, called.

"You're not leaving are you?"

"No, but don't tell nobody."

Later that day he called Rita wanting to know where their family pictures were and she wanted to know which pictures in particular he was talking about.

"All the pictures, the roofs starting to come off the house and I want to get everything and anything that I can find of our past life that I can save."

Rita was crying and wondering about the safety of her husband now that she knew he would not be joining her in Texas.

"She told me where some of them were at. I was able to save my wedding photo album, my twenty-fifth wedding anniversary album, went around the house in every single room and took every picture off of every wall, every picture off of every night-stand and dumped all my hunting gear out my totes, filled my totes up and put all of that in the boat."

His friend Bob Roberts called to tell him the levees had broken and his seven-year-old dachshund, Peanut, may have been the first to know.

"I looked outside, didn't see any water and looked for my dog and my dog high-tailed it into the back room," said Colletti. "He must have heard the wave coming. I went and found the dog, and when I got back into the living room the water was already four feet up the door, and it was pouring in from all the cracks in the house. I opened the door and it washed me and my dog through the living room, through the dining room into the kitchen, into the game room in the bedroom where . . . I got back on my feet [and] got out of the house; by that time the water was up to the gutter cans of the house and I got in the boat."

Colletti's neighbors directly across the street were Pitre and his wheelchair-bound mother, Joyce.

"Let's go, we got to get outta here," said Pitre. "Donald's gonna be outside."

Mrs. Joyce shot back, "You got to put my brand new comforter up high, so it don't get wet."

Pitre could hardly believe his mother's priorities at that moment.

"Don't worry about that comforter."

"I'm not leaving unless you do that comforter."

Agitated, Pitre placed the comforter on top of a wall unit and they hurried out of the house.

"You can hear as we're going out the stuff turning over from the water floating it up and turning it over," said Pitre.

When Colletti made his way outside, he saw them hanging on the gutter cans floating in the water and hollering for help.

"I immediately cranked up the boat, pulled across the street, this was in the eye of the storm which the winds died down to about sixty miles an hour," said Colletti. "I got across the street; meanwhile, they got cars and trucks coming up the street eight to ten feet of water, cars and trucks didn't even have time to sink yet, and they're coming up the street pounding into houses and into my boat."

Pitre and his mother grabbed on to the twenty-two and a half-foot MAKO offshore fishing boat with the 225 horsepower outboard motor.

"The wind just took us four or five houses completely across the street in just a matter of seconds," said Pitre. "I couldn't get no footing cause I couldn't touch the ground no more and we got wedged between two houses in the front yard on the same side of the street as Donald."

Pitre was able to get his feet on a fence and positioned his body underneath his mother while Colletti pulled her from inside the boat and the men rolled her in. Mrs. Joyce although elderly and sickly was of sound mind.

"I grabbed my mom, and I looked at her, and Donald helped my mother get situated into the boat and he put life preservers on her back so she would be comfortable," said Pitre. "We started to make it back out to the street [when] we started hearing screaming."

The men saw several people stuck underneath a carport; Pitre dove in the water to help them, and he heard his mother yell his name. Colletti checked on Mrs. Joyce.

"I asked her if she was fine and she shook her head yes," said Colletti.

The boat had a turnbuckle on the trailer attached to the eye-hook of the boat next to the boat's wench.

"I need something to get this turnbuckle off," Pitre yelled to Colletti.

"He gave me the smallest pair of needle nose pliers you ever seen in your life. I straightened out that eyehook, and I had popped the boat loose; when that boat came up it really came up cause it lost the trailer and that's when I went to the back of the boat, I asked for a rope and tied the boat up."

After Colletti threw Pitre the rope he turned back to Mrs. Joyce.

"I asked her if she was alright again and she didn't answer me," said Colletti. "She didn't make any signals to me all she did was look up at me with her eyes."

There were three people trapped under a carport roof, and Pitre tried to hook their boat to the *Big Fish* in order to yank it out. Pitre remembered one of the men being "white and look[ing] like a statue." Colletti wanted to know if Mrs. Joyce needed anything.

"She was kinda shivering and next thing I knew I turned around and looked and she was at her end, that last little shake to her and she was gone; she died," said Colletti.

Pitre climbed into the back of the boat as the second half of Katrina was beginning to start.

"Jim your mother passed away," said Colletti.

"You wouldn't believe the first emotion that went through my brain was my mom's dead damn what am I gonna do," said Pitre.

Colletti grabbed his long-time friend and pulled him into his arms. Pitre was in a calm state of shock as he thought about his mother and asked her for guidance.

"Mom I know you're gone but what you want me to do, right then it came to me, it's like she spoke right out."

Pitre told Colletti their mission.

"Donald nobody else is going down; we're gonna get every-body we can."

"If it would have been my mother that would have passed away I would of went ballistic," said Colletti. "But Jimmy held it together and knew that we had a job to do, and he did it. Not one time did I see him cry."

The men rescued a few more people and pulled the *Big Fish* into the Chalmette High parking lot, right into the bed of the truck parked in front of the gym. They were greeted by Fire Captain Eddie Appel and several other firemen who had seen the bittersweet reality of Katrina. The firemen pulled the people out of the boat and over the truck's ceiling and hood. The men saw Joyce Pitre's body covered with life jackets. Since this was the very first boat to pull up to the school and it contained a dead woman, the firemen were concerned about this being a sign of things to come. They did not have any place to put the body.

"We told him we didn't have any place to keep her," said Appel.

"We didn't know how high the water was gonna get. I'd hate to put her downstairs and have her float off again. We told him we couldn't take her and he seemed to understand the situation."

"They were gonna find a place for her where it wouldn't upset the other people in the building," said Colletti.

With the second half of the storm kicking up violent wind, Colletti said a deputy told him he was going to commandeer the boat because it was too dangerous to go back out. Colletti and Pitre looked at each other.

"We made promises to people; I told 'em I'd go get 'em," Colletti remembered. "They got people hanging on power lines right now, hanging on light posts, hanging on their gutter cans; how long can they hold on?"

"I'm not gonna be responsible if y'all die."

"Fine, we didn't ask you anyway."

With Mrs. Joyce lying in the boat, the two men looked past the danger they were in to rescue others.

"We went and gathered up all the people that we promised and quite a few more," said Colletti.

However, saving lives meant exposing those people to the death of Mrs. Joyce, which made everyone emotional.

"You ought to seen the people's faces when they seen the dead people in the boat. When they found out it was my mother then they started looking at me like wow, damn," said Pitre. "They thought I was crazy too, but I wasn't crazy pulling people off of rooftops, breaking their way out of the roof seconds from drowning."

Pitre says despite his steady nerves it was Colletti who took charge, keeping people calm especially the children.

"We had this man and a lady, two girls, and a younger sister, and the younger sister she was the only one that was really, really panicky," said Colletti. "She was out the box, screaming and hollering we gonna die, she sees this dead lady there and she screaming 'we gonna die, we gonna die' and everybody in the boat started getting panicky too."

With the winds estimated in the triple digits, Colletti motioned for the girl he thought was about seven years old to sit by him.

"Come on you gonna help me drive the boat."

He needed to calm her down and a bit of child psychology may have done the trick.

"I have a captain's license, and I've never sunk a boat, and I ain't gonna sink this one. We gonna get to Chalmette High School safe, so you just come help me; if you see any debris in the water you let me know, so I can steer around it."

The girl's mind had switched from being fearful to wanting to help get everyone to safety.

"This little girl is telling me to watch out for that, and she quit crying, and she quit screaming, and she was pleasant to be with after that, and everybody else calmed down."

Many others turned to their faith when they saw Mrs. Joyce.

"They went to praying and next thing you know everyone in the boat is," said Colletti. "As bad as the wind was howling and the noise where you could barely hear yourself talk you could hear the prayers above the wind and the destruction and the debris flying and the waves. You could hear they were getting into it. Maybe that's what kept their sanity. Just about every boatload of people that we had it just took one person to start saying and they all said the same prayer, Our Father. It kept them going."

The wind on the side streets were rough; however, when the *Big Fish* turned onto the wide-open Judge Perez Drive the cross wind shooting across the boat sent a jolt through everyone.

"You'd have five- to six-foot seas on Judge Perez Drive and when we'd get to that point I'd tell everyone look when we enter Judge Perez Drive it's gonna get bad. Hold on to each other, hold on to something, and be prepared. When we'd hit Judge Perez Drive the cross wind was so bad, that it would almost flip the boat over, and then again when I'd turn into Chalmette High's parking lot the wind would grab me again, and as long as I had my back to it or front to it I was fine but when I turned sideways it was real bad."

After a few drops at the high school, the men started seeing more boats on the highway; then the firemen decided they had a place for Mrs. Joyce.

"Somebody had found a big, gray container on wheels," said Appel.

"Ever see those big things they'll push like a janitor, with a mop and a bucket like a big wheelbarrow."

Getting her out had been strenuous; it took about six firefighters, Colletti, and Pitre to pick up Mrs. Joyce and pass her over the roof of the truck and down into the rolling bin. Once they had gotten her into the bin, they rolled the body into the gym lobby.

"We put her in a little storage closet," said Appel. "Little, small room, keep her separate from the people. We covered her as best we could with what we had and just put her in the room and closed the door, and that's where she stayed for a few days."

And just like that they went off again and again to rescue others. The gym had been sealed off from the rest of the school by floodwater. The lobby from the school into the gym had filled up with water and the only way to get to the other evacuees at the shelter was to either go into the five- to seven-foot deep water or go outside in the elements and walk around. On the Palmisano Boulevard side of the campus, people looked out of the stairwell windows and watched as the boats docked at the end of the aluminum-covered walkway. They stepped out of the boat and walked across the metal awning. Someone had placed a yellow classroom chair just outside the hallway window, so people could step up and into the second-story hallway near room 224. This is where the science classrooms ended and the newer building, which for a long time used to be St. Bernard Community College, began.

This became another staging area for rescue missions. When boats pulled up to either drop off site at the school, the firemen would unload people, commandeer the boats, and head back out on life saving missions.

"We'd see boats floating, we'd jump on them get them started. Chalmette High kind of looked like a big marina on the Fourth of July, boats just coming and coming," said Liccardi.

*Donald Colletti, Jim Pitre, and Brad Tregle in the Big Fish on Judge Perez Drive. Photograph by Errol Schultz*

St. Bernard Sheriff's Deputy Russell Gelvin, who was assigned to the Lake Borgne Levee District, was one of the officers helping to unload people from the boats, guiding them into the building through a window in the stairwell. Gelvin wanted to retrieve two boats he had at the levee district's building in Violet, an airboat and a twenty-foot flatboat. Pump operator Joe Perry wanted desperately to get to his father who had stayed in his home on Munster Drive in Meraux.

"Come on Joe I'll bring you. I'm going that way anyway," Colletti said.

Perry, Gelvin, and a couple of prison trustees including Tarrance Armstrong, who volunteered to stay for the storm, jumped on Colletti's boat and headed down Judge Perez Drive toward Violet.

"We couldn't believe how high the water was around Murphy Oil," said Gelvin. "Eight-foot waves on Judge Perez coming over the boat . . . kept spinning the boat around. The trustees thought the boat was gonna capsize."

"It was wild man, I was scared myself," recalled Armstrong.

"I'm just looking for the nearest tree or the nearest pole if the boat flip over."

Perry was very anxious to at least make it to Munster Drive; from there he would go it alone if he had to. With Katrina making it extremely difficult to navigate a boat and power lines blocking their path, the only thing the men could do was pull up to Ben's Pizza at the corner of Judge Perez and Munster and drop Perry off on the roof. Equipped with a life jacket, he hopped off the boat and went swimming toward his father.

Gelvin glanced around at the others in the boat and with all seriousness said, "We'll probably never see him again."

Colletti had questioned letting his friend off on that roof, but there was no talking Perry out of swimming into the floodwater of Katrina.

"That's how bad it was. There was nothing I could do; I couldn't force the guy to come; if it was my father I'd wanna try to get there too," said Gelvin.

The conditions were too rough to collect the other boats at the levee district office, so Gelvin asked Colletti to abort the mission.

"Turn around, we can't risk anybody's life trying to get these boats; let's go back to the school and wait till it dies down," said Gelvin.

On their way back toward the high school some people waved the boat down to pick them up from a second story apartment. So they cruised over to them, picked them up, and brought them to Chalmette High. Gelvin and the trustees returned to helping people off of boats and into the school.

Colletti and Pitre were headed back toward Meraux when a waterspout nearly wiped them out near the Murphy Oil Refinery.

"It came to the boat no more than fifty feet, the size of a lot," said Pitre. "I seen houses lifted up; one of them was turned around backwards and put back down, the other one was pushed out to the street where we was, and the third one exploded like it was nothing."

"We seen an eighteen-wheeler container not flying but coming through the water opposite way that the wind was blowing," said Colletti. "We saw a chunk of marsh like grass and mud the size of a room that came by and hit our boat, and it just threw mud everywhere. There was fifty-five-gallon drums, furniture, you name it, you saw it flying around in this tornado. There was a Jacuzzi® tub floating in the water and there was a bottle of soft scrub on top of the Jacuzzi®; how it could yank a Jacuzzi® out of a house and the soft scrub's still standing on top of it."

Back at the high school if they did not come in on boats then they walked in, and it didn't matter what kind of condition they were in. Not much surprised Carole Mundt, but one evacuee certainly caught her attention.

"He had a peritoneal port [a catheter disc surgically inserted into the abdomen] for his dialysis. He had gotten that bad water in there, which is an open thing on his body and he came in with only the clothes on his back and a flashlight," said Mundt. "We got him in and he sat and never complained. He started to shiver and we have a nursing assistance class and in there we found some hospital gowns and we let him take his shirt off and gave him a towel. Our biggest plea to the officials at that point was to help us get those people out, he needed medical attention we knew that he needed dialysis."

"I really got nervous about him," said Principal Wayne Warner.

Hundreds of people had started calling the Chalmette High shelter home, but Warner and those running the school had no idea what was happening at the gym. It was swelling with hundreds of residents and animals.

"Unbeknownst to us people were dropping other people off in boats at the gym," said Warner. "We're in the math area the gym diagonally across, we had no contact with those people. There were actually two shelters at Chalmette High School, the one we were running officially and the other over there."

For a man who has spent nearly all of his adult life running Chalmette High, he had no control over this particular section of the school. He also had no idea how many people had been dropped off there and how bad conditions were getting. Although they had limited supplies inside the school, there was nothing in the gym.

"They're getting to a place they think is a shelter and there's nothing to offer there," said Mundt.

Most of the arrivals were not going to the side of the school where they could receive attention from officials; instead they were going to the most visible place, which was the gym at the front of Chalmette High. Of course, the boats would follow each other and when one boat dropped off someone, the next followed suit. Most had harrowing stories of survival; there were

*Boats line up outside of the Chalmette High gym. Photograph by Wayne Warner*

entire families intact; the same could not be said of everyone who had arrived.

"There was a guy, I was by the gym getting people off of the boats," said Liccardi. "The guy said he lost his wife."

One of the other firemen responded, "Where is she, we'll go try to get her." "No, I lost her; she got caught under a carport when the water came up."

He could not reach her and she died. It was the second death Liccardi had been made aware of in such a short period of time. Katrina was a killer and everyone attempting rescues knew it.

Many people refused to leave behind their pets. No matter what happened or how much it may have hindered them getting rescued they were not going to abandon their pets. A boat pulled up to the side of the school; an elderly man, his wife, and pets stepped out and attempted to walk across the raised levels of the aluminum corrugated top of the walkway. This was not the easiest task for them to accomplish, especially guiding two dogs, carrying an exotic bird in an expensive looking birdcage, and hauling life saving oxygen tanks. The woman was visibly exhausted and told her husband to slow down.

"When we finally get him in the window, we got the two dogs and he has a leash on this arm with a dog, and a leash on this arm with a dog, and he's carrying his birdcage, and he's got an oxygen tank on his shoulder and attached to the oxygen tank is his wife, and she's following behind him because she has a heart problem," said Mundt. "He's very hyper and nervous and we get them fed and get them water cause they'd probably been isolated for a while."

With the mounting shortage of food supplies and water, the elderly man walked back to Mundt with a special request.

"You got any bird seed here?"

"No, but I have some bread," Mundt replied.

"My bird don't eat no bread."

"That's all I can help you with."

The further into this tragedy the more of a circus it had become.

"I think he really thought that I was gonna be able to produce the bird feed," Mundt remembered fondly. "He's exhausted and grumpy but that's O.K. He wanted bird seed more than he wanted cereal for himself."

Animals were being plucked from deadly situations. As the pet conscience of Chalmette High, Warner did not want any of them left behind. He and many of the volunteers who had stayed to run the shelter had their pets with them. Someone could see a small dog doing a balancing act to save its life.

"There was a dog on Veronica Street, a little, wire-haired dog, who was standing on a cage chain link fence," said Warner. "How in the world he could stand on that pipe?"

"All four feet," said Mundt.

"We saw him from a window and somebody went out and got him," said Warner. "We put him in a room and gave him food and water and ultimately we had two of those rescued dogs and a cat. Somebody had let their dogs out in the stadium and they fed the dogs and they were fine."

In spite of all the human suffering inside of the school, Warner still had an eye out for the animals. He was curious to know what was going on with one of the feral cats that lived in the main school campus courtyard.

"We had a colony of cats in the courtyard and over the years I've trapped and exported fifty of them," said Warner. "I had them all spayed and found homes for them, but I could never get all of them. We had a couple of cats, several cats still left in the courtyard, and they were always in trees. One of the cats, an old, big cat, I couldn't get close to him, there was no way. He used to live in the tree all the time, he got in the oil, the water some kind of way and I saw him in the bottom and I just got my courage up again to go down in the water. He was gasping when I saw him and then I went to go downstairs to get him. He drowned; he went under; I kept him alive for like six or seven years."

Hundreds of wet, nervous, young, able-bodied, and elderly St. Bernardians lined the second floor halls and classrooms of the school. The myriad of problems in the school boiled down to hundreds of people making individual requests. They needed food, water, and, most unexpectedly, medicine. Once he realized there were people in the gym, Warner thought of trying to move them up to the second floor of the school.

"We didn't have enough to give the ones we had much less anybody else," said Warner.

They had a lot of cereal and some water but not nearly enough.

"We had very limited food and we didn't know how many days we were going to be there because there was no communication. The only phones we had were our cell phones and they didn't work during the daytime at all," said Warner.

"We had Fruit Loops®, and we had some cereal bars, and we had some jelly packets, some bread, and some peanut butter, but I vetoed using peanut butter because it was gonna make people too thirsty," said Mundt. "The demand for water could not surpass what we had."

A steady stream of people made their way to the school Monday afternoon; some estimate nearly 1500 went to the gym; while inside the school, Warner figures it grew to about 400 people. Warner and those at the shelter discussed how much food and fluids they had and how they would dispense them.

"We had some water, some bread, some jelly packs, and we had a lot of Fruit Loops®, can peaches," Warner detailed. "We had two meals a day they could come and pick up Fruit Loops® or maybe there's a half a glass of water. The water we had was sufficient for two or three days, but we could have been there two weeks; we didn't have a clue. We didn't know how many people we would wind up with, cause people just kept coming; there was sick people there and we didn't want to deplete the water completely. If we depleted it and somebody really needed it at that point there's nothing we could have done."

It was not much, but thirsty and hungry, the people went with the plan.

"People were very willing to take that and they understood and it was hot and it was miserable," said Mundt. "They'd take their napkin and go sit and eat it and put their trash away and sit for another six hours and come back six hours later for Fruit Loops® or Frosted Flakes® or another sip of water and they'd just accept it."

Aside from not having enough food and water, another critical hardship was the amount of people who did not have their medication or medical supplies. Many people started having breathing problems; Warner estimates at least thirty people at the shelter needed oxygen. One gentleman walked up to Warner with an update on his supply.

"I have oxygen enough to last me till tomorrow."

Three hours later he returned and said to Warner, "I made a mistake; I have two hours of oxygen left."

Warner remembers school superintendent Doris Voitier near a window when State Senator Walter Boasso pulled up in a boat and asked if there was anything the school needed. Voitier told him oxygen.

"Boasso got us some oxygen, and the firemen later kept getting oxygen for all the other people we had; they kept bringing oxygen to us," said Warner.

For most it was a struggle just to save themselves, much less grab an oxygen tank or medication that may have been submerged under the water in their bedside tables, medicine, or kitchen cabinets. Warner and his staff went to work getting medicine by any means necessary.

Warner: "People would ask questions, and we could work through the firemen to get their medications."

Mundt: "We made an insulin list one time and sent a guy in a boat to get to a drug store so he could find it."

Warner: "We found out there are different types of insulin and we got to the point where we could ask people what kind do you need. One gentleman who had access to a pharmacy, we didn't ask questions."

Mundt: "We just asked, 'can you get this for us.'"

Warner: "He went out and he got it and because of him a lot of people had insulin who wouldn't."

The grocery stores, pharmacies, and any place that had food or water were raided. In between rescue missions firemen, deputies, and civilians would pick up supplies and bring them back to the school.

"The firemen would try to bring back as much water and a few can items. In all honesty that was very minimal and almost unusable, but the things they did bring in were fluids," said Warner. "They would bring water that was under the mess, so we had to take the bottles and our cafeteria lady Mrs. Barbier made a bleach solution. We'd wipe the water bottles down so that when we handed it to somebody they weren't grabbing contaminated stuff."

Warner, and the others running the school shelter, felt the mounting pressure to survive. They were concerned not only for their own survival but for everyone in the parish as well. They knew nightfall was coming and that there was no way they would be able to get to all of the people on top of their roofs and in their attics. People in the shelters were letting them know of others who needed help, but they knew people were dying.

"When you walk in the school you had people coming up to you with addresses written on paper of relatives and friends, 'can you go check this house,'" said Liccardi. "Guys would go out and you couldn't really go check any addresses in the beginning you were just getting whatever you can get. People are looking to you to help and you kind of in the same situation as them really. Not really much better off. The kids, seeing all the kids."

Once the wind died down, Gelvin decided it was time to take another shot at retrieving the boats at the levee district office.

"We had a guy gonna give us a ride," said Gelvin. "We're on the back of Chalmette High on the overhang using like a dock, getting ready to get in the boat. I heard somebody yelling my name, when I turned around it was Joe Perry."

"I bet you thought you'd never see me again; I got my dad out, and I got two boats for us," Perry said.

"Where are they at?"

"Let's go get 'em."

They jumped into a flatboat and traveled to the U.S. Maritime in Meraux, near where they dropped Perry off on top of Ben's Pizza. A U.S. Maritime employee gave Gelvin and Perry two twenty-eight-foot flat boats with 150 Yamaha's on the back filled with gas.

"Take 'em, do what y'all got to do," he told Gelvin and Perry.

Gelvin immediately took off in the direction of his pump operators; they needed to get the pump stations to start pumping the water out of St. Bernard.

The boat that picked up Barry Uhle, like many already zipping

A picture of Chalmette High quarterback Norris Weese inside of the gym trophy case. Photograph by Mikel Schaefer

around his Golden Drive neighborhood, went to Chalmette High and pulled up to the gym entrance, riding past the submerged fire truck in the parking lot. Uhle helped some of the people off of the boat. He walked up the ramp into the lobby, which was filled with about two feet of water. The first thing he saw was the huge trophy case that spanned the entire wall. The case held trophies, pictures, and mementos of nearly forty-five years of the school's athletic history. The centerpiece was a picture of quarterback Norris Weese, who guided the Owls to the state semi-finals in 1968 under legendary coach Bobby Nuss. Weese eventually made it to the NFL, playing four years for the Denver Broncos, who made it to Super Bowl XII. In that game, played in the Superdome, Weese led the team to a touchdown although the Broncos ultimately lost to the Dallas Cowboys.

"I can remember looking at the trophy cases there and some old friends of mine that had played ball there and remember seeing their pictures," said Uhle.

Uhle walked up a few more steps into the gym and nothing that he had seen up to that point had put the event into perspective like walking onto the Owls hardwood gym floor.

"That's when I realized what a catastrophic situation it was, not so much seeing all the water and the boats going up and down Judge Perez just when I walked in there," said Uhle. "It was so many people there that didn't have anything. Some men just had their shorts on, some people just had their underwear, most everyone was wet, and it smelled. People had their animals there; God bless 'em that's all they had left, they kept their dogs. I don't mean to sound mean about that; it smelled like freaking animal crap and piss all over the floor it was terrible."

The broken windows allowed the rain to get in, soaking the floors and chairs. The evacuees looked ragged and beaten. Many had staked out their spot on the gym floor and the wooden seats in the stands.

"Never once thought they had that many people as dumb as I was to get caught in the situation that needed to stay. God, why are they here? I know why I was there it was stupidity I guess."

Despite the chaos the people had managed to survive, Uhle said they reacted calmly.

"[I was] most proud of being there because there was a fifty-five-gallon drum in a corner behind the door where people were going to use the bathroom. An orderly line, it was disgusting but nobody was asking for something they knew wasn't going to be there like a port-a-let [portable bathroom]. People were functioning, no meanness."

There was no food or water provided in the gym, so people went out to secure whatever they could find to eat and drink. That meant breaking in to the I.G.A. store across the street.

"People coming in with garbage bags of stuff they were getting from Steve Fecke's store, and the firemen would say, 'O.K. people make a chain.' People would make a line from the door to the stage and firemen carried in a chain and handed food all the way up to the stage. The firemen came in, this is the way we gonna do it, not gonna have freaking mayhem."

The firemen set up sections and handed the food out making it as efficient a process as possible, especially with wet people sliding on the hardwood basketball floor and the heat making everyone sweaty, hot, and irritable.

"They were handing out a diet 7UP® and a Slim Jim® or a can of Vienna sausage and a Gatorade®," said Uhle. "No ice, no nothing and everybody took it. Certain people took charge where if people couldn't get down to the food, the older people would take too long; they would take it to older people."

Outside the situation was nearly the same as the boats pulled up to the gym. People made human chains to unload the supplies. It was not the same people with each load; many different men, women, and children pitched in to do their part.

"Nobody was like seven year locust feeding, everybody stood in line very orderly," said Uhle. "What I saw when I got out, I saw on television. I was proud of how we were."

Alan Clomburg could only see rooftops peaking out of the water in every direction he turned. He was not sure what he was going to do or where he wanted to go now that the home he and his family had lived in since 1992 had only its roof sticking out of the floodwater. Since he put it on the back of his boat, he had been having problems with his motor. He assumed he had set it down in the mud in the excited state of trying to get the boat operational and clogged the intake. He did not know how far he would get without help.

"Where did you bring those ladies at?" he asked a rescuer.

"They knew somebody over there had a two-story house, they went over there."

"Can I follow you?"

The rescuer tied Clomburg's flatboat to his boat and they slowly coasted through the neighborhood; they even picked up some people near St. Mark Church on Charles Drive. The two boats had a tough time navigating in the wind. He would try to make it on his own even if it meant tearing up his motor.

"If I'm gonna burn it up, I'm gonna burn it up on one run to save my parents and put them somewhere," said Clomburg. "We got tangled up in some trees, started the motor up and it worked, it was pumping."

Almost immediately he spotted a man doing the backstroke with a life jacket on heading toward Judge Perez Drive. The man was stripped down to only a pair of shorts.

"Where are you going?" Clomburg asked.

"Man you think you can bring me up to Chalmette High School?"

"What you think I'm gonna do, tell you no? You'll drown, come on get in the boat."

They helped the nearly naked and water logged man into the boat. The motor did not give them any more trouble as they made the nearly mile long trek to the school. Idling into the school parking lot, the stark, grim sight hit Clomburg and his companions. There were boats docked at the ramp and boats drifting in and out of the parking lot. The people, shirtless and wet, were helping unload the others from the boats. Clomburg graduated from Chalmette High and had not stepped foot in the school since the day he left in 1974, and now it was under water. Mickey and Elva were safe; he helped them climb out of the boat and walked with them into the gym.

"If that storm didn't kill them, the only thing they gonna die of is old age because they went through hell with that storm," said Clomburg.

He did not see them for the rest of the day; instead he took his flatboat to join the highway flotilla rescuing his neighbors. Judge Perez had become a heavily trafficked water artery and boats were everywhere. Clomburg had a sixteen-foot flatboat with a seven and a half Johnson to power it. He was on Judge Perez Drive about two blocks from Chalmette High when he came across someone with a brand new eighteen-footer loaded down with people.

"The water was still deep and people were trying to get on it and they were panicking. He was telling them to 'get off, get off,'" said Clomburg. "They wind up sinking the boat. One of the guys on the boat had a family on there and they had a boy I guess was eight years old. He's standing up with his head just barely above the water and he's got the kid up and we come riding by."

The man says, "Take the kid."

"Throw him in the boat," said Clomburg. "Where's his parents?"

"His parents are in the boat in front of you."

"Hang on side the boat and I'll bring you to where you can walk or get in the boat," Clomburg told the man in the water.

"I'm alright. I'm gonna stay here with my family, but take care of this boy."

So Clomburg turns to the boy, "Where's your daddy at?"

"He's up there, right there," pointing to the boat ahead of Clomburg.

"You scared?"

"No, not really."

"This is something you'll never forget son."

They pulled into the Chalmette High parking lot.

"His daddy was watching us; I never knew who his daddy was but he was watching us, watching he wouldn't lose his son."

They pulled up to the flooded ramp leading into the gym and the man approached Clomburg.

"Thank you, thank you, thank you!"

Clomburg seemed surprised by the reactions of those he was helping. It just seemed so natural to him.

"You can't let a kid drown, anybody, not even a dog."

With every person Clomburg plucked from a roof or out of the water, he instantly felt the bond that connects people when tragedy brings them together, as if you had known them all of your life. Those he rescued may never forget his face. Clomburg picked up so many that he knew he could never remember them all. When he dropped them off to safety, he thought about seeing these people again, and he still wants to see them again but knows he probably never will. Their images are burned in his brain but always slightly blurred. He rode around his parish until nightfall, saving his neighbors and thinking about how Katrina made everyone equal and joined them together in survival.

"It didn't discriminate; the rich and the poor were all in the same boat; I met the guy that owns a truck stop off of Paris Road, he's nothing, same thing I was in, a pair of shorts, this and that."

Like the many who luckily survived Katrina and boldly admit it was foolish to stay behind, Clomburg knows it was a colossal mistake that he would never make again, but he also knows that it was a life saving mistake for others.

"If I would have left, my parents would have stayed, and they would have drowned, so it was worth it in that sense," Clomburg said. "You can't save nothing; you can save the clothes on your back and your ass and that's about it. In fifteen minutes time you had six-foot of water, fifteen minutes."

David Defranza and his family saw the boats coming and a man guided his nearly full boat to their home.

"We can't take all of you."

"Go ahead and take my mama and my brother's girlfriend," said Defranza. "Where are y'all gonna bring 'em?"

"Chalmette High School."

A short time later, the Louisiana Department of Wildlife and Fisheries came by and picked up Defranza and his brother, Mike. When they arrived at Chalmette High they walked into the disheartening gym, looking for their mother and Mike's girlfriend.

"They had a lot of people, but you could just walk up and

down if ya mama sees ya she's gonna start yelling your name," said Defranza. "It didn't take long to find them in there."

In a bit of shock like everyone else in the gym, Defranza remembers a frightening moment when it appeared a man was having a heart attack.

"It was an elderly guy these people were trying to bring this guy back," said Defranza. "They had a whole bunch of paramedics on one side of the gym and they were sitting there talking to the St. Bernard Police and the next thing I know they're saying, 'oh my God, he's having a heart attack.'"

"Ma, look at all them police and paramedics over there."

"They've got to do it,'" said Emma.

"Ma, I've got to go; I've got to go get them right now."

Defranza ran up to the first responders.

"I said look I don't know if y'all know it y'all have someone over there dying."'"Where?"

"You don't see the big ring of people all the way around?"

Defranza remembers grabbing the man by the arm to guide him to the sick man but it did not matter.

"They went over there and the guy wound up dying of a heart attack right in front of my ma."

## St. Bernard High School Shelter

Several of the evacuees had their boats at the school, and even though Katrina was still kicking up quite a bit some of the men went out to save those in the surrounding neighborhood.

"We could see the people on the roofs from the school," said fireman Rodney Ourso. He and another man jumped into a boat and fought the tide to get to the back of the school and into the flooded St. Bernard High Eagle football field. They wanted to check on a group of people they saw that had made it to the stadium and had holed themselves up in the press box.

"I went out in a little boat with the cabin on it and we made it to the stadium but that was as far as we could go, because the wind was pushing this little boat with this cabin on it all over the place," said Ourso. "We barely made it over there."

Ourso was eager to know if they wanted to come to the school or needed anything in the meantime, but they did not want to leave the press box and opted to ride out the rest of Katrina there. Ourso climbed back into the small boat and headed to his next mission. St. Bernard High is in a rural area with a wooded section butted up against the school grounds, and as Ourso battled the wind and the surging water he saw something swimming ahead of him.

"I'm watching a doe swim across the football field, it had six, eight feet of water over the field."

The boat he had decided was too small to beat the power of the elements.

"We can't do this, this is too dangerous because we're being pushed all over the place by the winds," Ourso recalled.

They made it back to the school, tied up the boat, and waited for the wind to slow down before making another run.

In lower St Bernard most of the residents have boats. They are related to the water and probably feel more comfortable behind the power of a boat than a car.

A couple of those people turned out to be Chuck Thurman and Frankie Asevado. After watching Katrina destroy Kenilworth, Thurman received a frantic call from his younger sister in Utah.

"Chuckie, the water's coming; I'm looking at it on the news. The water's coming; the levees broke."

The news seemed so out of place compared to what he was seeing, but then again he was a few dozen miles from that Industrial Canal breach. He thought that maybe he was not in trouble anyway, because during Hurricane Betsy the water never got out of Chalmette.

Pacing back and forth, Thurman tried to explain the situation to her, but she was hysterical. He told her he was going to let her go and hung up the phone.

"When I got off the phone with her I could see the water coming in the trailer park and at that point it didn't look like much, little white rapid like coming down the trailer park," said Thurman. "I told Frankie, let's get the boat ready, the water's coming."

They had an eighteen-foot V-hull with an outboard motor. They started untying the boat from the trailer, but before they could get the boat untied the water was up to their waist.

"Vehicles floating by, campers floating by, quick like within five minutes stuff was floating," said Thurman. "We got the boat we brought it to the front of the house, got everybody in it, got all of the dogs, but we lost one dog at that point. It got caught in the water, we couldn't go after it, the current was so bad you couldn't go chase down something in it. So we got the dog food, as much supplies as we could and we went about three houses down the road, and we brought everybody and put them on the porch there."

The house became their temporary shelter. The wind had started picking up strength again, but this time the wind was blowing from the other direction; Katrina was moving out. It was a stressful wait because everything as they knew it had changed.

"When the winds started slacking off me and Frankie got in the boat and we went around to all of the houses trying to get people out of their attics," said Thurman." We went beating on people's attics on their roofs, getting them out."

No rescue was the same. They eventually got another boat and doubled up.

"They had a couple of elderly French people in a barn way in the back, we could hear them 'hey, hey, hey.' We go back there, we had to rip the front of the building off to get them out of the building, an old wooden barn," Thurman describes. "They were upstairs of the top loft of the barn. There was two middle-aged guys and there were two elderly people, I guess it was their mom and dad."

Asevado had already picked up some people in his boat while Thurman was in a boat by himself with the pit bulls.

The lady asked him if his dogs bite.

"The dogs don't bite, they fine."

Nonetheless, Thurman understood their hesitance to jump into a boat full of pit bulls.

"You come up to five pit bulls and you're gonna definitely worry about them biting. But I got the two elderly people in the boat and the two middle-aged guys wouldn't leave [the barn].

Thurman and the couple, who could not speak English very well, drove down to St. Bernard High School

"We got them down there and got 'em on top of the school," said Thurman. "We did that all day Monday after the wind stopped; we brought people back and forth."

In spite of the fact that the only rescue boats anyone would see this far into the parish were those of civilians like Thurman and Asevado, even begging would not convince these storm troopers to leave their homes.

"People in their attic, water up to the gutters, and still didn't want to leave their house, It was rough," said Thurman. "We'd bring them food and water, three days after the storm, we were still bringing food and water to some of them, asking them, begging them to leave, and they wouldn't leave."

Monday night, after bringing everyone they had with them to St. Bernard High School, Thurman, Asevado, his girlfriend, B.B., and six pit bulls found an open and abandoned home to settle into.

"We spent the night in a house right there in Kenilworth, a two-story house; we just crashed on the floor, cause we was exhausted."

Meanwhile, at the high school the healthier and younger residents went out to commandeer supplies. They grabbed anything they could find, because the more people at the school, the greater the need for food and water, a necessity the firemen didn't think they had enough of. Fireman Michael Lebeau, a paramedic, set up a triage area, so he could check the sick and injured. He was only equipped to handle minor injuries such as cuts and to administer oxygen, but he had no medicine to hand out. Many had come in with pre-existing health problems, and the storm had only exacerbated those issues.

"We had forty-two or forty-three people that were over the age of sixty-five. That was one concern during the height of the storm," said Lebeau. "We didn't lose anybody, with their age and medical problems we were being hard pressed."

"Their conditions were starting to deteriorate," said Ourso.

Lebeau and another paramedic determined they had fifteen who were becoming critical.

"We had to get those out quickly, starting to look bad," said Lebeau.

Lake Borgne Levee District foreman Troy Douglas, Sr. had instructions to get to the pumping stations as soon as he could after the storm. The water had already reached a capacity that was by far greater than he had ever dreamed would come into the parish. He thought about all the people in trouble and his goal was to get out of St. Bernard High and get to the boats at the levee district office in Violet, just like his friend Russell Gelvin was trying to accomplish from Chalmette High.

"I had orders to gather up the boat and pick up all the men from the different shelters, so we can all be together and when the water stopped, break off to stations," said Douglas, Sr.

The floodwater had changed plans dramatically, and he had

problems getting out of St. Bernard High. Douglas, Sr. was also worried about the citizens in the gym because they were sealed off from the rest of the school. Before he made his break out of there, he wanted to get supplies for the people in the gym.

"My operator said wait up I'm gonna take this man and gather up some pirogues. We had guys that went start looting the stores to feed the people," said Douglas, Sr. "They had plenty bread there; they had like cereal and no meat."

There was no feasible way to get the people in the gym back inside the school, without them submerging themselves in the water, so the levee workers gathered up food and brought it to the gym.

"We were just making sure they was able to get food and the only thing you can go through that gap with is a pirogue by laying down in it, " said Douglas, Sr. "You couldn't get to them, all you can do is throw stuff in the water and push it to 'em."

Hauck swam back and forth from the gym to the stairwell that led to the other group in the school.

"Early on I would be underwater I would just hang on to it and swim and kick from the north side of the school to the south side of the school, which was some distance, and went up another stairway," said Hauck.

After some time he began to move people out of the gym into the school, a process that lasted a couple of days.

"I tried to move people who were healthy enough to do it. If a son got separated from his father, a husband and wife, I'd try to take the healthy person and move them cause there was no medicine, people were depending on medications and not doing well."

In the meantime, Douglas, Sr. wanted to get out.

"Two of our men swam to the pump station, recovered a boat we had in the building," said Douglas, Sr. "From there they come back and picked me up. We tore off [to the levee district office] and get the big flat boat that will carry everybody."

While others looted stores for goods and brought them back to the school, the firemen devised a plan for the storing and handing out of food and water. A plan was needed because the supplies that were coming in were not staying in one spot.

"The first couple of loads of stuff that came in was disappearing in the rooms, never made it to our room," Ourso said. "We had to set up the deputies with us watching and get all of the stuff in one room that we designated, so we could ration it out, if not we would have lost people. They were hoarding all the stuff they could."

Once they had maintained control of the goods, they portioned it up for a school holding an estimated 250 to 300 people.

"When it was time to feed everybody we let Homeland Security be in charge," said Lebeau.

"We went to each room with carts and gave out food and water to all of them and we did that for the whole time," said Ourso.

As the hours ticked away, health concerns rose due to the number of animals inside the school.

"We couldn't keep the dogs out on the roof. We had so many, some dogs on the roof, some dogs in the rooms, defecating everywhere it was getting very unsanitary," said Ourso. "I impressed on them [parish officials] we need to get out as soon as possible. And they were waiting for the flood waters to come down in order to get to us."

## CHAPTER TWELVE

# Saving One Another

## Monday, August 29

### Day Two

After Sheriff Stephens set the example for his department by rescuing his men from the Arabi substation, deputies went out around the courthouse and beyond with whatever water vehicle they could get their hands on. They risked the elements to rescue citizens, and when Katrina's destructive wind slowed, more officers ventured into the flooded streets. These men had to think for themselves and quickly make things happen, because there was no command center to call in to.

"Here we were getting people out of attics and off of rooftops and within a short period of time we knew communications had been totally degraded," said Stephens. "We couldn't talk to anybody, and we had more and more evacuees that were coming in to the courthouse."

In order to deal with the mass amount of people deputies began creating makeshift shelters at other buildings around the parish. They broke the large glass windows on the second floor of the three-story Regions Bank on Jean Lafitte Parkway and Judge Perez Drive, across the street from the civic center. This is where they brought Glenn Sanchez from Arabi.

"We started putting people in there because it was at least above the water line," said Stephens. "You can imagine what the conditions were; the human waste and people getting ill. They were compromised because of age or health or exposure."

Stephens ordered the St. Bernard Jail open to triage the sickest evacuees. The jail, which holds about four hundred people, escaped the floodwater and was empty because the sheriff had sent all of the prisoners out of the parish before the hurricane. The jail sits in the shadows of Chalmette Refining at the intersection of Paris Road and St. Bernard Highway.

Directly across the street in the median sits the ruins of the De La Ronde plantation, fenced off with black iron. All that is standing of the original early 1800s structure are partial walls made of smooth, weatherworn, red-orange bricks. It was once a sixteen room, two-story mansion built by Pierre Denis de la Ronde, who also planted a double row of towering oak trees using slave labor in the late 1700s. Known as the De La Ronde oaks, the oak trees sit directly across the highway from the ruins behind the jail and run back to the refinery.

"That was the only place we had any medical personnel," said Major James Pohlmann.

In a short period of time the jail had become overrun with people needing medical attention and anyone else who managed to make it to the one dry spot in the parish with the exception of the levees. Whether they walked to the jail or were dropped off in boats, the people were exhausted, frightened, and in shock.

"There were people laying in the hallways on top of each other, most of them elderly," said Stephens. "It was a scene described something out of Hotel Rwanda; you didn't think that you were in the continental United States."

They eventually figured out a way to get one channel inside of the parish to communicate between the government officials and first responders; however, there was no connection outside of the parish borders.

"We had no radio or any type of communication outside of St. Bernard Parish, no way to contact anybody," said Pohlmann. "The system is designed to work that if there are any needs we have then it needs to be directed toward the Office of Emergency Preparedness on a local level through Larry Ingargiola. He then communicates to Baton Rouge whether it's by radio or telephone. But the phones and radios don't work. We couldn't get any supplies; all the supplies we had were things we had to get on our own."

The sheriff's department became responsible for more than just law enforcement.

"It became evident that we're in the rescue business now; we're in the sheltering business, and then we had to supply the shelters with medical supplies and food and water," said Pohlmann. "Not only are we sending boats out to perform rescues but now we need to send boats out to try to locate supplies, so any store we can find and we can get in we're taking the water, food, medical supplies, and we staged that at the jail."

"When you're picking them up they have nothing and neither did we," said Col. Forrest Bethay, who held down the chaos at the courthouse. "You need everything to survive, and it's more than you think."

The men had to make quick decisions based more on common sense than training; the strategy was to get to the ones who were in the most deadly of situations first and pray until you can get the next group.

"Sometimes you go into an area, and there's thirty people needing rescuing and you have one boat," said Doran. "If there's a kid or an older person you got to get them first, hoping the others will survive if they're strong enough. If we had water in the boat we'd give it to them. It was a nightmare."

The troops had orders to go until nightfall; they were not allowed to put themselves at risk in the darkness.

"We had asked all boats to be in for 7:00 P.M., so we can account for all personnel," said Pohlmann.

It was an order Pohlmann found out first hand he would have to obey after Katrina passed.

## Just Enough Headroom

Chief of Field Operations, Major James Pohlmann and Captain Mitchell Roussell left the courthouse in a boat headed for the government complex to pick up the head of the Lake Borgne Levee District, Bob Turner, and Constable Tony Guerra. Turner needed to reach the district office, so he could get their boats. He needed to get the pump operators to the pumping stations. Turner's boats had been jammed under the overhang of the complex; he and Guerra climbed out of the window they had rigged with ladders into Pohlmann's boat.

"Jimmy we've got to get over to our offices and try to get our boat because we've got to get this water outta here," said Turner. "We've gotta open up the Bayou Dupre control structure and try

*The side of the flooded government complex. Photograph by Donald Colletti*

to find out how we're gonna get this water outta here fast."

The boat ride was several miles long and the entire way they saw people on their roofs trying to flag them down. The guys could not pass up the ones who needed immediate help, but they had to be selective. It was imperative they get to the locks to drain the water out of the parish, otherwise lives could be lost.

"We tried to get people off of roofs and on to second story buildings because we had no place to bring them at that time," Turner said.

Driving down Judge Perez drive through Chalmette, Meraux, and Violet, they were getting close to the levee district boats.

"We took a right turn on Colonial Drive, kind of putt-putting down Colonial. Probably got about midway and we hear cries for help," recalled Pohlmann. "We looked to our left and you could see probably had about eight inches of a window that was exposed, wasn't under water at that point yet and they had some people you could see the hands and the faces up against the glass beating and yelling for help."

They steered the boat toward the window; they saw three people peering out, an elderly man, a woman, and a mentally-challenged woman, possibly their daughter. The plan was to crash the window and pull them out.

"We're gonna get you out," said Pohlmann.

But when they got close to the window they noticed burglar bars; they would not be able to break through the bars. Pohlmann and Roussell glanced at each other with that what should we do now look.

"Can y'all go to the front door? The window's right next to the front door just go right to the front door I'm gonna get in the water and open the door," Pohlmann said loud enough for them to hear through the window.

"We can't; we're standing on the bed, if we get off the bed we'll drown," one of them shouted back.

Pohlmann gave that look to Roussell again.

"We gotta do something, give me a life vest," Pohlmann said.

So Pohlmann jumped into the water, landed in the hidden garden bushes, lost his balance, and fell over.

"I'm able to go under water, turn the knob and just by feel I was able to get the screen door open and push the door open."

The furniture was floating; several pieces were touching the ceiling. Pohlmann had to push a sofa and other furniture out of his way.

"I get half way in and it turns out that they're in the bedroom next to the living room, so I got to go through the living room to a hallway," Pohlmann said. "I make it all the way to the hallway, and I stop, and I yell for the other guys, 'I want one of you other guys in the water in case something happens.'"

Guerra put on a life jacket, grabbed his flashlight, and jumped in the water to help Pohlmann.

"Here take my flashlight," said Guerra as he tossed it to Pohlmann.

The flashlight careened off of the ceiling, landing out of Pohlmann's reach, and disappeared under the muddy water.

"Son of a gun, I'm gonna go back, just stay close in case something happens to me, and you can kinda get me outta here," Pohlmann said to the other men in the boat.

Pohlmann had extra life jackets with him to hand to the three trapped people. The extra vests helped him stay afloat because the one he had on was cheap and kept floating up to his neck. Because it was so dark in the house Pohlmann had to feel his way along the walls to find the room they were in. He turned into the room and all three people were standing on the bed with their heads just above the water line.

"I see the fear in these people's eyes, particularly with the girl.

She was mentally-challenged, and she was big, and you could see she was nervous."

Pohlmann, unable to touch the ground with his feet, looked at the three from a safe distance.

"I'm gonna throw you a vest."

He looked at the younger woman and said, "I'm gonna take you out first."

"I can't, I can't," she said.

"Just grab the vest; don't grab me; grab the vest."

She grabbed the vest and struggled to stay afloat.

"I just grabbed the other end of the vest and kind of towed her all the way out of the bedroom, down the hall into the front door. We had a time but we got her in the boat."

Worn out, Pohlmann said, "Tony they've got two other people in there; let's go in there together; let's take 'em out together and get it over with."

Following the same procedure, Pohlmann guided one out while Guerra grabbed the other. Roussell and Turner were in the boat and helped pull the elderly couple in. Having saved three people in danger of drowning, Pohlmann tried to complete his first mission. He flagged down another boat so that Turner and Guerra could get another ride to the levee district. Then Pohlmann and his new crew headed west down Judge Perez Drive towards the courthouse.

"This little old lady is shivering, and she's cold and I'm trying to cover her up with whatever I can find, a rain suit, and the old man was laying in the bow of the boat" said Pohlmann. "The lady was sitting in the lap of the daughter and she kept looking in my eyes saying, 'thank you,' that's all she kept saying. She knows we saved her life."

Looking at his watch, Pohlmann turned to Roussell, "We're getting close to seven o'clock, come on let's pick it up a little bit. We're passing Meraux's field and she's still looking at me, 'thank you' and she's cold, nice old lady. Well we hit something in the water, boom; Mitch hits his mouth. That old lady's laying there and she yells out 'F&@K!'"

Pohlmann turned to the woman and said comically, "You watch your language in my boat."

He could not believe this little lady had just dropped the F bomb.

She looked at him and said, "Thank you."

"We brought them in, and I don't know what happened to them; I wish I knew where they were; I wish I could find those people."

### From St. Rita's to Beauregard Middle School

As Gene Alonzo, his brother, Carlos, and the residents who were saved from inside of St. Rita's nursing home sat on top of the roof getting whipped by the wind and rain, a boat docked. The group was loaded and taken to the second floor of Sal Mangano's daughter's house a few hundred yards away.

"We're trying to transfer them to this house, we carried 'em up the steps in this house, trying to put some dry clothes on 'em," said Alonzo. "But everything was a mess, trying to give 'em something to eat, all of this is taking hours, not doing this fast. We've got all these people most of them can't walk, can't talk."

Employees of St. Rita's, the nursing home owners, and Alonzo were now caring for the survivors. The boats were going back and forth retrieving people off of the roof and looking for others who may have made it out alive. All of these people were in rough shape; they were old, and many had debilitating problems. Medicine was needed most of all, but there was not any. By three or four in the afternoon the situation had become critical.

"We realize we got people here that need insulin and seizure medicine, so they tell us to go to Beauregard School," said Alonzo.

After another stressful boat ride, they docked at P.G.T. Beauregard Middle School on St. Bernard Highway in St. Bernard.

"That's where they brought us and by that time the wind stopped. We get there, they really ain't nothing there," said Alonzo.

Since the only two designated shelters of last resort in the parish were St. Bernard and Chalmette High, Beauregard did not have any provisions. There was no food; others who had evacuated to the school with meager supplies shared what little they had with the nursing home survivors. Alonzo believed there was a total of thirty-five nursing home patients.

"The nurses was trying to set up a little care for them, the ones that was really, really sick," said Alonzo. "I was thinking my brother needs that seizure medicine he takes in the morning and evening. He's probably gonna start getting these bad seizures without no medicine."

The people were cold and wet. The only dry clothing they could find were the costumes used for plays.

"They had old costumes and put that on them. Must of had some kind of play or something; at least it was dry," said

*The inside of Beauregard Middle School after everyone had evacuated the school. Photograph by Mikel Schaefer*

Alonzo. "It was like Mardi Gras costumes or something; the people were shaking, and they was soaking wet. We stood that night, slept on the hard floor, everything was a mess, toilets was overflowed, stinking."

After rescuing his brother, Chris, Don Robin passed the back of St. Rita's and through the chaos the word was out about the deaths at the nursing home.

"That's when someone had told us that a bunch of the elderly

that was in the nursing home had drowned and they were evacuating the survivors to Beauregard School," said Don.

As they passed the school going toward the Violet Canal, the
boats separated. Chris took a boat to check on a couple of his
friends; Pete took some people to St. Bernard High School. Don
and his cousin wanted to check his mother's home on Kelly Road.

"We were getting close to my mother's home; there was an old
man hanging on a boat, and the boat was kind of turned up on the
side, and he was hollering for help. We went over there and picked
him up. I guess he was about eighty years old; disoriented as can
be, he had a couple of licks on his head, and he was just hanging
on this boat. I don't know how long he would have made it"

They got the man into the boat, and he asked a lot of questions
about where Don was taking him. He wanted to go back to his
house to shut the front door.

"Sir don't worry about your house; your house is gonna be
O.K." said Don.

"I just don't want nothing to happen to the inside of my
home," he responded.

Don brought the man to Beauregard Middle.

"That was a sad sight to see these older people laying down
in boats," said Don. "We pulled up to the front of the school, and
there was a couple of boats dropping off the elderly people from
the nursing home. That's when we dropped off that old man and
that's when we took off for the Violet area."

### Pumpers Save Lives on the Way to Pump

One of the trustees with deputy Russell Gelvin was Tarrance
Armstrong, who was assigned to the levee district earlier in
August when he applied to be a trustee. The thirty year old was
caught shoplifting in a Dollar General Store in Meraux and
admitted to the crime. When Katrina bore down on the parish,
Armstrong was given the option to leave.

"I really never experienced nothing like this, so I wanted to be
there, because I wanted to help, so I stayed, and I helped,"
Armstrong said. "I felt obligated; I had to be here that was our
job. I knew it was gonna be a lot of people panicking and a lot of
people dying and a lot of people gonna be hurt, and I knew I had
to be there to help. I couldn't just let nobody die, suffer in pain. It
was life threatening."

Gelvin, along with trustee Steve Edgett and Joe Perry, picked up two boats from the U.S. Maritime and headed back to Chalmette High to get Armstrong and some others. They were supposed to pick up other crewmembers at other sites around the parish and then get to their designated pump stations.

"We went out and was going to look for the rest of our crew, the pumpers and the ground crew, to pick them up, so they could get everything started, but they done already left," said Armstrong.

Gelvin hoped the Lake Borgne Levee District offices were dry; he wanted to use it as a base of operations, if they could ever get down there. All they saw for miles was water, and although the water hid the massive destruction from the naked eye, the rooftops revealed the full picture.

"You might see a few rooftops but everything was under, cars, you had boats on top of houses, you had sheds on top of houses, I even saw a dump truck on a house." recalled Armstrong.

They picked up several people, like every other boat on the water, but not everyone felt the need to be rescued.

"They was undecided and they wanted to stay. They wanted to go, but they wanted to stay," said Armstrong. "But you had to let them know, man you gotta get outta here; it ain't worth staying; you gotta leave, gotta get to safety, gotta get to higher ground."

Then there were those who just flat out refused.

"We had a few that didn't come; they put up a fight to leave, so we had to go to the next one."

The rescues that really stuck in his throat were the ones where families still had their children with them.

"They was thankful; the people was crying and everything; they even had little kids still here," said Armstrong. "They really didn't know what was going on; they didn't know we just rescued them to put them in the boat and bring them to Chalmette High too."

From a jail cell to the flooded houses of a parish he never lived in, who knows where Armstrong would have been if he had not been caught shoplifting. Even though he knows he did all he could, the faces of those he passed up are permanently burned in his mind.

"I just wished I could have helped everybody out, but you know the ones I did save, I feel good about it. I know I did something."

Meantime the head of the levee district Bob Turner picked up his boat and offered Tony Guerra an airboat to use to check on his family. Turner tried to launch his boat across the highway from the office into the Violet Canal, wanting to get to the Bayou Dupre locks.

"The boats were all smashed and we couldn't get through there," said Turner. "So we wound up having to go the long way, in and out of the streets, wires down, gas bubbling up out of the ground. You couldn't even see where the levee was."

They found their way back into the Violet Canal near the Violet Canal Bridge overhead. When they got about half way into the canal they ran into Douglas, Sr. and crew and together they went toward the locks to see what they could find. However, the sunlight had disappeared and the clouds allowed very little moonlight.

"The flashlights weren't working so we got about two-thirds or three-quarters of the way out there and we couldn't figure out which way to go to get to the locks, no landmarks, at this point the water was so high everything was covered," said Turner. "Everything was blown down."

With no light, they searched the sky for a marker, something to help guide them back to the Violet Canal. They spotted a light they figured was coming from a refinery across the Mississippi River.

Turner told the others, "We're not gonna be able to make it out there tonight; let's go back and tie up in the Violet Canal and at first light we'll go out."

They made their way back to the Violet Canal Bridge; Douglas, Sr. went in one direction, while Turner went deeper into the canal.

"They tied up a little further up the canal than us, and we tied up right close to the bridge to an oyster lugger," said Turner.

Constable Tony Guerra searched for his mother, aunt, and uncle who had decided to ride out the storm.

"I went to Creedmore Drive and parked the boat on my mama's roof of the house and was beating on the attic trying to see if they were there," said Guerra. "But they weren't, so I figured they drowned or they got out, it was getting dark at this time."

All he had was a flashlight to shine in the darkness; he navigated the airboat along St. Bernard Highway to Beauregard, hoping his family had walked over there before the water got too high.

"I went in there and it was already night. I went up in there and I went through the whole building," said Guerra. "I went up the steps, shined the light looking for my aunt and uncle. I couldn't find them, and I talked to one of the nurses, and she told me where they were from, from St. Rita's and that they evacuated, and they had no medicine, no water, no food, a lot of these people use diapers; they couldn't get up to go to the bathroom."

Guerra told the nurse, "Look it's dark I'll come back in the morning. I'll come pick you up and we'll go to the drugstore." There was Bradley's Pharmacy nearby in Poydras. "If we can get in, we'll see if we can find any insulin. If you know the medicine you need, I'll bring you there and we'll go get it."

Surprised to see people from the nursing home stranded at Beauregard, Guerra did not think to ask any other questions. He left with his flashlight and began the trek back to the levee. The ride was dangerous and he traveled slowly, trying to avoid hitting leaning power polls and power lines that could clothesline him right off of the boat.

Alonzo and the others tried to rest as best as they could. He worried deeply about getting the seizure medication for his brother. Alonzo had no idea how many had perished in the floodwater, but he was grateful he and his brother had survived.

A fisherman, Alonzo and the water of lower St. Bernard were like family. He remembered a story his mother repeated to him and his brothers, Carlos and Alex.

"I fished all my life and I never thought water would come like that. But I could remember my mama saying, they had a big double house in the front and they had the schoolhouse [Old Sebastian Roy School in Hopedale]. When she was little that they had a storm and they didn't know a storm was coming in them days. The water started coming up, before they could walk to the schoolyard, they couldn't, the water was over their head. I said the water couldn't come up that fast. She said, 'I'm telling ya that water came up that fast with that storm.' I remember her telling me that; it must have been the same kind of storm surge."

## CHAPTER THIRTEEN

# A Day to Forget, a Night to Remember

## Monday, August 29

### Day Two

*Sunset, the evening after Katrina blew through St. Bernard. Photograph by Donald Colletti*

Dozens of firemen had combed the parish all afternoon and evening saving people, communicating as if it was the early twentieth century, not the modern twenty-first century.

"To call one boat, they would call another boat and send a message all the way down the line like a relay race, that's how we communicated," said Fire Chief Thomas Stone.

For first responders it was a Herculean effort all day long.

"I didn't realize the amount of rescues our guys at Chalmette [High] were making during the storm, here we were [government complex] stranded with no boats, at the sugar refinery no boats, civic auditorium no boats, but as people came into the shelter they were just commandeering these boats and going right back out and bringing in boatload after boatload of people to the shelter," said Stone.

The chief may not have been in communication with most of his men but his captains, who chalked up a quarter century of experience apiece, performed like they were trained to and did not need a command to make life saving decisions.

"I don't think any fire department ever faced what we faced," said Stone. "We were one hundred percent inundated with floodwaters; everybody knew their homes were flooded; we found out our cars had been flooded. The next thing I know I was the fire chief in charge of the largest fire boat flotilla in the history of the United States."

Their boats ran into debris, and one firefighter was tossed into the water when his boat hit a dumpster. The worst disaster to ever hit St. Bernard Parish or just about anywhere was ending its first day, and Stone's flotilla had to call it a night.

"Coming in at night we just had to go so slow, and we had spotlights, and we'd be in a line, kind of like you see in the movies where the people going through the mine field and you're following the guy in front of you; that's what it was like because there was debris everywhere you couldn't see what was in the water," Stone said.

The firemen at Chalmette High discovered there was only one way to beat the stifling heat inside the school. They climbed on to the flat roof and found it much cooler than inside, and that is where they slept if they could manage to relax long enough. Some of the men had blankets to spread out, while others took broken-down cardboard boxes and created a layer between the roof and their bodies. Liccardi lodged in the classroom his wife taught in.

"I slept in my wife's room. I had my dog with me in the classroom in the kennel, and I'd go sleep in there," said Liccardi. "She's [her room] where the corner of the roof kind of came off, so she had water; it leaked and it was wet in there."

The firemen were not the only people using the roof at night.

"We'd go on the roof about eleven o'clock and try to reach

*One of the destroyed fire stations in St. Bernard. Photograph by Thomas Stone*

people on our cell phones," said Principal Wayne Warner. "Some services worked better than others; some people never got through to anybody. Some people were lucky and it would hit, and they would get on and they would be talking for a few minutes and then it would go off. We were trying to talk to our family to let them know we were alive."

"When I would get my sister, [school board member] David Fernandez would say here's my mother's number could you call my mother," said Mundt. "That's how many of them communicated with their families through someone else's family."

To conserve battery power they would only use their phones for a short time because on Monday night there was no way to recharge them.

Inside the school was like every other place in the parish, hot, stuffy, pitch-black, and miserable. Mundt thought about the elderly couple with the two dogs and the bird and the woman attached to an oxygen tank.

"We don't have any accommodations, that poor woman, who's on oxygen, is trying to sleep in a student desk with her head down and she's exhausted, she'd been on her roof somewhere for a day."

If there was any place worse than the school, it may have been the school gym. Conditions were tough and the putrid smell of animals that were urinating and defecating was difficult to bear. It was hard to control the animals, and there was no plan to do anything about it. Barry Uhle remembered one person trying to provide energy by starting up a generator inside the gym.

"Man are you crazy; you'll kill all of us!" Uhle said.

There was one nurse in the gym, and she was extremely busy all night, helping the hurt and sick. She had a little table on which she handled scrapes and cuts. The only light she had was from a flashlight.

"Somebody would yell nurse and all the flashlights would go to whoever was hollering, the lady would attend to whoever," said Uhle. "You hear somebody fall or crying they would shine over there like a beam. During the night people crying, dogs barking, it was kind of hard."

**Wildlife & Fisheries Arrive**

Monday night the first outside agency into St. Bernard Parish was the Louisiana Wildlife and Fisheries Department. Leading the way was Captain Brian Clark, who is the head of Region 8, a five-parish area that includes St. Bernard and Plaquemines.

Brian, who lives in the parish, grew up in St. Bernard and graduated from Chalmette High. His brother, Chad, is a captain with the sheriff's department. Brian was on his way down into the parish earlier that day but could not get any farther than the St. Claude Bridge in the Lower Ninth Ward because of all the people who needed help there. His mission, once he hit St. Bernard, was to visit as many places as he could to check on the condition of the residents and help them get whatever he could to sustain them.

"We knew we had calls from the government complex; we received messages from [State Representative] Nita Hutter and Larry Ingargiola that they needed help; they needed boats," said Brian.

They finally reached the complex after dark to see what their needs were and to see what they could do for the people trapped there. Brian talked to the firemen. From there his next stop was the Chalmette Medical Center.

"We heard the hospital was asking for help, so we went back to the hospital and met with some staff back there, that was a chaotic scene," said Brian. "They were out of power; they needed supplies; they were flooded, [there were] sick people there that needed care."

The hospital asked if Brian could provide them with more security.

"People were trying to get into the hospital from Village Square [the neighborhood surrounding the hospital] and other areas," said Brian. "They were trying to get in there, cause they thought it was a safe haven. They couldn't let any more people in; they had to stop it; they had limited medical supplies, no communications."

So Brian boated over to the courthouse.

"We met up with all the deputies and went and talked to the sheriff," said Brian. "We picked up a couple of deputies from the courthouse and brought them to the hospital to provide security for the night to relieve the one guy who was there."

Brian and crew then left to check on Chalmette High School.

"We started transporting some medical supplies along the way, trying to get supplies to bring to Chalmette High School; to try to get to the different shelters we had to try to assess what needed to be done; it was too big for us to handle in one night," Brian said. "With downed power lines, safety issues, everywhere you stopped the boats you heard people screaming and hollering asking for help."

Once they arrived at Chalmette, Mr. Warner asked Brian to bring him oxygen for the nearly three-dozen people there who needed it.

"We went back to the hospital, got some oxygen, went back to the school, dropped it off to them and started moving around from there again," Brian said. "We went back to sheriff and said we'll be in here with you. We worked all the way until four o'clock the first morning then we returned to the St. Claude Bridge and we slept in our trucks on the bridge."

## Hospital in Critical Condition

Housing patients, evacuees, and animals, the hospital was in dire straits.

"We had all ages young and old, children, babies, a few animals, people were bringing their dogs," said Dr. Domangue." I think we even had a chicken at one time."

They moved all the patients into one section of the facility while the evacuees, staff, and staff family took over the rest.

"Most were in the halls and some were in some rooms that were still open," said Dr. Domangue. "We tried to get as many of the staff into rooms as we could. Many of the people who came in from the community quickly overran all the rooms, so we had most of those people focused in specific hallways so they wouldn't interfere with the flow of nursing and physician movement into the patient rooms."

Even with the organization, the nurses still had issues with the people in the pitch-black hallways.

"We were tripping over them in the halls because you had the refugees lining the hallway," said nurse Barbara Warren. "It's kind of unnerving trying to make it through the halls without a flashlight cause you didn't know what you were gonna trip over. We had family members of staff and the patients and the refugees, trying to make everybody as happy as possible."

Nonetheless, Dr. Domangue felt things were under control.

"There was a certain amount of calm despite the tragedy that was engulfing all of us, and I think that was rather remarkable. Obviously, there was anger and a lot of distress and depression and crying but people would listen; they were not unsettled enough to create havoc; they were contributing to the calm, which was nice to see. With the numbers of people we had at that point in the facility under duress if there would have been a major upheaval it would have been a huge problem."

And everyone had to be fed something.

"A meal consisted of a cup of water, two pieces of ham, a tablespoon of banana pudding, and three vanilla wafers," said Warren. "And it didn't matter whether you were a physician or a refugee or a patient that's what you got."

The portions, already divided, were brought out to the people, but the servers did not have to go far.

"They saw the food coming; once the cafeteria person brought the cart out with the trays the people would flock to it," said Warren.

The sweltering heat caused a few nurses to bow out with heat exhaustion; those seeking relief found their way up to the roof, escaping the cramped building. Warren figures about thirty made it up to the top of the Chalmette Medical Center Monday night.

"Asphalt roof with rocks, it wasn't all that comfortable but it was better than being inside the hospital," said Warren.

"It was comfortable; I was actually sleeping between the Chief Executive Officer, Jon Sewell, and the Chief Operating Officer, Tim Coffey, and I think Dr. Bryan Bertucci," said Dr. Domangue. "Jon Sewell had only been on board for about five or six months. He came from Colorado and didn't have a lot of experience with hurricanes, so I think he very wisely solicited the help of others who had more experience with hurricanes. He'd always ask questions not just to me but to others in groups because there was things that had changed in the transition from the previous administration to his and they weren't all good. Some were financial; others were issues having to do with the medical staff. One of the questions he would often ask physicians in groups, 'Is it me? This place was working so well before, and why is it I'm on board now we're having this problem or this problem; is it me?' We'd always say no Jon it's not you. As we were laying on top the roof of the building and looking up at the stars I happened to say Jon, maybe it is you. We all laughed."

The evacuees laid down sheets, mattresses, and pillows for bedding. Under the star filled sky, flat on their backs, they took in the celestial show.

"It was the most awesome sky with the stars I have ever seen in my life, because there were no lights at all to reflect against them," said Warren. "That was kind of comforting to see that but we had brought what we had in air mattresses and bed mattresses, and we'd stick them all together and have staff laying however they could fit on those mattresses when we put them together, and we got a couple hours sleep."

It was a sky most never would have seen if not for Katrina. Would they have traded the experience? Absolutely, but it brought them a semblance of peace they had not felt in days. Many had gathered on top of the government complex. Earlier, they opened the hatch in case the water kept rising; now they could go up of their own free will and sleep up there with the rocks.

"You ever sleep on rocks? Not a very comfortable feeling on your back, it was a beautiful night stars in the sky and you could see across the river," said Larry Ingargiola. "There was some lights on down in New Orleans and down here black as anything. No noise, nobody out there, every once in awhile you see a light flash across the sky somebody with a flashlight or something, so we still had some people in the neighborhoods."

Councilman Kenny Henderson joined Ingargiola and others.

"That particular night, probably was the prettiest night I ever witnessed. There wasn't a light in St. Bernard Parish, the only things that were lit were the two refinery flares and that's all you could see for as far as you can see. A beautiful, cool night, looked up you could see every star in the sky."

Judy Hoffmeister was one of those who did not quite like the thought of having to go on to the roof, but to escape the heat of the complex she made the trek up the stairs to the roof.

"I couldn't hear helicopters, but you could see helicopters with the search lights and, I was looking to the west and I'm thinking where are they going," said Hoffmeister. "But when you would see the helicopter with the search lights you could look into the St. Bernard section and you could see the flares going off the roofs cause they saw it too. I knew they weren't close."

Hoffmeister has volunteered for years at the Red Cross and went to Homestead, Florida, after Hurricane Andrew to help with relief. She went to the office to gather supplies, cots, blankets, and toiletry kits with shaving cream meant for soldiers in Iraq, she had brought with her to the complex before the storm.

"We brought the cots upstairs on the roof and that's how we slept but then you had to go to the bathroom on [top of] the government complex and go on the roof; it was a separate section of the roof that was the poo poo potty; we called it the poo poo roof."

A councilwoman for less than two years, Hoffmeister had planned to retire in 2006.

"I said Lord I'll make you a deal, don't let the big one come until after I retire, I think that got miscommunicated, I think he heard me say let the big one come now and then I'll retire," Hoffmeister laughs.

The agony and chaos of a full day of survival turned in to a frighteningly quiet night in St. Bernard. Bob Turner had to maneuver his boat in the dark to secure it in the Violet Canal. It had been a brutally intense thirty-six hours or so and many had not slept at all in that time; if they were going to get any rest, it would have to be in the spot they were in when the sun flickered its final rays. Turner and his boat mate, Norbert Billiot, a heavy equipment operator, curled up in separate nooks in their flatboat.

"Raincoats for covers and life jackets for pillows," said Turner. "It was kind of cramped."

Food was as scarce as light, and some were lucky to have a little something tucked away. Turner dug deep into his pocket and pulled out a snack to share for dinner.

"We had Skittles for supper; one bag of Skittles, and I split it between me and [Billiot]."

The other group of levee district men, led by Troy Douglas, Sr., docked closer to the Violet Canal Bridge and hopped onto an oyster boat to try and get their first bit of sleep since before Katrina struck.

Deputy Gelvin and his trustees had to end their run toward the levee district and as they approached pumping station #7 at Bartolo Drive in Meraux, he didn't expect to see much, since he was told Katrina destroyed the station.

"Pumping station seven was still standing," Gelvin said. "I can't believe this; two people told me it was gone."

So he decided that was where they would spend the night. Normally, to get to the station you would drive down Bartolo Drive, cross a small bridge over the 40 Arpent Canal, and then turn right onto the flattened, dirt road at the base of the canal levee and drive about a block or so to the elevated station. This was all underwater, so Gelvin docked the boat at the station; the water had stopped about six steps below the bottom of the building. Looking out behind the back of the pumping station, the men had an uneasy feeling about the merging of Lake Borgne and St. Bernard.

"The safest place to be is gonna be at the pumping station for the night," said Gelvin. "We made it to the station, cranked up the generator, the roof was gone off the building but me, three trustees, and five other employees, we stayed there that night because it was too dark to ride around. You'd be taking a chance riding around in the dark."

When Tony Guerra left Beauregard Middle School, he just wanted to get to the levee without running into any of the power lines that draped St. Bernard Highway like a country clothesline. He used his flashlight to guide him through the black night. He made it to the levee district in Violet sometime between 9:00 and 10:00 P.M. and parked the airboat, not bad for a man who had never driven a boat like that before. He saw a dry vehicle on the levee and was glad to see it belonged to his friend, Donald Mankin, who was inside the car.

"Man can I sleep in the back seat?"

"Yea."

So while Mankin slept in the front seat, Guerra climbed in the back seat soaking wet from head to toe. He had nothing to dry off with and nothing dry to put on. He was cold and crunched up with an uncomfortably wet shirt, pants, socks, and shoes clinging to his skin. Guerra's mind wandered in the dead silence of the moment.

"I didn't know if my wife was alright; she didn't know if I was alright, cause we had no news coverage," Guerra said. "She went to Picayune [Mississippi] with my mother and her mama. I'm assuming they made it all right. I talked to her a couple of times during the night [Sunday] but once that wind hit, we lost all cell phones and couldn't talk to anybody. We had all this water and all this devastation and Picayune's not that far. You've got tornadoes; she was wondering if I was alive I'm wondering if they're O.K."

He eventually passed out.

The evacuees inside St. Bernard High School were trying to rest as nightfall came. Firemen Michael Lebeau and Rodney Ourso, along with the other first responders, tried to stabilize the group by calling a lights out and providing a bit of calmness to the school. They were exhausted, and this was a chance for them to get their first rest in nearly two days. Despite the absolute hell everyone had suffered through, some were in a disruptive mood. Sergeant Greg Hauck refused to let the situation get out of hand.

"I took weapons from people; I had to delegate people to make 'em deputies, I had to do that with the firemen; I armed most of the firemen," recalled Hauck. "There was fights. We took weapons from people; there were people that came in intoxicated, under the influence of narcotics."

"This was a night where everybody was tired and exhausted," said Lebeau. "It was nice and quiet, and I was contemplating going to lay down myself, and this guy was warned once about being rude. The second time was when I got involved, and I actually knew this guy, and they came and got me and I went down to the room; me and the deputy pulled him outside and tried to talk to him again."

The officers were trying to reason with some people who had

made supply runs that afternoon; they picked up and brought back to the school the one item no one needed, alcohol.

"So they're drunk; you got people in the shelter trying to get some sleep and surviving, and they're being stupid getting drunk," said Lebeau. "We had two deputies and I was armed; I'm always armed when I go to a shelter cause you never know what's gonna happen. Being in the drunken state he was in, there was no talking to him, we had no other recourse but to incarcerate him, it was a shame. We handcuffed one of them first then the girl that was with them, we had to handcuff her too."

Lebeau remembered that one of the men was spitting on people and that the woman was fighting; then the woman's husband began acting out of control, and the officers handcuffed him as well.

"We had three people on the roof screaming and hollering all night cause they were drunk," said Lebeau.

"The guy's telling the girl he loves her," Ourso adds.

"We had thrown all the booze out the window, and this particular guy we're talking about went to the second floor on the roof and dove off head first into all this water and debris and whatever else may have been down there to try to find a bottle of booze in the middle of the night," Lebeau said. "That was just one of the stupid things, he swam back in, we take the booze away from him again and empty it."

Lebeau thought it all started when the man tried to steal some pills out of an elderly woman's purse and when she screamed they responded.

"It escalated from there, and we didn't need that with all these people trying to survive," said Ourso.

The man stayed handcuffed on the roof of the school all night.

"We had to stay up with him, dealing with that all night," said Ourso

Lebeau did not want to give the name of the man he knew.

CHAPTER FOURTEEN

# Second Verse, Same as the First

## Tuesday, August 30

### Day Three

Just when people around the parish were starting to get a sliver of peace, the quiet night air was pierced with the shocking sounds of automatic gunfire. They could hear them clearly at the Domino Sugar Refinery, which sits just blocks from the Orleans Parish border and its Lower Ninth Ward. The gunshots seemed to be coming from the Lower Ninth Ward, which has experienced its share of the infamous New Orleans crime rate. Some fire district chiefs stationed at the refinery called Chief Stone.

"I was on the roof of the [government complex]; it was about 2:00 A.M. Tuesday, and they were hearing gunshots in the city, and they thought they were coming closer to them," said Stone. "They had [heard] all the rumors of the civil unrest and they were very concerned for their safety."

After talking to the three district chiefs at the refinery, Stone contacted Sheriff Stephens, who had just lain down on the floor of the courthouse, on one of the police radios. With dozens of evacuees and more than thirty firefighters at the refinery, the last thing they needed to handle was lawless criminals.

"Sheriff Stephens sent deputies down there," said Stone. "They could travel the levee and after, he brought them weapons. The situation lasted from about 2:00 A.M. to 5:00 A.M. before they felt secured in their location."

Stephens decided he would keep a few men at the refinery.

213

"We left people staged in that area in the event there was any attempt to move up the levee," said Stephens. "There were all kind of stories circulating that people thought we had a stockpile of food and water and medicine, and that's the thing we were concerned about we didn't have any of that but didn't want somebody to do something crazy that thought we may have that."

Stephens realized his ability to enforce the law was compromised in the destroyed parish; therefore, the firefighters had been deputized on Monday.

"It was an executive order from the sheriff that deputized all firefighters," said Stone. "It was brought to me by presidential attorney Alan Abadie, who came to me and said that everybody was deputized."

Tuesday morning was the first time deputies issued weapons to the firefighters. Extra guns were tough to come by after the flood but over the next few days all the firemen had been saddled with some sort of firearm.

"They were shotguns or something like that and people went and signed out handguns," said Stone. "We tried to keep a real strict accountability of the guns. We had them with the person's name that signed them out."

### Marina Time Is Not the Same as Bank Time

Around four o'clock, not long after the gunshots frazzled those huddled at the sugar refinery, Glenn Sanchez popped up from his few hours of exhausted sleep. An owner of the Breton Sound Marina in Hopedale, he was still on "marina time," while everyone else in Region's Bank was, for the most part, resting. He got up and talked with some of the sheriff's deputies there.

"They had about ten guys keeping it under control, otherwise it would have been total chaos," said Sanchez.

He believes there were fewer than sixty people inside the sweltering bank. They broke open windows for ventilation, but they did not provide any real relief. Sanchez had to wait until sun up before anyone could get the boats running. Out in the water the amount of people that needed help seemed endless.

"Somebody was screaming for help and we went over there," said Sanchez. "In Chalmette, off of Packenham [Drive], this guy needed dialysis, and he hadn't had any dialysis in five days and it was his brother screaming. We put him in the boat and took him to the hospital. They checked his vital signs; they said they knew him and had to airlift him outta here."

They loaded the man back into the boat to take him from Chalmette Medical Center to Paris Road; they dropped him off in front of Our Lady of Prompt Succor Church, only a couple of blocks from the jail, which had become a medical staging area.

"They were gonna medevac him out," said Sanchez. "We brought him up there and I got out the boat and stood in a foot of water on dry land, put him in the back of a Blazer so they could medevac him out. I stepped back in the boat and went back to Region's Bank, and that's the dumbest thing I ever did. I could have got out right then and there."

Instead he forged ahead with the search and rescue. While Sanchez saw many people lucky to be alive, he came across a few people who made the best of the dire situation.

"They had people on rooftops; they were barbequing; they had a two-story, might have had porch on the side of it; stuff in their freezers, it was dry; they were cooking what they had to eat," said Sanchez. "One guy asked us if we had any ice to keep his beer cold."

Sanchez stayed with the crew, thinking this would be the day the cavalry would ride in and rescue them from that sweltering bank. When he got back to Region's, the population there had doubled to around 120 people.

### Getting The Water Out

The crack of dawn was a busy time around the parish for Bob Turner, Troy Douglas, Sr., and the other levee district employees.

"We started heading out and the other boat met us, and we went out, and I stopped right by the bridge, cause there was a group of people on a boat right there that had been rescuing people during the day," said Turner.

Looking for help to work on the Bayou Dupre lock structure, Turner wanted to recruit extra men.

"We might have to open up the Violet locks manually, anybody want to volunteer to come help us?" Turner offered and three or four volunteered.

Russell Gelvin and his crew were on the water at first light, heading out to meet Turner.

"I knew I had to get to Troy [Douglas, Sr.] and them, and I

knew I had to get these boats out," said Gelvin. "I started coming up the Violet Canal and I ran into Tony Guerra, and he told
me Bob had already come down here and got the two boats the
night before, and they were out at the locks."

Guerra had run the airboat the night before, but Gelvin let one
of his trustees, Steve Edgett, take the airboat to go with Guerra
back to Beauregard Middle School. Guerra informed Gelvin that
at the school were St. Rita's Nursing Home evacuees with no
medical supplies and barely anything to eat or drink.

"Y'all go do what y'all got to do," Gelvin told them.

From there Gelvin drove down the Violet Canal to join up
with the men and when Turner got to the locks he was struck by
the condition of the structure.

"We got out there and the place was destroyed, the locks were
still closed but all of the doors and windows were blown out of
the block houses," said Turner. "There was trash everyplace.
The generator [was] hanging out of the building, holding on by
the exhausts pipe through the roof. We knew we had to open it
manually and it wasn't safe for these volunteers to be out there,
so we had to ship those men back and got some of our people
together from the shelters and started opening it up manually."

The job was tedious and strenuous.

"It took us about six or seven hours," said Turner. "You can
only crank it a quarter turn at a time with four people pulling on
the wheel and every quarter turn it only moves like a sixty-
fourth of an inch. You got thirty feet to open so it took a long
time to do that and we finally got it opened up that afternoon."

It was the first step in getting the water draining out of the
parish and going back toward the Gulf of Mexico through the
marsh and the MR-GO waterway.

### St. Rita's Evacuees Need Medication

Guerra and Edgett went immediately to Beauregard Middle
School to pick up the nurse from St. Rita's. They were going to
the closest pharmacy, the long standing Bradley's Pharmacy in
Poydras. Guerra went inside the school and found the nurse
who had the list of medications needed for the St. Rita's survivors. When they arrived at Bradley's, the backdoor was open,
so they walked in.

"We [were] walking in water and anything that wasn't in the

*St. Rita's Nursing Home after the floodwater receded. Photograph by Mikel Schaefer*

water that was up above on the shelves that stayed dry, she took it," said Guerra. "Like the insulin needles, the insulin that was in the refrigerator, whatever medicines they needed. We got diapers; we got water, whatever we could find that wasn't contaminated with the water, and pills that was up on top; she got everything she needed, and she said she was satisfied."

Guerra felt uneasy going into Bradley's, like he was looting, but he realized there was no way he could not. The law would have to bend to help those suffering at the school.

"We got in there before the druggies hit it, just in time," said Guerra. "We brought it back down to the nursing home people and left everything at Beauregard until we was able to get them out cause we had no way to get all these old people out."

The sick and infirmed seemed vastly out of place in the surrealistic nightmare of Katrina.

"I might see some young people that stayed at their homes like my uncle might have been there, but I never believe I would see people from the nursing home still there," said Guerra.

Gene Alonzo was hoping the nurse would come back with something to stop Carlos from going into convulsions.

"They had some seizure medicine, but it wasn't the kind he takes, so we just giving him a different kind anyway it was better than none," said Alonzo.

Fortunately, the medication served its purpose and Alonzo was not even sure what his brother was given. Then others at the school went out to loot stores for food to help feed everyone. For the first time since the storm had hit Monday morning, someone official had made it to Beauregard. They arrived in the early afternoon, Alonzo believed around two o'clock.

"The Wildlife comes with these airboats and said they could take people to the sheriff by Paris Road," said Alonzo. "They came in two airboats, driving them to the jail. They brought us up there, but they ain't had nothing up there neither, a mass of people. They said they was gonna have helicopters to fly these sick people out. We got there and waited, and they said they got a helicopter coming. They said they had medical care, but they didn't have nothing."

Alonzo began to tear up as they pulled away from Beauregard.

## Checking on St. Rita's

It had been nearly forty-eight hours since Steve Gallodoro went to St. Rita's Nursing Home to check on their evacuation plans; he was worried about what had happened.

"I figured they didn't have electricity, they may have needed food and water," said Gallodoro.

His mission was to go to Blue Dot Marine on Paris Road. He had been told there were two party barges there; they were both to be used for search and rescue and for hauling supplies.

"The party barges at Blue Dot were upside down, none of them had motors on them," said Gallodoro.

After leaving the Blue Dot, Gallodoro finally had time to check on his father, Tufanio, at the nursing home. He picked up fellow fireman Lee Gonzales and long time friends councilman Ricky Melerine and Raymond Couture, better known as "Bozo" and headed toward St. Rita's. This was the first trip the councilman had made to his district since the storm, thus affording Gallodoro the chance to check in on his father.

"We made it down to the eastern end of the parish crossing the [Violet] Canal, dragging the boat over the levee, underneath the [Violet] Bridge and then put it back in the water and continued down Judge Perez Drive," said Gallodoro.

Once on the other side of the Violet Canal they could see there was more water at this end of St. Bernard.

"When I saw the water there I was thinking three foot of water," said Gallodoro. "Of course the water had already receded some at that point. I wasn't feeling real comfortable, I thought that the nursing home most probably received or endured a lot more misery than I thought prior to seeing that."

It was not much longer before they reached St. Rita's.

"When we got down there, there was six feet of water in the parking lot," said Gallodoro. "I thought that at the last minute they evacuated until I saw the owner's Hummer in the parking lot. When I saw that I said if they would have evacuated, she would have taken her Hummer; she wouldn't have left it; it was brand new. At that point I figured they were all inside drowned."

The men were so quiet you could hear their Adam's apples contracting in their throats. Gallodoro's mind was foggy with the overwhelming fear of the death of a loved one. He stepped out of the boat and swam over to the front double glass doors.

"I tried to get in, they were locked," said Gallodoro. "I tried to break through those doors but swimming in the water, trying to break through doors, that wasn't working."

He figured the water was around seven feet by the steps because the wooden deck that would have been there had floated away.

"I swim back to the boat, and I tell them to bring me over to the patio, there was a patio of the north wing and the south wing," said Gallodoro. "They brought me to the patio; I climbed over the rail and stood up on the patio, and the water was about three and a half-foot deep on the patio in the front. I noticed the double doors there, one of them was broken, so I knew I was gonna be able to get in. As I walked to that door, I was thirty feet away from it, I noticed a body floating on the patio. I walked over to it, and it was an elderly lady."

He did not recognize the woman.

"I crawled underneath the handle of the door and walked into the hallway, and right inside the door I came across another floating body. It was another female. I was in the TV room at that time; I walked to the main hallway, and before I got to the main hallway, I came in touch with another floating body. All three were females."

He quickly assessed each body he came across.

"I was checking to see if it was my father, once I identified that it wasn't him then I didn't go look to see who it was. When I got to the hallway and looked down the hallway, the furniture, the mattresses, and everything that was floating I couldn't get over that to get through the hallway to my dad's room; I hollered 'fire department is anybody in here? Anybody need help?' It just echoed through the hallways, there was no answer. I hollered again, again it echoed through the hallways and no answer."

Since the hallways were cluttered with wheelchairs and other furniture, Gallodoro decided to leave the building.

"I went outside, got back in the boat, and called for assistance. I told them we were at St. Rita's Nursing Home, we had multiple fatalities, and we needed assistance at this site. At that time I thought everybody had passed away."

The men with Gallodoro were at the scene of the largest concentration of dead bodies in St. Bernard; they could feel the pain emanating from their friend.

"Councilman Melerine and I have been best friends for forty years. But I had a rookie firefighter with us, six months on the job, I couldn't [n]or did I want to put him into a situation of being the only two to go in there, and I didn't want to expose him to that. It's not a pretty sight; it's a sight that lives with you forever. You will burn that into your brain and your memory and you will be haunted by that and I am, but there was no need to put him in that. Had I heard an utter of communications or sound of help then I would have brought the other three in immediately. What I was asking for help for was a recovery of bodies."

They pulled the boat away from the facility to East Judge Perez Drive and over to a sheriff's deputy.

"I pulled up to the sheriff's office amphibious vehicle and was going to tell them about St. Rita's, and they said they already know; they've got thirty-five floaters in there."

Shaken, Gallodoro questioned the deputy further.

"What is your plan of action?"

"We have none."

"O.K. I just stayed there looking and wondering why they had no plan of action."

"The survivors were at Beauregard," the deputy told Gallodoro.

"Upon hearing that I told Lee Gonzales [to] drive the boat over to Beauregard, let's go see who the survivors are and if my dad's there," said Gallodoro. "We went over there and upon arriving at Beauregard, there's a boat in front of us and they're trying to get a lady out of the boat. She's screaming and hollering she doesn't want to get out the boat unless her husband comes with her. Her husband is in a sheet, he has passed away. They were not gonna take the body inside of Beauregard, but she didn't want to leave her husband, so they convinced her to go inside, and they took his body and put him on a piece of wood and tied him to the fence."

Gallodoro walked inside the dark school and down the hall until he saw one of the nurses from St. Rita's who had taken care of his father.

"When she saw me, she looked at me and said, 'I'm sorry' and put her head down. I continued to walk over to her and she looked at me and said 'I'm sorry,' and looked away. When I got close enough I said, "Are you telling me he didn't make it?"

"I'm sorry," and she started crying, and she couldn't talk anymore.

"After further checking, my father wasn't one of the people who survived; I left and went back to [the] sheriff's office boat that was on Judge Perez."

When he arrived there he saw the owner of St. Rita's, Sal Mangano, in a flat boat tied to the sheriff's office vehicle boat. Gallodoro forcefully confronted him, asking Mangano what he was doing riding around in a boat.

"You've got dead people in your building and you're out riding around in a boat bullshitting with people."

"'They've got people floating dead all over the parish,'" Gallodoro recalled Mangano saying.

"But those people had a choice, yours was your responsibility; you told me you were getting everybody out!"

Gallodoro could feel his temper rising to the point of no return; he knew the storm had taken all of his material possessions, and he was still in shock from the news that Katrina had taken his most precious father's life.

"I didn't want to do anything that I would regret later; I don't know if I would have regret it, I may had to pay a price through the courts," said Gallodoro. "I was an emotional wreck."

"I don't know specifically, having talked with Sal, that conversation took place," said Mangano's attorney, Jim Cobb. "You mean he's questioning Sal about what's he doing in a boat when he's got dead bodies in his [place]? All day Monday and into the night Monday night and then again on Tuesday morning, Sal [Jr.] and Sal, Sr. and others worked feverishly to save the people that he had saved, went back and found people after he got the initial people out, saved as many lives as they could. To the folks that unfortunately died, died within minutes, and what they were concerned about were taking care of the living not recovering the dead. So he's accosting Sal about riding around in a boat, he's on the property doing what he can."

Gallodoro called for command and asked for thirty-five body bags.

"They said stand by and came back an hour later and said they didn't have thirty-five body bags," said Gallodoro. "If you don't have thirty-five then send me one body bag; I'm gonna do a recovery of one."

They all knew who he was talking about.

"They came back and said there were no body bags in the parish at this time. The only thing they could provide me with was a plastic bag, but that I was to be advised that if I made a recovery that no one would accept [a] recovered body from me."

The sun was going down; all of the boats were ordered in, and Gallodoro went back to the government complex.

"When I got back to the complex, Deputy Chief Raleigh Richards met with me in a boat and we talked for about an hour or two on what my options were. Neither one of 'em was gonna be pleasant or easy to live with. In an explanation and bringing me back to reality at the time of me discovering St. Rita's we were still very much in a rescue mode. I was attempting to start a recovery, while rescue was still going on. Many years of service with the fire department, never before have I tried to break that chain or do recoveries before rescue was completed. However, the person was never my father. So I was somewhat able to come to grips with that, and they told me I could be part of the recovery team not recommending that I go and do the recovery of my dad but that I could be part of that team that went to the nursing home to do that."

Every time Carlos began to have a seizure, Alonzo would give him the medication.

"When he start getting those little seizures, I start giving him some medicine; I didn't know what to do cause that was not the kind he took," said Alonzo. "The nurses was with us and said that was all you could do."

The jail took on a much more ominous feeling once several of the nursing home survivors arrived, because they represented some of the most critical patients to seek refuge at the severely undermanned facility. Several could not even walk.

"They ain't had no place for them to lay, it was hot and the toilets was all over flowing, I wished we had stayed at Beauregard, this is critical here," said Alonzo. "We couldn't stand it, it was so hot in the jail, must have been 115 degrees in there. We moved some people out; you couldn't breathe; we put them on the sidewalk."

That included Carlos and some girls trying to drag their mother out of the overheated jail.

"They kept getting more and more people and they say helicopter's coming. I never could get on a helicopter with my brother, always somebody else getting on. We did that all night only had two helicopters," Alonzo said with exasperation in his voice. "They had workers trying to get water for the ones from St. Rita's but they had other sick people. We're trying to change these people; we had a couple of diapers they gave us. All of them all messed, nothing to clean them with, the bathrooms you couldn't even go in."

**Word Gets Out**

It did not take long for word to filter out about the dead bodies floating inside of St. Rita's Nursing Home. The head of the office of Homeland Security and Emergency Preparedness Larry Ingargiola remembers hearing the news.

"I was one pissed off mother f@!ker. A lot of those people I knew, a lot of their family members were friends of mine, still are. I knew we did everything we could possibly do to evacuate people out of the parish. Hindsight, maybe I could have called all the nursing homes."

While St. Rita's had a plan to evacuate, Ingargiola stated there was nothing in Louisiana state law that gave authorities the power to make a nursing home adhere to their plan.

"When I usually give speeches to the elderly there's always a few that say I rode out Betsy, there's nothing worse than Betsy. I always carry little toe tags with me and I say do me a favor and fill one of these out and when the water comes up tie it around your toe for me. [They ask] 'What's that for?' So I know who you are; so I can identify the body. I used to bring body bags and stretch it out on the floor, and I would say that's for people who don't evacuate."

A state trooper walked up to Sheriff Stephens to tell him about St. Rita's.

"She came in and they were bringing some people that needed medical attention and she was down there with some wildlife agents and a couple of our guys," said Stephens.

"Sheriff, we've got casualties at St.Rita's," she said.

"How many?"

"Over thirty."

"What happened?"

"They didn't evacuate them; they couldn't get out; they drowned."

It was a jolt to Stephens psyche.

"Man as bad as things were I had to take a minute just to absorb that, think about it," remembered Stephens.

Stephens compared St. Rita's decision to stay against his decision to evacuate prisoners.

"I had 350 inmates at the parish jail, and I was in a much safer position than they were, and I evacuated them, if I exercise that degree of care for criminals, why wouldn't they do it for senior citizens who couldn't really take care of themselves. It was just a horrible decision."

Cobb responded to Stephens reaction, "How many of your 350 prisoners are unable to walk; how many of your 350 prisoners are on oxygen; how many of your 350 prisoners are on feeder tubes; answer, none. You shackle 'em up and shuffle 'em up, and they're ambulatory and you put them on a bus. So to compare 350 prisoners to 70 folks in a nursing home who can't walk, who can't sit up, can't breathe, who are on oxygen feeder tubes is a disingenuous comparison."

Cobb, Sal and Mabel Mangano's attorney, said if parish officials, such as Stephens and Ingargiola, received calls before the storm from the National Hurricane Center informing them that the parish was facing such a catastrophic situation, why didn't they call the nursing home.

"He [Stephens] didn't call St. Rita's to tell them, neither he didn't nor anybody else didn't. The only phone call that anybody says they had with St. Rita's is [Dr.] Bertucci, and Bertucci says [he] didn't tell them it was a mandatory [evacuation]. Everybody in the parish knew they were there; Gallodoro knew they were there; Ingargiola knew they were there; why didn't somebody tell them."

## CHAPTER FIFTEEN

# I've Got to Get Out of This Place

## Tuesday, August 30

### Day Three

Sunrise did not come soon enough for Charlo as he climbed off of his shipping container into the water that was between his "knees and his waist."

"But I ain't walked passed my neighbor's house I done stuck a nail in my toe," said Charlo in his sweet countrified twang. "Oh, Lord this ain't gonna work."

He searched around and found two sticks about three feet in length; he placed them ahead of each foot, so he could feel anything that was hidden beneath the surface of the water. He stepped down on the sticks to keep from stepping on all the debris splattered from destroyed homes. Scattered in Charlo's path were power poles, crab nets, fishing gear, and just about anything that one would find inside of a home or camp. He walked the 1.6 miles toward the old steel drawbridge that crosses Bayou La Loutre connecting Yscloskey with Hopedale and Shell Beach.

"I got to the Yscloskey Bridge and it was about five foot higher and cocked sideways where the wave knocked it up and jammed it up that way," said Charlo. "I gotta climb up there and get on top that bridge to cross it. I was worried about it falling as soon as I touched it, offset it or something, naturally my skinny ass didn't offset it, but I had that in my head; I got to cross it."

Charlo climbed up the steel beam located under the circular

wheel pulley at the top of each end of the bridge and pulled himself up on the bridge, he walked across the metal-gated plank and
climbed down the extra five feet off the other raised section. He
was now on Florissant Highway in the shadow of the Yscloskey
water tower. It was the road out of there, but just like on his side
of the bridge, Katrina had smashed everything. All the houses
were either mangled into a mash of unrecognizable pieces or
washed away down to the pilings or slabs. Homes were now
only shells of their vibrant life, a single set of steps to nowhere or
a flagpole standing with a shredded American flag jostling in the
wind. The trees were naked and the tops had been sheered off as
if ravaged by a ten-mile wide buzz saw.

In the opposite direction, on the road to Shell Beach, homes
had been tossed off their foundations, a stainless steel, double
sink hung from tree branches, and shrimping boats had been
tossed on to the roads and into the marsh. Charlo had walked
through the valley of death, and he was alive, and there was
only one thing on his mind.

"I'm looking for a pair of shoes all that time cause since I left
my house I couldn't see nothing. I'm barefoot with a nail stuck
in the toe, and I kept walking."

He approached the destroyed Dynegy Gas Plant to his right
on the other side of the bayou; he said he saw and heard a hissing sound.

"They got a mess there, gas squirting everywhere."

He said to himself, they are gonna have a lot of work to do to
clean that up and put that thing together.

"You could hear it very loud, sssssssssssshhhhhhhh gas blowing at high pressure."

He lost track of how long he had been walking on Florissant
Highway, but he walked gingerly because his feet were
swollen and he was still holding on to those three-foot sticks.
Charlo looked down into the soft, brown mud and saw signs of
an alligator.

"I seen where they had big alligator bellies walking on the
road; you could see it was large alligators, six- to ten-foot alligators easily. You could see their bellies were going through the
mud. While I'm walking I only see one alligator, he was at least
six-foot to ten-foot alligator. I don't believe that on TV they can
jump on their back and wrestle them; they got to be giving them
Valium or something; it don't work like that. When I seen him

looking at me I just hollered like hell and beat my two sticks together, and he left. Alligators don't like all that noise and ain't going after people; I ain't on their diet."

## Unlikely Sight

Chuck Thurman and Frankie Asevado spent the early morning hours making their way around lower St. Bernard; they rescued people who wanted to leave and brought them to St. Bernard High School.

"The whole time we were down here, we was going to get supplies to make sure we had enough food, water, and fuel for the generator and that type of stuff cause we knew there was no help," said Thurman. "There was no one down here trying to rescue nobody; the community down here is what rode [around] in lower St. Bernard."

They rescued a couple from their attic in Sylvia Estates, but by now they knew the water level would have dropped significantly outside of the levee protection system, so they also wanted to check on their properties off Florissant Highway. When they arrived by boat to the levee, right across from the Verret Fire and Sheriff's Department building and a stones throw from President Junior Rodriguez's house, the water had gone down so much they had to leave the boat right there. So while the couple went into the station, Thurman and Asevado walked the nearly desolate four-lane highway. The forests of trees on both sides of the road were bent toward the southwest with the tops butchered. After about a two-mile hike, they reached the junction where you can go either right toward Delacroix or left toward Yscloskey, Shell Beach, and Hopedale. The main marker was shattered to smithereens and the Junction Food Store was a collapsed conglomeration of cinderblocks and smashed food. It was almost unrecognizable.

"They had a bunch of debris and pirogues and boats," said Thurman. "Right there we picked up two pirogues and we started paddling our way down to see what we had left. My house was gone, I told Frankie, 'you're house is gone too podna.' We wanted to come to our own property, figuring hey at least we'll be home: we'll set up shop at our house: there was nothing down here left."

They were paddling toward Asevado's house when Thurman saw something that was more shocking than the total destruction of his house. He said to Asevado, "Is that somebody walking up the highway?"

Up until then the only sounds Charlo had heard on his nearly five-mile walk were the sticks splashing into the water, ambient wildlife sounds, and his breathing. For the first time in more than two days he heard humans.

"I heard two men talking; voices travel well over water, especially when there's no wind and it's calm," said Charlo. "I don't have a lot of frog in me just to jump out there when it comes to another human being, so I eased upon them."

Thurman and Asevado rowed toward Charlo.

"Man y'all look like angels," said Charlo.

"Man you look like you've seen God," Thurman shot back.

Charlo leaned into Asevado's pirogue and fell right on board.

"We were both amazed to see anybody or anything coming from down here," said Thurman. "He was solid white; he looked like a big scab. He look like he came out of a prize fighting championship. He was beat up all over, legs, knees, everything beat up; he was so weak; I don't think he would have made it very much further cause he had no water, no nothing for days."

"They didn't expect any human being to come walking out of there." said Charlo. "I told them I couldn't paddle; I know how to paddle a pirogue; I know how to ride in a pirogue, but I don't know if I can paddle it without flipping."

They turned the pirogues around and headed back and about a half mile later they reached the Highway 46 junction. Thurman and Asevado scoured the area for something to drink, knowing Charlo would be in trouble if they did not get some fluids into him quickly; they found soft drinks and beer.

"The Junction store was all busted up, so there was free beer," Charlo laughed. "I didn't drink any. I'm just beat up, wore out; I knew not to drink a beer; I'd probably fall out."

They also found a rolling garbage can and helped put Charlo inside of it. Thurman and Asevado rolled Charlo, who was sucking down a hot Coke, down the highway. There wasn't much debris; the road was pretty clear. The men ended up back at the Verret substation.

"We got to the substation he [Charlo] just laid on top of an ice box that was laying down, and he went to sleep right there," said Thurman.

That night they ate well; Thurman had saved a freezer full of big, white shrimp; he had taken it out of his house before the storm. They peeled the shrimp and fried them without any batter.

"I had a stove in the back of my truck up in Kenilworth off of my boat, a little propane stove; my bottles all floated off, but down here I found a bottle hanging over the power line, and I got that bottle and that's what we had gas to cook with," said Thurman.

Thurman and Asevado also figured out a way to generate power.

"At the substation they had a broken generator up high on the shelf that didn't get wet, and they had a brand new one down low that got flooded, but it was brand new, so we took the parts off the new one and fixed the broken one, and we ended up with a generator."

### Medical Center Meltdown

By Tuesday Chalmette Medical Center had reached critical mass. Supplies were low; they could not reach anyone outside of the parish; and the situation was not going to get any better. Finally, the decision was made to empty the building.

"We were running low on essentials and our supplies were not gonna last much longer," said Dr. Domangue. "We realized the water was not going down; we weren't able to get in touch with a helicopter transport system to land on the roof. The sheriff's department advised us they had the jail, had generator power, and they could take patients if we needed to move them from our facility to the jail."

Because the jail had generator power, Dr. Domangue was asked to check it out to see if it could receive the hospital patients and what supplies would need to be transported there. Dr. Domangue and nurse Keith Bradbury boated over to the jail and found a third world country awaiting them.

"What did I do? I've gone from the pot into the fire, and it was so bad and so intense neither Keith Bradbury or myself had time to stop and communicate with the hospital and say look we better rethink this for right now; we've got to get things under control right here, and I need help," said Dr. Domangue. "It was really a mess. A lot of people in need of medical care already there, it was overwhelmed, and there was a couple of people who had some paramedical training who were there trying to take care of all these patients. Packed to the gills with people, nursing home patients as well as people injured from the sheriff's office, local residents who needed care."

In the Chalmette High gym a woman, pregnant with her first child, went into labor and was rushed to the jail. Nurse Janie Fuller was taking care of her when Dr. Domangue arrived. Together they helped deliver the baby while the expectant father watched.

"She and I concentrated on delivering this child, which delivered an hour or so later, young girl, who the family named Katrina," said Dr. Domangue.

A child delivery notwithstanding, Dr. Domangue and the nurse were hit from all directions.

"We were absolutely engulfed with all kinds of medical problems, people were bleeding, people were having chest pains, in diabetic comas, and we began addressing all these needs," said Dr. Domangue. "I had communication with the hospital and I told them on multiple occasions I need help, I need physicians over here, and I asked specifically for Dr. Bertucci and Dr. Al Lemerande; I was asking for them and nurses."

Dr. Domangue said the hospital didn't quite understand what he was requesting; however, doctors and nurses did arrive at the jail. It took another twenty-four hours before they had completely emptied the hospital of patients.

"I ended up with a select group of nurses, and we still had to deal with the other injuries and illnesses going on from people who were injured from the storm or evacuated from their houses and were massively dehydrated," said Dr. Domangue. "Some of the [nursing home patients] were very sick, dehydrated, exposed to the elements, often times with multi-system issues to heart, to lungs, to kidney."

They did not have time to think; they could only treat as many patients as possible. Dr. Domangue thought this had to be what it was like in Iraq.

"I can't imagine a war zone being much different from this, and everybody has visions of *MASH* and how things occurred there it seemed like that *MASH* unit was much more controlled and calm. The patients were very calm often times very sick or severely injured but not making unnecessary demands of anybody which was nice."

When Brenda Ingargiola heard from a Wildlife and Fisheries agent that the hospital was filled with people she was extremely surprised; she thought they had evacuated. There was only one thing she could think to do, climb down the ladder suspended from the broken government complex window and take a boat to the hospital to check on everyone. She went with Wildlife and Fisheries agent Colonel Richard Baumy and parish president assistant Charlie Reppel. They took the short ride down Patricia Street toward the hospital. Although Brenda had her mind set on helping her friends and coworkers at the hospital, she could not help but let one of her fears surface.

"I'm terrified of snakes and that's all I kept thinking was all these snakes," said Brenda. "I remember the May 3 flood [in 1978] and being in a flat bed boat doing CPR on a patient, trying to get to the hospital and snakes are just swimming along side of the boat, and that just creeped me out, and that's all I kept thinking of."

They docked at the overhang of the emergency room area and came across a boat carrying a man who she says had gone into cardiac arrest.

"He had a heart attack; he was down for a while because he was blue," said Brenda.

Brenda climbed into the building through a second floor patient room. Everyone was congregated in the emergency room part of the hospital, which had just opened a couple of weeks

*Brenda Ingargiola helped evacuate Chalmette Medical Center. Photograph by Mikel Schaefer*

*Chalmette Medical Center submerged. Photograph by Errol Schultz*

prior to the storm. Wet, sweating people were everywhere; they were lying in the beds and on the floors, gutting out an existence not comfortable for the human soul.

"The nurses were running around, and it was very hot and humid, and the floors were very slick with condensation; you had to be very careful when you walked; it was dark and hot and there was two doctors, Dr. Bertucci and I want to say Dr. [Bong] Mui," recalled Brenda.

Seeing the hospital in such critical condition was a hard pill for Brenda to swallow.

"I was so close to everybody at the hospital being there so long it was a family type of facility," she said. "We all took care of each other; we all knew our kids as they grew up, the things that we went through [with] the graduations. I knew which managers would still be there because in prior times when we had to have a hurricane there were certain managers that always stayed, that were always reliable, and I knew they would be there and sure enough they were there."

One manager saw Brenda.

"I'm so glad to see you; now you can take us away and everything will be fine."

"I'll take you away, but I can't guarantee it's gonna be any better, other than you're gonna have lights and power," said Brenda.

She asked one of the nurses where she could find administration to see who was in charge.

"She directed me to the Director of Nurses, so I asked her how many patients they had, how many people she estimated that they had. I was going to move them all over to the jail. Because I knew that the jail was cleared out and had generator power and at least it was dry."

The nurse estimated there were a total of fifty-four patients and three hundred people inside the hospital.

"Because people were just coming into the hospital from all over and I spoke to [Colonel] Baumy and we started the evacuation that afternoon," said Brenda. "And we took the isolation patients first; those patients had to be isolated from the rest of the patients based on their disease."

These patients, with respiratory problems and on prescribed special antibiotics, had to be isolated to keep the general public from compromising their immune systems. Brenda's coworkers must have been glad to see her because she said they let her take over. At one time She had been the nursing director for critical care in the ER for eleven years and had years of administration experience.

"The newly appointed administrator CEO was there, but he was despondent, Jon Sewell. The other administrator [Tim Coffey], I got word from one of the nurses that he had left the night before on a helicopter and hasn't come back, so we didn't know where he was," said Brenda. "They all looked at me, for years; I've always been in management, and I was always involved in the disaster preparedness for the hospital."

The tricky part was moving the many patients who could not walk. They fashioned sheets into sling carrying stretchers, and despite the heat, they wrapped up the patients who were in hospital gowns or in diapers tight in the sheets, so as not to expose their skin to the sun.

"It was very traumatic for the patients because it was hot," said Brenda. "One of the issues we had to deal with was balancing the patients on the boats. Because a lot of them were bed bound, you had to put them in a position where it wouldn't tip the boat along with the nurses and make them comfortable but also shield them from the sun because it was very hot. "

It took four people to carry a patient; each person grabbed one corner of the sheet and lifted the patient out of the window and onto the overhang. Two people went into the boat on either side of the patient, and the mummified person would be slowly lowered down into the boat. Depending on the size of the boat, they would try to send more than one person but far too many had only room for one. Each patient had a nurse who rode with them as close to the jail as the water would allow; then a vehicle would bring the patient and nurse the rest of the way.

"Once we got all the patients to the jail we had separated the other patients in isolation," said Brenda. "Then we set up ER patients that were more critical in another area and had ER nurses that stayed."

Brenda knew she had to get back to the government complex to take care of the people that were going there and President Rodriguez. She also knew that eventually her husband Larry would wonder where she was, and her instincts were right. By the time a group of firemen came to rescue parish officials and their loved ones from the government complex, Ingargiola could not find Brenda. He did not know where she was or where she could have gone. Feeling somewhat frantic, Ingargiola finally found her as she disembarked from a Wildlife and Fisheries boat.

"He thought I was with Junior [Rodriguez]. He saw me changing the dressing on my leg because it was wet, and he asked me how'd I get wet, and I had to tell him, I was trying not to; I told him I had to go to the hospital; I couldn't leave them there," said Brenda. "I was just so mad because I kept stressing to them for years we're gonna get a big one and you're gonna have to evacuate, and they wouldn't evacuate."

## Maintenance Yard Rescue

The maintenance yard workers were stranded on the second floor of their three-story, concrete, cinder block structure. The aluminum siding had been partly blown away and pieces of the roof were all over the flooded yard. Some of equipment they needed to work with after Katrina was under water; luckily, they had parked a number of their heavy-duty equipment high above the floodwater on the top of the Violet Canal Bridge. The calmness and stillness of Tuesday was nerve wracking because they had no way out. Martin Onidas and some of the other men climbed on to the third story roof and saw that the water from the marsh and the parish had become one.

"You could look around the parish up on the third floor, all you see is water, see rooftops," said Onidas.

Sitting in an industrial area off Paris Road, on the fringes of a neighborhood, the men were alone and had not seen anyone.

"Everybody was so worked up and wanted to get outta here and get to a real safe place where we could get some dry clothes," Onidas said.

Usually after a storm the men were on the road cutting down trees and clearing debris as soon as the weather cleared. The hard reality for the men was that it was more than twenty-four hours after the storm and they were not out doing anything. With all the water covering the ground they didn't know what they would have been able to accomplish anyway.

The men were also very worried about the stability of the building, which had walls torn away.

"We had twenty feet surrounding us and the building we was in; we heard all kinds of noise like the bricks was cracking and moving," Onidas recalled. "Some of the concrete was breaking off; we didn't know the building was all collapsed or what, but we had no where else to go."

Suspended over the water in a compromised structure, the maintenance yard men wondered anxiously if anyone was coming. Officials in the government complex were well aware of their predicament and wanted desperately to rescue the men. Everyone had their own set of problems, and it would take time before anyone would make their way to the garage. Councilwoman Judy Hoffmeister was worried about the men.

"I kept thinking are they alive; did they make it," said Hoffmeister.

The men had only a little bit of food to eat.

"We had Vienna sausage, potted meat, bread, crackers, chips, and water," said Onidas. "We rationed it, cutting it in half so everybody can have a little something in their stomach. It was the only thing that kept us going."

Almost worse than being stranded was being stranded wet.

"We was soaking wet; we didn't have no dry clothes; we all got wet." Onidas starkly remembered.

About an hour or so after the men had climbed on top of the

third floor roof to survey the submerged area a man came floating by in a canoe, saying he had come all the way from Arabi.

"I got no control," he shouted to the men on the roof.

"The current had him and brought him to us," said Onidas.

At the government complex someone in a boat pulled in next to the *Big Fish* to talk to Donald Colletti and Jim Pitre.

"Junior [Rodriguez] just came over the radio," someone said. "He wants the men out of the [maintenance yard]; could y'all go get those guys?"

Colletti and Pitre went back out this time to pick up Onidas and the men.

"We never knew how many," said Pitre. "We thought it was just a few men."

"We see a rescue boat come with a few guys and that's when they saved us," said Onidas. "When we seen that boat we was like in heaven, but before then we didn't know what to expect."

The emotional relief came just in time; the men jumped up, screaming "let's get outta here."

"We started cheering, everybody happy cause we had some guys just insane like they were in shock," said Onidas.

"They were trying to direct us to the yard," said Pitre. "When we got to the thing we were on top of a bucket truck; you couldn't see it."

The men piled onto the *Big Fish*, and in spite of being over-loaded with people, Colletti still grabbed water, cots, and any supplies he could salvage, tossing them on to the men's laps and wherever he could find space. Colletti knew he better save what he could because goods were hard to come by. The workers warned Colletti that it was dangerous near the fence surrounding the yard due to submerged equipment and because the fence was topped with several feet of barbed wire. But Colletti carefully maneuvered the boat over the drowned equipment and over the fence without hitting the bottom of the boat. The only noise anyone heard was from the boat's motor.

"They was the quietest bunch of men," said Pitre.

Their destination was Chalmette High School. The men got off of the boat and walked inside the gym; Onidas's immediate assessment was that being at the school was not a good idea.

"We can't stay here."

Onidas approached one of the firemen he knew.

"Eddie, y'all got a boat?"

*Maintenance yard rescue by Donald Colletti and Jim Pitre. Photograph by Donald Colletti*

"Yea."

"Bring us to the complex."

"The gym was filled up," said Onidas.

So they boated down Judge Perez toward the government complex. Cruising down the highway, they passed the skating rink, the fire station near Jackson, the old Village Square shopping center, McDonalds, Home Depot, Region's Bank, and the civic center. Finally, they saw the complex, noticing they had a welcome home crowd. Hoffmeister along with others spotted the boats standing on the roof of the complex.

"Here comes the public works guys coming up Judge Perez in a boat," said Hoffmeister.

"We thought we lost y'all," came the catcalls from above.

"They were all yelling, hooray the road crew, they made it, they made it!" Onidas fondly recalled. "We was giving peace signs and had our hands raising; we was happy to see them too."

"We were so glad to see the guys, and they're so glad to see us," said Hoffmeister.

The boats pulled up to that same ladder the firemen had rigged to get people in and out of the building.

"We had to go up a ladder to get up to the second floor," said Onidas. "We went up there and they was able to get us some hot food, dry clothes. When the water went down, it didn't go down much, we got in boats and started rescuing people."

The first stop was the Violet Canal Bridge to pick up their heavy equipment. The bulldozers and trash trucks were high, dry, and intact. There were also dozens of people who had escaped their homes and had made their way onto the bridge. Without shelter from the sun, they were burning up and were relieved to catch a ride off of the bridge. Onidas and his crew loaded up as many as they could carry on the trash trucks and began hauling them to the jail.

"We had loads of people going back and forth."

They would drive in the water down Colonial Boulevard and hop on the levee near the Lake Borgne Levee District because the water was still too deep on St. Bernard Highway. They drove the trucks on the levee until they could see where the water had receded from the highway, and then they caravanned down the highway to the makeshift triage area at the jail.

In a matter of hours, the maintenance yard workers had gone from stranded victims of Katrina to receiving dry clothes and hot meals and were at work clearing people off of roads and bringing them to safety. However, Onidas would receive a disturbing phone call about his mother.

### Getting Out of The Complex

Parish CEO Danny Menesses found the Exxon-Mobil building on the site of Chalmette Refining dry. The decision was made to get out of the complex and commandeer the Exxon-Mobil building, making it the base of parish operations. Unfortunately, the only way out of the complex was through a busted window and then through the storm protection that covered the window. That was a rough chore for seventy year old parish President Rodriguez, who is a big man and recently had a major surgery. His wife, Evelyn, had also undergone a surgery of her own.

"Me and my wife crawled down the ladder," said Rodriguez. "Everybody did things they didn't think they could do, it was amazing."

In her younger years, Judy Hoffmeister would have gladly scaled that ladder down to the boat, but not quite as young or as limber as she would like to be, she was hesitant to make the trip.

"That was the scariest part; I could have faced the water but this makeshift ladder, to go down in this boat, and they had firemen in the boat helping us," said Hoffmeister. "When I climbed out they actually took my legs and went this is a step, this is a step, each rung cause you couldn't judge. That was just to get out of the building."

As they launched the boat, the magnitude of the event became more focused. To watch it from a building or a rooftop was bad enough, but to ride through it and feel the devastation close-up brought the horrifying situation full circle.

"The strangest feeling, you're riding down Judge Perez Drive and you got to duck to get under the signal lights; that was really strange," said Ingargiola. "We seen one or two bodies on Judge Perez floating that you just left behind."

The body was in front of the St. Bernard bureau of the *Times Picayune* newspaper building in Chalmette. Even though Ingargiola saw the body he couldn't tell if it was a man or a woman. He didn't care to investigate further because it was something he was used to, having spent twenty years in charge of EMS.

"Body recovery was not part of my job at that time," said Ingargiola. "In a disaster of this magnitude I was surprised that I didn't see more."

When they got to Paris Road near Prompt Succor Church the water had become too shallow to go any farther. They walked through the water to the dry part of the road and hiked from there to the Exxon-Mobil building.

"This is the firemen and you got to remember I'm the director of the American Red Cross down here," said Hoffmeister. "The firemen and policemen pretty well know me and said Mrs. Judy you have to get out."

She hesitated.

"Guys, I don't know if I want to walk," because she knew the shoes on her feet were the only shoes she had, and she didn't want to get them wet.

"We're gonna carry you."

"No son, you can't carry me; I'll break your back."

"No, no, no we're gonna do the firemen ladder."

They carried her down Paris Road until it was dry, and she

walked from there. Once they got to the building, they had to "bust open the doors" because no one had the keys. Once inside the building, in an effort to find the keys that would unlock the doors to the offices, they continued to break down doors.

"The office with the keys is the very last one we opened," said Hoffmeister.

They had a dry building but they still had no electricity, air, or water. Then someone from the plant offered a generator.

"I could get y'all a generator for the first floor, I don't know if it's gonna work everything but it's gonna work the lights," the man said.

Now they had lights, and the firemen used a fire truck or two to replace their flooded pumpers.

"One of my firefighters got the gate open to one of their fire stations [at the refinery]," said Chief Thomas Stone. "I waded into water up to my waist and took their fire trucks out of their fire station. We rode down the street to Murphy Oil and took the one fire truck they had. They were smart; they took their good one out of the parish. We took the one fire truck they had and a fire department vehicle and that was the vehicles we started using."

Brenda Ingargiola immediately created a makeshift emergency room area in the waiting room of the office building.

"We had two stretchers with a crash cart that we needed, and we took care of a lot of injuries, skin infections, cuts, we had a couple of heat exhaustions that we had to medevac out."

Because civilians and rescue workers were spending so much time in the contaminated waters, Brenda knew everyone would need tetanus shots.

"We were giving out tetanus shots to a lot of the rescue workers. We didn't have a whole lot, so I had to go to the jail and pick out what they had and then we commandeered a whole bunch of stuff. We went to all the doctor's offices, pediatricians mainly because we knew they would have tetanus."

She also designated a room to create a pharmacy from the supplies they were pulling out of the flooded doctors' offices and stores. Brenda's daughter-in-law coordinated cataloging the medicines so they could be dispensed as the doctors needed them.

"As people were in boats going to different places whenever they found medicines they knew to bring it to Exxon-Mobil and they just dropped it off," said Brenda. "If it was still sealed I used it, if it wasn't then I had to dispose of it. We made use of what we had and it worked out pretty well; I was surprised how well it all came together."

Due to the amount of cuts and scrapes, antibiotics, antibiotic ointments, and diaper rash creams were in great demand, especially for the men working in heavy waterlogged boots.

"The firemen with their heavy boots, their socks were wet, and they had no dry socks to use," said Brenda. "So their feet were staying wet constantly and they were coming in with open sores and ingrown toenails and cuts and raw edges from their boots up around their calves. What I did was found diapers, baby diapers that we scooped from Wal-Mart when they were floating by. I took the diapers cut them in half and lined all the guys boots with diapers and then took the other part and padded the edge of their boots so their skin wouldn't rub and it kept their feet dry."

At night fall the men made their way to the mini ER to receive treatment.

"They were lined up like soldiers taking care of them, dressing them, and cleaning them up."

Tuesday night, once the chaos had calmed down, Ingargiola climbed to the third floor of the roof of the Exxon-Mobil building and looked out at the parish.

"There was nothing left, there was not a light on; it was total darkness. I don't say it was scary; it's just a very sad feeling. I'd seen myself take my times where I had to just go by myself and do my little cry and come back downstairs and do my thing."

### Moving On

Bubby Bodden's not so sure he wanted to hang around A.J. any longer.

"It was getting kind of odd, more people were coming up, not shady but people on the verge of I'm gonna do whatever I want, and I didn't like that without thinking of the consequences," said Bubby.

One of the men who had been riding around picking up people was getting low on gas when Bubby approached him.

"My neighbor has a full tank of gas; you can bring me to my house, I'll give you his tank," said Bubby.

So they went to Bubby's house to get the tank out of the boat that had saved his life.

"I see the boat kind of bobbing up and down; I reach down, unhook the boat, so now I got my neighbor's boat."

Since Bubby would now have use of this boat, the man told him he would go somewhere else to find gas.

"I'm gonna go back to the school," Bubby replied.

After getting back to Andrew Jackson, a man, his wife, and teenage son float by in what Bubby described as "some kind of apparatus they concocted." They had come from their home on Old Hickory Avenue, which was quite a ways from where they were now. Looking exhausted, they told Bubby that they had heard the jail was dry.

"Y'all want to go to the jail; I'll bring y'all right now," Bubby said.

They climbed off their homemade floating device and hopped in the boat.

Bubby drove the boat down Chalmette Avenue, ducking under compromised power lines; they saw a couple of people in a two-story home and offered them a ride as well.

They refused, "which is kind of weird for me cause I knew that the water wasn't going down," said Bubby. "Between Monday and Tuesday morning the water may have went down eight inches to a foot at the most so I knew it was gonna be there awhile."

Bubby turned the boat onto St. Bernard Highway and doing so left him with an indescribable feeling.

"We're going down St. Bernard Highway with a boat. Never, ever thought that would happen or ever see that," Bubby remembered, feeling numb. "Like riding down the bayou down in Delacroix going fishing, this is where I drive my car or ride my bike; this is not a boat area, surreal, assessing, knowing total devastation."

They passed the courthouse and the farthest they could go was the entrance of Chalmette Refining; the water had receded at that point on St. Bernard Highway.

"We pull up there, see two state troopers, one of them used to be a good friend of mine, Ronnie Tardo. I see [Lt. Governor] Mitch Landrieu's there; Jack Stephens and [State Senator] Walter Boasso are sitting right there just talking. Landrieu has a satellite phone, and I see an army helicopter come down. Bomp he's gone, I'm sure he was assessing the refinery. It struck me odd [that] the first person of any kind of significance I would see in the government would be Mitch Landrieu."

Bubby and his passengers discovered that the jail was dry and saw that there were hundreds of people around the complex, many trying to cool off in the shade of the big De La Ronde Oaks. He went to the jail to register his name, so it would begin a trail on his travels.

"They were taking people's names, and I walk in and it was like the death came over you. It really reminded me, if it would have been during the black plague time, when you're walking down the street and you see death that's exactly what that was. There were people dying right there, mentally retarded, mentally handicapped, physically handicapped people just on their last gasp and breath it was incredible."

Bubby saw hundreds and hundreds of people stuffed in the jail.

"I knew this wasn't a good situation; it was sheltering dogs, had them in the courtyard where the inmates would walk."

As he checked around someone told him they were ferrying people to Algiers Point, which is several miles down on the other side of the Mississippi River in Orleans Parish. From there buses were taking people out of town to Baton Rouge. Bubby's family was in Baton Rouge, so he wanted to get on a ferry and head across the river. This would be his next move.

"The only choice I had for my cat was to leave him there. He was in his cage. I left him with his cage open with some food and water cause he wasn't gonna be able to take a ferry ride. I left him in good shape and prayed he would make it."

## al-Katrina

Eric Acosta made a check of the people at the St. Bernard Port, making sure the facilities were in order for people to settle into. He and some others cleaned things out and set up bedding. He walked around performing semi-physicals to make sure there were not people who needed medical treatment, especially small children and the elderly.

The decision was made by a group of parish officials to open up the Arabi facility for the St. Bernard Port as a staging area to begin evacuating people out of the parish. There was no way to travel by land, so people would have to be placed on boats.

Acosta said he informed Sheriff Stephens that it was dry and brought him down to the slip. It was a loading area for ships for the port on the Mississippi River, and it had a huge warehouse

*Eric Acosta calls in a terrorist attack on St. Bernard because of Katrina.*
*Photograph by Mikel Schaefer*

stocked with plywood from Indonesia and China. Most people called it the Chalmette Slip because that's what it used to be called when Kaiser Aluminum owned it, but it's technically in Arabi. Before too long they were calling it Camp Katrina.

Acosta used a four-wheeler to run down the levee from the Port to the slip. Acosta, like everyone, was frustrated by Tuesday afternoon that there was no sign of any outside help. There were no supplies being shipped in, and the entire parish was crippled with floodwater.

Acosta wondered why help was not coming to St. Bernard after being devastated by Katrina; he believed that someone from the federal government would have already been on the ground if this had been a terrorist attack. As the facility security officer for the St. Bernard Port, who had been through all types of terrorist training, he had an idea how to get someone's attention.

"I activated us a terrorist attack, by doing that, it was Katrina instead of al-Qaeda, and it was flood water instead of biological, chemical, or nuclear, everything plays the same all the way down to the toe tags," said Acosta.

He got on his marine radio and made the call.

"This is Eric Acosta, F.S.O St. Bernard Port, and I'm activating a terrorist alert. We [are] using Katrina as a terrorist attack; we got massive evacuations, and we gonna have deaths and massive destruction throughout the entire parish of St. Bernard, so I need any assistance coming in, and I need food and water."

Acosta trains a lot of people involved in the maritime industry on terrorist attacks; he figured his people along the river would hear the Mayday call and bring some desperately needed help to St. Bernard. The radio signal would only go as far as the Orleans-Jefferson parish line, but he believed others would relay the call from there. He would have his answer in the next twelve to twenty-four hours.

### Chalmette High Surviving

The first plans Warner had heard of moving people came on Tuesday when Sheriff Stephens sent a deputy to the shelter with a radio, the only line the sheriff had working, for Warner to communicate with.

"This is when they started to work the ferry," said Warner.

Warner just could not understand how communications in St. Bernard could be so crippled.

"We live in a world of satellite phones, in Iraq they can put somebody on television and immediately beam it back to the United States and not only can you hear them you can see them. In St. Bernard, you couldn't communicate in any way with anybody I mean it's unthinkable in this world we live in."

There was hope of getting people out of the school; however, the day was one of chaos and uncertainty. They had their routine of breakfast and dinner to serve. Those cans of peaches off the commodities truck helped feed the people inside the school and they were able to spare a little more to drink.

"We started giving them a whole glass of water," said Mundt. "And we were giving peaches."

Not all the food and drink came from the shelter. Some evacuees had brought their own water and food and the misperception set one man off.

"One guy, the stress had gotten to him and he didn't understand, some people brought their own things and some people had water; they were quite willing to share with other people, that wasn't a problem, but they weren't going to give all their

water away," Warner explained. "Every now and then somebody would walk out with a whole bottle of water."

To be fair, Warner and his staff "ate exactly what everybody
else ate, drank exactly what every body else drank."

As the day went on, the shelter received additional people
and the mood deteriorated.

"All we kept getting from the outside was how terrible it was,
so there wasn't any hope; it just got worse and worse," said
Warner. "People were coming in, and they were dazed because
they were on top of roofs and dehydrated."

"People are dehydrated and not making good decisions, you
had to try to work with everybody," Mundt said.

Everyone was just trying to manage; the really sick were compromised to the point of near death.

"One lady had cystic fibrosis, and she looked like she was on
her death bed, and her father was taking care of that lady, and
he did so much for her," Warner said.

"It was valiant, he worked so hard to keep her comfortable,"
Mundt said.

A question many started to ask was when were they going to
get them out?

"We had no information; 'sure they'll come;' we smiled a lot,
but we had the same questions, are we gonna get out? These
people are telling us they got to have these things or they're
gonna die; are they gonna be rescued," Warner said.

The answer people wanted the most appeared to have come
from State Representative Nita Hutter and Councilman Joey
DiFatta.

"They came and talked to the people in the gym, and I could
hear a cheer from the gym," said Warner. "I didn't know what
that was all about; I was kind of worried about it but then found
out it was a good thing."

Then they came over to the school and talked to Warner.

"They told the people they were going to get out, were going
to a nicer place," said Warner. "It would be clean and dry and
fans and hot food. What he said is they'd be out of there by midnight Tuesday."

By early evening, Warner had received a message saying that
if anyone wanted to walk out of the school that a bus would pick
them up.

"The water had gone down at that point," said Mundt. "If you stood on the roof and looked out at Palmisano [Avenue] from the roof, from where the band room and cafeteria are it was all still flooded toward Judge Perez, but from the band room to St. Bernard Highway it was dry, dusty and muddy, but dry."

In order to get there you had to walk through the parking lot behind the school along the backside of the football stadium; it was covered with thick, brown, pasty muck. Some of the firemen tested the route by walking through it, and this helped create a path for people to walk on, making it as safe as possible.

"About twenty-five people left but when they left though, it was starting to get dark," said Warner. "In all honesty I didn't want people going out on Palmisano. You have a ditch on one side, you've got snakes; it was pitch-black."

But as time passed the rescue operation still had not reached the school.

"The people were happy, and I believe he [Councilman DiFatta] meant what he said," said Warner. "It started to get late and we had these people start asking us when are they coming to get us."

Nobody came that night, and it was an anxious time for people in the gym and in the school who had gotten their hopes up; they wanted to get out of the waterlogged parish, to get to their families, clear their mind, and shake off the shock of losing everything they owned and the reality that their parish had been destroyed to the point of possible extinction.

## Camp Katrina

The day after Katrina, parish leaders realized that while most of the parish had evacuated, far too many of them had stayed, and they were now responsible for thousands of people at the shelters, the other buildings people had escaped to, and those trapped in their own homes. Deputies, firemen, and civilians had saved thousands already and with the parish waterlocked how would they get them out. They wanted to centralize everyone and everything, so they could triage, feed, and shelter thousands of St. Bernardians on their way out of the parish.

With the help of the Coast Guard, the sheriff's department commandeered a "four hundred-foot Norwegian freighter" they had ordered to dock at the St. Bernard Port's Arabi Terminal on the Mississippi River. The slip, which dates as far back as the

*Some of the thousands of people who passed through Camp Katrina on their way out of the parish. Photograph by Pete Tufaro*

early 1900s, is a channel nearly seventeen hundred feet long and three hundred feet wide.

"I thought we might have to evacuate the entire population on the deck of that ship and go up river," said Stephens.

The boarding of vessels along the Mississippi River by St. Bernard Deputies became a common occurrence as they collected everything from deck barges to tug boats to even an historic paddlewheel boat.

"The Creole Queen was moored at the foot of Canal Street," said Stephens. "We got a pilot on board and brought it down and moored it here, and the deputies lived on that for three months. There was another quarter boat facility that we commandeered and brought to port ship services down here where most of our rank resided for almost three months."

Also with the help of the Coast Guard, these vessels were used to get people out of St. Bernard, and the port was one of the most logical places to begin to make that happen.

"We had to start, the sheriff's department and parish government, we had to do something about sheltering," said Major James Pohlmann. "We can't have everybody spread out, that's why we came up with Camp Katrina."

Camp Katrina sits on the riverside of the levee protection area and from the dock you can see the skyline of New Orleans in the distance and the Domino Sugar Refinery immediately to your right. Directly behind the facility, the peak of the Chalmette Battlefield Monument can be seen sticking out above the levee. The huge warehouse was stored with loads of plywood stacked dozens of feet high. It would be a huge undertaking to get it ready to house people. They needed help and it took deputies, firemen, parish officials, and residents. Some of the volunteers came out of the Chalmette High gym.

Barry Uhle said some of the men at the gym "made a little band, troop of ten to eleven" that would come together. Amidst the crowd in the gym, Uhle ran into a man he has known for thirty years, and the man told him he had lost his wife. Uhle didn't understand exactly what he meant and said he would help find her.

"No, I lost her," he said again to Uhle. "He was trying to get out of the house, and he lost her; she drowned right there."

The man managed to escape with his son.

"This guy we shared beers together, traveled overseas together, and what do you do; you just sit there and you look at 'em, you hug 'em and his wife's still there; she's still in the freaking house with the water in it; what do you do? You got to move on. We took him and his son into our little band," said Uhle.

Tuesday evening Uhle listened as State Representative Nita Hutter and Councilman Joey DiFatta said they needed nine to ten people to help at the slip to get the warehouse ready. They were looking for strong guys between eighteen and twenty-six years old to volunteer. Uhle and the other men approached DiFatta, who he graduated with from Holy Cross High School, and Nita Hutter, who lives three houses down from him.

"Look I'll outwork any eighteen- to twenty-six-year-old kid around here; I'm going now. You need some help I know the guys," Uhle said to DiFatta and Hutter. "We'll go over there and we'll get the stuff ready."

Uhle was going to leave his friend, who lost his wife, behind but the man asked him to take his son.

"Get him out of here and get him to Shreveport to his sister."

"Alright," Uhle replied.

The men boarded a boat that took them west to Paris Road where they got out in knee-deep water at Our Lady of Prompt Succor; the men walked to St. Bernard Highway and approached some deputies staged at the jail to tell them they were headed to the slip.

"We get up there, it's mayhem, people walking everywhere they going to the ferry, they going down St. Bernard Highway, some walking around in circles," Uhle said with a tone of disbelief.

The men walked down to the ferry landing, thinking they could just hop on a boat and ride up river to the slip.

"We're just about to get on and the guy says it's going to Algiers," said Uhle. "We're hearing horror stories about people shooting at the ferry; 'I ain't going to Algiers!' We walked back to the refinery on the levee."

One of Uhle's band made like a bandit, went into the refinery, and stole a pickup truck.

"We all jumped in the pickup truck and we're heading down the levee. We run into Senator Walter Boasso," said Uhle.

"Where y'all going?" Boasso asked

"We going to the Chalmette slip."

"Good they need your help."

"We looked like a cross between the Keystone Cops and Beverly Hillbillies going down this sloppy, bumpy levee in this old truck," said Uhle.

Their trek was less than two miles. They jumped out of the truck and walked down the levee and into the warehouse.

"A guy driving a forklift comes toward me; when he turns and looks its [Councilman] Mark Madary," said Uhle. "I knew Mark since I was a little kid, grew up in the same neighborhood, and we worked together with St. Robert's fair. His brother, our kids went to school there together."

Madary looked at Uhle, "Look what God done sent me."

"He knew what we could do together, and we hugged for a little while," Uhle said.

The men drove forklifts all night and into the morning. They were moving the stacks of four-by-eight sheets of plywood and creating spaces about two feet high that one family could climb on top of and claim as their own. There would be hundreds spaced out and a clear runway right down the middle of the warehouse from one end to the other, so they could drive an ambulance or emergency vehicle through if they needed to. Uhle ran into another man he grew up with, who lives six houses from his parents.

"How was the water in the old neighborhood?" Uhle asked.

"He gave me his line, and we cried and hugged and got over that event and just started working."

The sheriff's department handled security in the building and barely had any gear to protect the people with. Colonel Bethay assigned Major John Doran and Captain Chad Clark to oversee the warehouse.

"We have one of our armory guys clean up which weapons we had," said Bethay. "Not that we were gonna use them but it kind of intimidates people into behaving when you're outnumbered like 50:1, 70:1. We had some automatic weapons just to have them on their shoulders. There was no time they were gonna shoot anybody, but you have to keep some type of order."

CHAPTER SIXTEEN

# Hanging On

## Tuesday, August 30

### Day Three

Tuesday saw the first group of people evacuated out of St. Bernard High School. A Coast Guard helicopter was able to hover above the roof of the school; they lowered a basket, and the firemen helped load some of the sickest people into that basket. When the chopper was full it flew off, and they did not know when another was going to show up. But as soon as they would get someone out, more evacuees would show up in their place. They needed a mass evacuation and Rodney Ourso managed to get one transmission to Chief Stone.

"We've got four hundred people here; we're short on water, short on food."

And that was all Ourso could communicate to Chief Stone.

"I tried to impress upon the chief we need to get out of here cause we had people that had come with dogs, conditions were getting very bad," said Ourso. "Mentally, physically, health conditions, people were gonna start dying because of disease. They were waiting for the floodwaters to come down in order to get to us."

The number of dogs in the facility worsened the conditions.

"We couldn't keep the dogs out on the roof," said Ourso. "We had so many, some dogs on the roof, some dogs in the rooms, defecating everywhere it was getting very unsanitary."

Mitch McDaniel understood why the school was burdened

with animals but tried to stress to people to take care of them, especially the waste.

"A lot of people had pets; we were letting them keep their pets around," said McDaniel. "A lot of them thought that was their life, their child, so we couldn't tell them anything different. If their pets made a mess we told them they had to clean 'em up, otherwise the pets had to be put outside."

Lebeau and Ourso wanted to see how bad it was farther away from the school, so they drove their boat toward the Violet Canal Bridge. On the way they cruised through the Southlake Subdivision in Violet.

"A lot of people were on their second stories," said Lebeau. "The ones that wanted to leave had already made it over to us by boats, civilians bringing 'em. There were maybe twenty or so people in houses altogether."

"We're good; we'll leave when we're ready" was the response from some of those staying put.

Lebeau and Ourso had no idea what was happening in the rest of the parish because they had not talked to anyone, except for a brief conversation with Chief Stone, since the storm hit.

Lebeau: "It looked like a normal navigable waterway, a large bayou; it looked like a great fishing place."

Ourso: "We did see fish."

*View from the top of the Violet Canal Bridge, looking east. Photograph by Thomas Stone*

Lebeau: "Fish, deer, when we got to the top of the bridge there was actually a horse walking on top of the bridge."

Ourso: "With a bail of hay, somebody threw a bail of hay."

Lebeau: "We walked to the top of the bridge and the sight that we seen from the high school, when we seen Judge Perez was the same on the other side of the bridge, I did just about anything just short of falling to my knees. If I didn't see how bad it was on the east side of the bridge I probably would have fell at the sight; I grew up on the area on the west side of the Violet Canal Bridge, so there was a lot of stuff that went through my mind there. I grew up on Kenneth Drive [in Francke Place] that was an emotional sight to see there, and then we thought as soon as water recedes we'll be able to get some of these dump trucks [that were stored on the bridge] and bring them over to the school."

The men returned to the school to let the other firefighters, deputies, and other parish officials like McDaniel in on just how widespread the flooding was and to formulate a plan to get out. The best thing to do was to be patient and to get as comfortable as one could. McDaniel brought enough clothes to last a couple of days but they got wet along with his shoes.

"You would kind of alternate days, you'd wear one set of clothes one day; I walked in water so much, my shoes and socks got so wet my feet were just cracking, chaffing, "said McDaniel.

Then they got creative.

"My boss came up with the idea; we had some baby diapers down there so we used them for socks to keep our feet dry," McDaniel remembered. "Used the baby diapers like booties and put them inside the shoes. Just stuck 'em in there and used the two-sided tabs to tape and we took plastic bags and wrapped 'em around our feet before you put 'em back in your shoes."

Come Tuesday night McDaniel had decided to do what others around the parish had discovered on Monday, get up to the roof.

"You could feel the cool breeze outside, at first one person was out the window on the second floor, walking between the buildings. You'd see them sitting on the roof, another person got the idea it was cooler out there, might as well go out there. All of a sudden it snowballed, probably seventy-five to one hundred."

Getting out of the miserable heat brought badly needed relief to the stranded.

"They were having a good time," said McDaniel. "Some were laughing and joking like nothing happened. It just felt good to

get out from that stagnant air smell in the gym and in the classrooms. The sky, I've never seen the sky so clear, I think cause the
hurricane just came and took away all the smog and pollution.
There were millions of stars, and the number of shooting stars I
had seen that night I counted six, clear as day. We had this terrible storm and God said you need one good night; you deserve
this; you kind of knew everything was gonna be O.K. eventually, this is his sign, time to move on. It's not as bad as it coulda
been, cause we all could have perished down there."

## Old Arabi Unites

The water had gone down enough that Kevin Reichert and
his family could move back into their Old Arabi home on
Angela Street. Compared to Glenn Gallo's house, which was
one of only a handful of houses or structures in the entire
parish that did not get water, Kevin Reichert's neighborhood
may have been in the next best shape. The homes along the
levee in Old Arabi were probably the only homes in the parish
that after twenty-four hours no longer had water inside.

Knowing this area was one of the highest in St. Bernard,
Reichert feared others desperate for dry land would overrun his
neighborhood and that "chaos may break loose." After the storm
he ran boats, saving as many as ten people at a time in his neighborhood. He watched people swimming toward the levee until
they could walk themselves up. When nightfall hit, he was
unable to size up just what could happen next.

"Monday night was the darkest night of my life, there's not a
single light anywhere to be seen. The moon was very dim; you
could see every star in the sky, and if you knew anything about
them you could probably point out stars you've never seen
before. You couldn't see your hand in front your face," Reichert
said. "There was a little fear of that as well as who's around the
corner; who's gonna be walking up; what about the animals that
may or may not have made it, stray dogs, hungry dogs; so there
was a real eeriness about that night . . . there was no protection."

Reichert's thoughts had calmed somewhat by daylight
Tuesday. Others in the neighborhood were also able to get back in
their homes, and there were those who were staying on the second floors of their homes as well. He and his neighbors formed
their own little survival crew and pitched in to help each other.

"The community actually came together; most people already know each other in Chalmette, very family oriented," said Reichert. "There were about a hundred people mostly men that formed this family, that basically our job was go and bring any supplies people may need."

One of the community's saving graces was a four-foot high above ground pool in the backyard across the street from Reichert's house. The floodwater had not gotten high enough to pollute the pool, so the water wasn't contaminated; it was fresh and chlorinated. That made the non-existence of running water a bit easier to deal with. They used the pool water to wash clothes and to clean themselves.

"We used that pool water, bucketed out; no one was to go in the pool at all to contaminate the pool. You bucket it out, bring it to where you need it, put it in your trucks, letting people from all over take it," said Reichert. "Go home and you'd wash your clothes or transfer the bucket for a smaller bucket so you can bathe in it. That was your only water source that anybody had for all these days and it was neat."

They had even placed people in charge of sanitation, laundry, and the cleaning of certain areas.

The old Arabi crew was self-sufficient and did not burden the first responders who had more than enough people to feed, house, and evacuate. The old Arabi crew even coordinated its rescue. With the help of a sheriff's department satellite phone, they organized supply boats out of St. Rose, Louisiana, in St. Charles Parish, to go to Camp Katrina to pick up the people from this neighborhood.

"We would get as many people on this barge as possible. It happened twice on Thursday and again on Friday," said Reichert. "We had to coordinate this; people were staged in different areas at this time, and see who in fact wanted to go, when they could go, how many people they would be able to take, and we got about ninety percent [of the] people out from the old Arabi area in those two days. This was completely civilian coordinated. This was solely individuals doing what they had to do to help other individuals to get out. It was the only way out; the roads were still flooded."

**Relief Trickles In**

Fire Chief Thomas Stone did not realize the amusement park

thrill ride he was already on would spin his head faster than a whirl-a-whirl at the annual Crawfish Festival. He had received the good news that BellSouth was going to give him the keys to their building and that he could house his firemen there.

"They said if we can keep diesel and oil in their fifty-year-old generator without it stopping that we could have a building that would be as cold as a refrigerator," said Stone. "I called it the Bell Hotel."

The building had something that could help the men ease some of their tremendous personal and professional stress, air conditioning. Chief Stone says he also received good news out of Lake Charles, Louisiana, from his son, Thomas, Jr., who was attending McNeese State University. He wanted badly to be home helping his father and fellow neighbors, but since that was unrealistic he helped in other more creative ways.

"He called the Calcasieu Parish Sheriff's Office and spoke to a lady name Kim," Stone said. "He got heavily armed Calcasieu Parish Sheriff's Deputies and police officers from Lake Charles and Sulphur, Louisiana, here to help take up security in St. Bernard Parish on Tuesday night."

Calcasieu Sheriff Nick Mancuso remembered the calls that came in for St. Bernard.

"It was actually the second person saying St. Bernard is not getting any help," said Mancuso. "We had already sent people down there, but they really didn't have a mission yet and that's when I directed my people to go there and help."

He sent thirty deputies to the parish, and they caught a ride with the Coast Guard from a warehouse in New Orleans near the Riverwalk Shopping area on the Mississippi River downtown.

"They were godsends," said Sheriff Stephens. "They were armed; they were equipped; they were a lifesaver."

Stone's son also used his girlfriend's cell phone to text message information out as well.

"He was at a 337 exchange and that was how we communicated, cause at three o'clock in the morning my Alltel telephone would be able to make or receive a call," said Stone. "They brought us satellite phones; they brought us special cell phones; none of that worked. He would put things out on the Internet and then would get contact numbers for our firefighters to family that was checking on them. He would text message me and I would go to that firefighter and say here this member of your family is at this number and give them a call."

Stone noticed that the first state agency to make it to St. Bernard was the Louisiana Department of Wildlife and Fisheries, who came in Monday night. With Calcasieu deputies finding their way into the parish, he figured the federal agencies could not be far behind.

Some of the firemen assigned to Chalmette High found themselves back on the roof for a second night of sleep. The men took off their wet fire suits and heavy boots and ripped off their wet socks and underwear. Since there was neither running water nor the prospect of getting any in the near future, one of the men improvised with a pool of water that had collected on the roof.

"We clogged up the drains to collect the rain water," said Captain Eddie Appel.

"I don't know the first to do it, but they went up there with a little bucket, a can, or cup, wet themselves down and showered up," said Liccardi. "I did it and it was probably one of the best showers I took in my life under the circumstances, but it was good to do it in the evening cause you couldn't see the water too good; you couldn't see how dirty it actually was but it was fresh water after getting in the muck all day."

If you were in a helicopter you could catch some of the firemen stripping all the way down and taking a gravelly roof shower.

"I didn't go all the way down, but they had some guys went el natural with helicopters flying above and everything," said Liccardi. "About dusk take a cup, wet yourself down, and lather up some soap in your hair. Some guys had shampoo they had brought, rinse off, then dry off with towels, and get back dressed in wet clothes. I only had two sets of clothes. We wouldn't wash the clothes in the same water we bathed with, we'd take water in buckets and moved the buckets away, get soap and wash clothes out and let them dry out on the roof; they had air condition units we'd hang them on."

Captain Appel made the mistake of trying to shower in the daylight.

"It was fine when you took a shower at night, but when you took a shower in the daytime you seen how dirty that water was in the cup," said Appel. "That was bad; I only took one in the daytime."

## Pump It Up

Bob Turner and his men churned that crank for hours, trying

to open the Bayou Dupre locks. Their next mission was to get to the stations and turn on the pumps that would push the rest of the water to the other side of the levees. Turner and the others made a list dividing the twenty-four men in to stations. He sent boats to pick up the men still at shelters as he attempted to check which pumping stations survived the storm.

"We started placing our people at the drainage pump stations to assess damage there and what was operable and what stations were not operable. I set up my base of operations at station #7," said Turner. "It's centrally located to all of the pump stations. We had no roof; most of the roof was gone."

Russell Gelvin went back to the levee to rendezvous with Steve Edgett who had helped get medicine for the stranded St. Rita's Nursing Home survivors. While Turner went to station #7, they checked on elevated station #4 at Guerra Drive in Violet.

"As soon as the water level dropped below the levee, we could start pumping," said Gelvin. "The biggest challenge, we started scavenging for drinks and water and food. We were pulling stuff out of the floodwaters, potato chips that had floated out of stores and stuff."

Troy Douglas, Sr. wanted to make sure all of his men had food and drinks once they were set up at the pumping station. If you had a vice he got it.

*Levee district men—Doyle Dardar, Jr., Troy Douglas, Sr., and Jaurell Aisola.*
*Photograph by Mikel Schaefer*

"I made sure you had cigarettes; if you smoke cigars, I'm the only one, I made sure I had cigars or whatever you told me; whatever habit you have or whatever I made sure you had that with you," said Douglas, Sr.

Their job would be monumental and once they started pumping it was going to be a 24/7 affair.

"We had food from day one I made sure," Douglas, Sr. said. "I made sure everybody was able to survive. I went out and done whatever it took to get food and drink. It wasn't ice cold drinks; they had drinks maybe room temperature, and I made sure what I ate, they ate. Mostly Vienna sausage, can stuff the water hadn't got to. Wash it off, open that up, and eat, survive. I'm a woodsman; I hunt, and I'm a survivor. I felt nobody's life period, ever in danger."

"He took care of everybody," said one of the pump station workers, Doyle Dardar, Jr.

Douglas, Sr. and Gelvin got in a boat to find food as the men made their way to the pump stations Tuesday afternoon.

"Never once we went in the store, I got it from looters from different people," said Douglas, Sr. "I come from the streets; I'm pretty much street smart; I can finesse too, and I done whatever it took for my guys to survive."

Douglas, Sr., Gelvin, and his badge wheeled and dealed their way to survival for the pumping crews. Douglas, Sr. explained how it would go down.

"Hey man I need half of that; if they don't want to give it to me, I step my officer in there, he looting, that's a crime right there, so one hand washed the other. You give me something; I don't want it all; I just want some to give to my guys. I determine how much I need cause I might say I just need a quarter of that you got three quarters go ahead with your business. I got to give it to the public out there; they help us."

By Tuesday there was not a store in St. Bernard Parish that had not been broken into for food and fluids, but when Gelvin saw otherwise, he went into deputy mode.

"People have to eat and in a time like this I saw things out there I didn't like. We attempted to get in the Winn-Dixie [on Paris Road] and it was actually so high we couldn't get the big boat in there, and while we were trying to wait for a smaller boat to come so we could try to go in there and try to find some chips and snacks, a boat came outta there with three guys and boat was loaded with rocking chairs. I went crazy."

Gelvin yelled at the men, "I could understand y'all going in there for water and food, nobody is going to begrudge you that, but you going in there and stealing rocking chairs, what the hell are you gonna do with rocking chairs!"

At one point Gelvin's temper got the best of him and he tried to jump in their boat and "whip their asses". He pulled his gun out of his holster and tried to hand it to Douglas, Sr.

"No, you're gonna get in trouble," Douglas, Sr. reasoned.

He ranted and raved, but they did not say anything to him. "They were dumbfounded," said Gelvin.

"Get the hell out of here before he jumps in your boat," said Douglas, Sr.

Gelvin still bothered by the encounter said, "I don't think I would have done anything like that [jump in their boat] but it's just ridiculous. People shouldn't be doing stuff like that; we lost everything, and they're in there stealing from other people, and I mean it's just not right."

One of the levee district men was trying to get supplies to St. Bernard High School and Gelvin made his way to the Violet Canal Bridge to meet a supply boat. He had the keys to a Jeep on top of the bridge and backed it down to load it up.

"There was maybe thirty to forty people on top the bridge; we were giving them water, but they were getting greedy," Gelvin said.

Some of the guys wanted cases of water and Gelvin told them they couldn't have that much.

"Y'all shouldn't be on the bridge; why don't y'all go to St. Bernard High too; they'll take you over there by boat," Gelvin told the people.

A couple of them offered to help load the supplies on the truck.

"They were loading them on the truck; well, I turned around and I caught this young guy sneaking over the side of the bridge and stashing supplies that were meant for the people stranded for St. Bernard High in a pirogue," said Gelvin. "I grabbed him and I handcuffed him; then I got to thinking, what the hell am I gonna do with this guy, there's no jail to bring him to."

He let the guy go, but it sent a message to the others on the bridge.

"The people that saw me do that went and retrieved the supplies and brought 'em back to the truck," said Gelvin. "A lot of the people that I saw on the bridge, I don't think they wanted help, some of them were up to no good, trying to get boats and ride around to see what they could steal themselves. I saw a lot of them; you could tell they weren't helping people because they were passing people up that were begging for help, and they were just riding around. I mean if you're just riding around, what are you looking for? You're looking to see what you could steal and not what you can help."

While Douglas, Sr. and Gelvin ran boats up and down the 40 Arpent Canal to drop off supplies to all the pump stations, the pumping crews were cleaning and cranking up the stations that worked. There are eight drainage pumping stations positioned throughout the parish from Arabi to Verret. Once they had finally gotten all the men to the different stations they realized they had lost three stations. The ones not operable were land based and flooded; the ones they could operate were elevated. They were stations #1 and #6 at the end of Jean Lafitte Parkway in the Buccaneer Villa Subdivision in Chalmette, station #4 on Guerra Drive, station #7 at Bartolo Drive in Meraux, and station #8 in Verret. They had to relay messages with their radios because of the compromised communications system.

"Our radio repeater was out but we have a simplex channel, so at each pumping station we switched over to the simplex channel and it'll transmit four to five miles," said Turner. "We were able to then relay information from one side of the parish to the other by transferring it from pump station to pump station kind of leapfrogging down. Of course the message they got to station #8 from station #1 might have been a little bit twisted, but it would come close."

The men had seen the human catastrophe and the homes engulfed with water. They knew about the people trapped in the attics; they had even pulled people from their attics. They knew that every minute the pumps were off there was a greater chance someone could die.

"Without those pumps they go under period," said Jaurell Aisola. "Once you crank them pumps it's steadily, gradually pulling that water down, making it safer and safer for you to get off that roof or evacuate out of here."

This is the reason why they stayed in the parish stationed at shelters close to the pumps, so they could get to them immediately after the storm, but the unprecedented flooding delayed the men a good twenty-four hours. Even so there was not much they could do until the Bayou Dupre locks were opened.

Doyle Dardar, Jr. went to pump station #7 while Aisola made it to station #1 and #6 just down the street from where he stayed at the civic center. Tuesday night Douglas, Sr. said the only pumps that could begin pumping water out of the parish were stations #1 and #6.

"They have sheet pilings up on the levees. You cannot pump if the water differential is even; you cannot pump water from here and put it there because it's gonna roll back over, so it has to be a differential," Douglas, Sr. explained. "Because of that sheet piling you can pump until that water comes to the top; that was it; after it get to the top you got to shut down, cause it will start coming back over."

The stations from Paris Road eastward had to wait because they did not have the same water differential; at stations #1 and #6 pumping became a delicate balancing act, so they could not pump at full capacity Tuesday night.

"Just cranked the pump, start pumping, and let the pump run," said Aisola. "Maintain 'em make sure all your oil pressure, air pressure, everything is all right and hope one thing—that the tide you pumping the water in falls. Tide was beautiful, just right, it dropped."

"They were taking it real easy, pumping at maybe 900 rpm to a 1000," said Douglas, Sr. "Full blast is about 1500, between 12 and 1500 rpm."

Dardar went to station #7, which had its roof partially ripped off and served as the base for the levee district operations. They could not pump but they were getting ready.

"We started cleaning up to get it ready, checked all the engines," said Dardar. "It was above the water, the levee; we couldn't pump yet because the water was still over the levee. They were just warming up the engines, cleaning up and get something over the roof so we don't get wet inside the building."

All the pump stations had generators and that meant air conditioning but everyone was wet with no change of clothes.

"All we had [was] what was on our back, that was it," said Dardar.

The stations were noisy and in spite of going nearly forty-eight hours without sleep, the pumpers were just beginning. The most rest they would receive until the parish was pumped out was a couple of hours of sleep at a time.

"With all that noise and all it was kind of hard," said Dardar.

"You couldn't sleep back there; sleeping was no where on your mind," said Aisola, who was born in Violet but had moved to Algiers a handful of years ago. He was not sure how his house had made out although he knew nearly all of his coworkers' homes had been destroyed. The men were also fearful of unwanted sleeping guests.

At night we would post guards to keep the animals off of us while we slept," said Turner. "Station four, the guys were really afraid of snakes there and so they wound up sleeping on the roof of the station; they were afraid to sleep downstairs. There were a lot of snakes at station four apparently."

While the men pumped, cleaned, prepared, and shared snake-watching duties, Douglas, Sr. and Gelvin made the rounds.

"As we going through each portion of the parish, bringing food and beverages to the stations, we also go through the neighborhoods," Douglas, Sr. said. "Hey, hey, anybody holler we respond to that and get them off their roof, put in the boat, and whatever high land would be. A few of them houses we had to bust through the roof."

The Lake Borgne Levee District men knew their jobs would save property, but after Katrina it took on a drastically different meaning.

"We did both, we did rescue and try to get the water outta here to save lives," said Douglas, Sr. "We wasn't trained for the rescue part but we was trained, if the water come, how to react to it to get the water away from here as soon as possible."

A life long resident of St. Bernard, Troy Spencer Douglas, Sr. took it to heart when he said he was responsible for his men; he felt it, and he would stop at nothing to do his job, plain and simple. It was such a serious matter to him; a situation like this had played over in his mind many times before.

"It really never occurred to me to save my life; my job was to save my men's life. I see this all in my sleep. I made it my choice to be dedicated to my job, and I have seen this storm but not the mud that came with it. I have seen this storm in my sleep several times. For me visualizing it through my sleep, through my dreams I reacted to it according to my dreams and what I been taught through training."

**Ferry Across the Mississippi**

Bubby Bodden left his cat Neo at the jail and walked to the ferry loading area at the end of Paris Road. He got on a ferry, thinking it was from Assumption Parish headed for Algiers Point. It was a car carrier ferry and he sat on the slick, hot, steel deck, and as they pulled away from the Chalmette side of the ferry landing, he wondered when he would return to the parish he grew up in and given so much of his life and time to. He crossed the river, and he could not wait to get to his family in Baton Rouge and to eventually see his wife who had evacuated to Mississippi. He knew his life had been altered forever. The ferry docked on the West Bank of the river and the passengers had to walk across a long, metal plank off of the boat into Algiers.

"They weren't able to dock as a normal ferry docks. It was a single line and took a while to get the people off. We stood at Algiers Point maybe an hour, hour and a half waiting for buses to come."

The school buses pulled up and he was surprised at how good everyone behaved getting on the buses.

"I fell asleep and next thing I know we're outside of Baton Rouge. Probably had eight hundred to twelve hundred people [get] off the buses. They had twelve buses, a lot of people that left."

The buses took everyone to the Pete Maravich Assembly Center at LSU, which is the university's assembly center and basketball arena, but they were told not to exit because they were going to the nearby River Center. It was set up as a shelter for New Orleans area evacuees.

"We all get off and we walk inside and there's three Red Cross people trying to take applications for twelve hundred people, plus people that were already there; it was total chaos. Elderly people, people who couldn't speak a lick of English, Spanish, Japanese, Vietnamese, had no idea what to do."

In order to get into the River Center you had to fill out a paper and go through a security check. When Bubby checked in, he knew he had a niece who was a member of a sorority at LSU, and they had a lot of LSU students helping out. He saw a girl with a Delta Gamma shirt on and thought that was the sorority she was in. Bubby approached the young ladies and asked if they knew his niece and one of them did.

"All I want you to do is get a word to her that her Uncle Bubby's O.K."

This way his wife and her family would learn he was safe in Baton Rouge. He went to get an MRE and met up with a guy who had helped save people at Andrew Jackson. Bubby, always watching and plotting, did not like the way some of the people were acting at the River Center.

"The LSU students were handing out clothing, and I said I just need one shirt, cause the shirt I had was terrible, and they gave me a shirt. They go to this other kid and the kid says 'I want one of those, but I want it in blue.' So it was like people weren't getting it, just take what they give you, cause you don't have anything else knucklehead. It was getting to that point where people were arguing over, well he got this meal, well I want this meal; I said this is a bad situation gotta get out.

## Not Only the Good Die Young

Major John Doran composed himself after being rescued by the sheriff at the Arabi substation, and after grabbing a flat boat, a couple of men, and hitting the flooded waterways Monday, he found that another day just brought more of the same.

"You couldn't go a block without somebody yelling for help," Doran said. "We hear these people yelling and there's five rooftops of people. The water's up over the roof and it's a couple of adults. They're telling us there's an older lady at one end of the block. We go down there, and she's real sick, and these people on the roof had already cut their way out of the roof, some kind of way; [there was] a young woman, two older women, and a really elderly woman that was dying inside the roof."

The attics were like boiler rooms and Doran hurriedly dragged the elderly woman out and into the flatboat. The women told Doran there were men inside the house, "There's two guys in the house that are dead; they drowned." When they told Doran one of the men's name it hit him in the gut.

"One of the guys I knew; I grew up with him, but I hadn't seen him in fifteen years or twenty years, but I knew him; I knew the name right away."

"You know him?"

"Yea," Doran said.

His name was Thomas Burke, but he was also called Tab Burke. The men got trapped in the fast rising water, trying to get a generator up into the attic after saving the women first. The name was familiar to the other officers because they remembered arresting him once.

"We arrested the guy on a search warrant with DEA," said Colonel Forrest Bethay.

But even they realized none of that mattered right then.

"He was trying to save those people," said Bethay. "Everybody realized this is the time to do some good, even people who did some bad in their life."

"He saved the older lady," said Doran. "I know him my whole life; I know him since I was a little kid, it hits home. That sets your mind into hey you don't realize people are actually probably drowning as we speak."

Nighttime at the courthouse was about as peaceful a place can be without electricity, steaming hot, no working restrooms, and overcrowded with people. The conditions were deadly for some. Colonel Bethay remembered hearing bad news from the only paramedic they had at the courthouse.

"I have a lady that died; she's in the back."

The elderly woman's husband had kept a vigil all night, holding her until she finally passed.

"Do we have any body bags around here?" Bethay asked the lieutenant.

"No."

"Do we have anything we can put her in?"

"I don't think so?"

"Do we have any large garbage bags?"

"Yes."

"Put her in a large garbage bag, a couple of them, tie it up, put her in a boat, and send her to the Deano Center, which is right next to the courthouse," said Bethay. "Bust the door and put her in there."

So the men picked up the woman, moving her away from her grieving husband, and took her to a place they could bag her up. They carried her body outside, put her in a little flat boat, and guided it to the building across the street that used to be the battered women's clinic.

"We can't let a body around us, we'll get sick," said Bethay. "We had to put that lady over there and that's where she stayed."

"Whenever you thought it couldn't get any worse it got worse," said Doran.

## CHAPTER SEVENTEEN

# 48 Hours, Is Help Coming?

## Wednesday, August 31

### Day Four

While many worked feverishly to get the slip warehouse ready early Wednesday morning, across town, Glenn Sanchez was lying down at the Region's Bank to rest his aching back around two o'clock.

"I was dying of thirst; my mouth was so dry I couldn't even breathe," said Sanchez. "I asked one of the cops for water."

"They're rationing the water, not giving it out until breakfast time," Sanchez recalled the officer saying.

"My mouth was so dry I couldn't deal with it anymore," said Sanchez. "I ended up cutting a button off my shirt and sucking on a button for about three hours just to put some saliva in my mouth."

A couple of hours later Sanchez was back on "marina time."

"I go outside and I need some water, I see a cop and he says 'nope not until breakfast time.'"

Sanchez had had enough; after saving people Tuesday, he felt like he had foolishly returned to the bank when he could have just left from there himself.

"I wasn't staying with all these people in there without knowing when help was coming," said Sanchez.

So he made a critical decision; he pulled out his knife, a Leatherman, and started trimming his clothes for a trip. He grabbed his life jacket, picked up his knife, and cut the sleeves

271

off of his jean shirt and then cut his jeans into short pants.

"I don't go anywhere without my Leatherman," said Sanchez. "I cut the corner of my jean shirt off and chewed it like I was chewing gum to keep saliva in my mouth. I walked down the steps, got in the water, and I swam."

In the black of the early morning he set out for the closest facility he figured people would have evacuated to, Andrew Jackson High. He swam across Judge Perez and down Jean Lafitte Parkway in the Buccaneer Villa South Subdivision. It was about a half-mile trek to the school and he thought it would be a jumping off point to get to dry ground.

"I was going to the river that's gonna be the highest land; I was getting on the levee. I was gonna go to Paris Road cause I knew they had the police station there and I knew it was dry."

As the light of the morning broke through the eastern sky, Sanchez was keeping an eye out for something very small and venomous.

"The thing that I was worried about more than anything else was swimming with floating red ants. They float and get in piles. I would not go by any trees, any debris, anything. I wasn't worried about snakes or alligators or anything else cause everything else was trying to survive."

With A.J. in close range his journey to avoid ants that could inject toxic venom, which can be deadly to some people, was nearly complete. Then he heard a boat coming.

"I yelled for help."

His life jacket was bobbing up around his dry head, and as the boat pulled up, he heard, "Is that you, Glenn?"

"A friend of mine I went to school with Mark DiMaggio. I got in the boat with him, and they brought me all the way up to the Chalmette Cemetery."

The National Cemetery sits right next to the Chalmette Battlefield where the Battle of New Orleans was fought in 1815, the last fight between the United States and England. Major General Andrew Jackson and his troops teamed up with the infamous pirate Jean Lafitte and defeated the British in the famous battle that marked the end of the War of 1812.

Part of the National Park system, the battlefield and cemetery sit between St. Bernard Highway and the Mississippi River levee. In 1864, the cemetery was opened for Union soldiers who had died in Louisiana during the Civil War. There are four men buried there who died fighting in the War of 1812, but only one soldier who actually fought in the Battle of New Orleans is buried in the cemetery. The soldiers buried in the cemetery's soil fought in conflicts ranging from the Spanish-American War to the Vietnam War.

Sanchez walked in water up to his chest to the back of the cemetery. He walked through the sacred ground unable to see the headstones lined side by side at equal length and near equal height under old oak trees that stretch across more than a dozen acres. When he reached the levee he walked to the port, and once there, someone drove him in the other direction to the slip where they began staging all of the evacuees.

"The guy said check this out, they had that concrete wall over the levee, and they had drift all the way against that wall, the river and the lake almost met," said Sanchez.

The sun already cooking, Sanchez believed he had arrived at the slip after nine in the morning and saw a man and his daughter talking with a doctor.

"She had the worse acne I'd seen all over her," said Sanchez. "They hung on the telephone poll by Lexington [Place Subdivision in Meraux] during the storm, and ants made a nest in her hair, and they ate her up; it was terrible. It was all ant bites."

While Sanchez's swim seemed dangerous enough, why do it before sun up? He would have certainly been able to see better and if he would have gotten in some kind of trouble, the chances of someone helping him would have been much greater. But he wasn't worried about drowning, "that wasn't an option." He was worried about something much more serious.

"I left so early cause I'd really look like an idiot if I'd got in the water and a boat came along and picked me up and grabbed me and bring me right back to that place," Sanchez said with a laugh and dead seriousness. "I had to get away before the boats started coming, I had to get far enough away."

It was a much more thought out plan than you would have figured, and he really did not want to go back there once he had jumped in the water.

"Especially soaking wet, I'd a really looked like an idiot," Sanchez laughed.

### Camp Katrina Overload

The men had worked through the morning to get the warehouse

ready, and people arrived Wednesday morning en masse. They walked in or were dropped off at the slip either by vehicle along the levee or by boat via the river. When they walked through the huge opening of the warehouse they saw the hundreds of plywood pallets of red birch and white oak spaced out across the facility. A family could climb on top of one of the pallets with their belongings, making it their personal space until they loaded onto a ferry or barge to head out of town.

"Everybody sitting, two to three adults and children, sitting on a stack of plywood," said Port Facility Security Officer Eric Acosta. "Look like they went through hell. They had a place to lay down; all I can tell you it was a safe haven."

Parish officials were arranging for ferries or barges, whatever large boats they could get to cross the river, to drop off as many people as possible in Algiers where buses would pick them up to take them out of town. Meantime the river was filling up with other boats. They heard Acosta's terrorist alert Tuesday and boats from all over the Mississippi answered his call for help.

"We had boats from the parish line all the way past my Chalmette ferry," said Acosta. "Every shape and size boats, from one hundred-something-foot Joe boats [to] ferry boats from all the way as far as Shreveport. They were all familiar with what we was doing. Thanks to the Coast Guard and the new code of federal regulations all this training has to be done on the maritime men, so everybody's pretty well in sync on it and it worked out beautiful."

Civilian and small business boats pulled up to the slip one by one.

"Eric, what do you want us to do?"

They grabbed water and threw it to the men on the boats.

Acosta would repeat his request over and over, "Start heading down river, anybody you see throw 'em a bottle of water. If there's five people, you throw 'em five bottles of water. Once you run out of water, turn around and pick them up, and bring them this way."

The boats began a river train of rescues, picking up the people who had traveled to the levee. Meanwhile, security at the facility fell upon Major John Doran and Captain Chad Clark. Before long they had recruited more volunteers to help make needed improvements for the people arriving.

"People started coming in by the hundreds," said Doran. "We just went through the crowd, does anybody have any medical background, we need help. There was six to eight of us at first.

We had a little civil unrest, fighting over food and space; we quelled that real quick."

The deputies no nonsense attitude caught the attention of the people coming in. Like the officers, most were fried and were not a problem, but there was no tolerance for trouble.

"They were bound and determined that they were gonna run this shit orderly," said Barry Uhle.

There were plenty of people more than ready to help the officers; one guy who used to be a nurse volunteered to help begin a triage area. They needed people to operate forklifts in order to finish bringing down the pallets and place them for bedding; many evacuees stepped up to help. They did not have any bathrooms, so another man who said he served in the army dug a latrine.

"We were working off the cuff and working with what you could find," said Acosta, who also said it was his idea to lay down the pallets of wood for the people.

Glenn Sanchez's swim to escape Region's Bank ended at the slip where a man working a forklift, pulling down pallets, assigned him a spot that he believes may have been heaven sent.

"I was third row back in the middle," said Sanchez. "It was funny, my son told these people, cause he was with their daughter up in Shreveport, 'if you run across my daddy, you don't let him go.' When I wake up I see these old friends of mine and it was the same people my son said if you see my dad, don't let 'em go. I truly believe God was with me a long way on this journey."

Councilwoman Judy Hoffmeister did not sit back and let the men do all the dirty work at the slip. They needed so many things that she went on a number of expeditions to get food and water.

"We finally found a truck and I'm getting pretty good at, I don't want to say stealing and looting, I think commandeering is a better word," said Hoffmeister. "When the people were on the slip, we had babies who needed diapers, needed butt cream, we needed feminine products, we had nothing. We needed food, so we did a pretty good job of commandeering things."

They drove down a mostly dry Paris Road to the Walgreen's at Judge Perez. Although the water had receded somewhat, it was still up to her chest. It was sloppy inside the pharmacy and everything had been moved around.

"I knew if I could get stuff that was on the above shelves, we'd be O.K." said Hoffmeister.

*Boats lined up outside of Walgreens, trying to get to the supplies inside.*
*Photograph by Al Clavin*

So she pulled up with her husband, Lloyd, who is a retired police officer from the New Orleans Police Department and is currently a Lieutenant in St. Bernard.

"There's looters in there," he told his wife.

"Oh, maybe we ought not go in."

Hoffmeister, like many in the parish, was aware of the trouble-makers in the city and did not want to run into anyone like that, but she went in anyway and stood by the door.

"Anybody in here?" she said.

"Yes, what you need," was the answer from inside.

"I'm with the shelter and I need baby diapers, I need feminine products."

"Don't move we'll come to you."

"[They] just start grabbing things off the shelves not affected, hand cream, cleaner anything we could use," said Hoffmeister.

Standing there in her knee high boots she could hear them slosh-ing around in the water, and they came up with loads of materials.

"They brought me everything I said I needed," said Hoffmeister.

They brought bags and bags of supplies to Hoffmeister and filled up her truck.

"Let me go bring this to the warehouse," she told her new friends.

"No, we got more."

"Would y'all just get it for me and bring it outside?"

By now she was on a first name basis with the "comman-deerers."

"O.K. put it out; look don't let anybody take it," Hoffmeister said.

"Don't you worry, nobody's taking that stuff."

An elderly woman who lived around the corner went to the Walgreen's to see if she could get some blood pressure medication for her husband who had ran out; Hoffmeister stepped in.

"You tell me what it is you need, you continue to help me gather stuff, I'll bring you back some medicine."

Hoffmeister and her husband drove the truck along the levee back to the shelter and unloaded it. She went to Dr. Bryan Bertucci to get the exact medications she needed.

"This is the deal I made with this lady," Hoffmeister told Dr. Bertucci. "She's gonna get me more stuff and I'm gonna give her some high blood pressure pills."

Hoffmeister said Dr. Bertucci provided pills for the barter exchange and she hoofed it back to Walgreen's to re-load the truck and drop off the medication for the woman.

Supplies were far and few between, but finally the sound of helicopters grew louder and louder approaching the slip. The large, green military choppers loaded down with MREs and water were finally bringing some relief into St. Bernard. Someone had painted a landing symbol to create an area between the levee and the facility for the helicopters to land and drop off goods. The choppers belonged to the military, Red Cross, and private owners; they were the first signs of help being flown into the parish from the outside with the exception of the Coast Guard, who had been involved in rescue missions.

As the helicopters landed, the men ducked underneath the pro-pellers, grabbed the boxes of heated meals and water, and ran away, hair flying all around, eyes squinted with grimacing faces. They carried the boxes into the slip to store them away from the people, so they could manage handing them out. They even came up with a system to distribute the food and Uhle and five others ran the food services.

"The six of us ran the little cafeteria," said Uhle. "They'd roll the door and close the door, twice a day. We'd hand out MREs and a couple of bottles of water to each person. Nobody fought in line and nobody took more than they needed. The older people went first and they took care of anybody with kids first. People that couldn't make it there we brought it to them. People that really needed it more we gave it to them. Bottles that fell on the ground and got muddy people put on the side and gave it to their pets."

A lot of people brought animals to the slip as the day progressed, and the plan was to keep them from coming inside the facility to keep it sanitary.

"Everybody with pets stayed outside, never once did they say why I gotta stay outside?" Uhle said.

People finally had a place that became the final stop in St. Bernard before leaving the parish. Conditions were uncomfortable and the heat of the August day was overwhelming. They rolled in big fans to circulate the hot air, but if you were not close to the fan you could not catch the breeze. The amount of people standing around the fan blocked any significant airflow in the building.

"It was kind of miserable; you learned to live with it," said Sanchez. "It was a lot safer than any place else in the city; you knew you weren't gonna die until you left there, and then you didn't know what would happen."

Hundreds of people walked on board the first boat, awaiting their destination, Algiers Point. Buses were said to be waiting on the other side and many prayed this was the beginning of the

Residents at Camp Katrina waiting for a ride out of the parish. Photograph by Errol Schultz

end of the hell they had been through. The ride was filled with anxiety, relief, and exhaustion. The ferry pulled up to the dock to unload the parish's first mass movement of evacuees.

"They had nobody to receive them on the other end," said Major James Pohlmann. "We sent five hundred people over there, and there's not a bus in sight, so what do you do? We're responsible. We feel a sense that wherever we send these people they're counting on us for them to be safe to get to somewhere. To dump them on the West Bank and just watch them with no place to go bothered us. We turned the boat around and made it come back. At least when they're here we'll do the best that we can."

When the ferry returned to the slip, the desperation grew stronger, but at least they were on familiar soil. The accumulation of people, the heat, and the feeble conditions of many people revealed the inherent flaws in the ability to take care of those who were seriously compromised or injured. With the arrival of helicopters to medevac people out, there was some relief to the dire medical situation, but there were deadly implications for some.

"People's medical conditions started to deteriorate," said Doran. "We didn't have insulin; we had pregnant women in the facility. It was a twenty-four hour, non-stop situation and who we're gonna medevac out? It was a logistical nightmare and evacuees kept coming with dehydration."

"I learned that the most necessary drug in the United States is insulin," said Sheriff Stephens. "We didn't have any."

The slip filled to capacity in a short period of time and was overcrowded by the time buses finally showed up on the West Bank. Under the eye of the Coast Guard, St. Bernardians boarded the buses, headed anywhere that was not under water.

"There was never any occasion where we didn't have probably 2000 and 2200 people on the Chalmette Slip waiting to be evacuated," said Stephens. "The Coast Guard was protecting the evacuees because they had some random gun fire and some civil disobedience over there. People would have to wait there sometimes eight, ten, twelve hours to get a bus or truck out of there. It was a horrible situation."

The thousands of hungry, hot, tired, and emotionally drained people all under one roof in the most extreme of psychological circumstances are a testament to human survival. Chaos did not break out, but deputies responded quickly when there was even a hint of foolishness.

"The troublemakers were such a small minority that they knew . . . my guys were fried," said Stephens. "They weren't in enforcement mode; they were in search and rescue mode, and they weren't about to put up with any bullshit from anybody, and I think they could sense that. They didn't look like the regular police, and they weren't acting like the regular police. There wasn't any humor in our voice or anything like that, and in addition to that just the general population we were helping was so cooperative; I think they would have torn somebody apart."

They occasionally did have to lock some people up who pushed their luck, but not in the jail that was overrun with evacuees, the deputies made one up out of a fenced in area outside under the boiling sun.

Colonel Forrest Bethay told his men, "If they're unruly take them over there and put them into that caged area and just leave them in there for an hour or so. Tell them when you want to behave just raise their hand and go talk to them see if they've been in there long enough, see if they want to behave and get back to the rest of the people."

Once he checked on a guy a couple of hours later and found three people in the cage.

"I told 'em look just release them on their own recognizance after about an hour if they promise to behave, so I pull up they had guys in there with their hands raised," said Bethay.

"It wasn't locked or anything it was like Mayberry," said Stephens. "One day I'm walking by and [he] said 'sheriff can I talk to you,' the man's in the hot sun."

"Hey man can I get out now?" he asked Stephens.

"What were you doing?"

"We were fighting over the MREs."

"Look can you control yourself now? I'm gonna let you get out of here, but if you start f@&*ing up again, you're getting right back in this cage you understand me?"

"Yes, sir."

"Let yourself out."

Stephens cracked up laughing at the thought of this.

"It was true, that type of thing [hearty laugh] it's like you're in time out, stay in there until we tell you to come out," as he bellowed another laugh.

People were getting out, and as they left, more filled their spots at the slip. They brought in generators to power lights in the dark warehouse. People tried to rest on the wooden pallets as they wondered when their ship would come.

## Burning Up

It did not take the morning sun long to start cooking Gene Alonzo and his brother, Carlos. The humidity was high and the sweat poured out of everyone. They still had people inside of the jail and it was critically hot inside.

"It's worse in that jail now; you can't even take it," said Alonzo. "We got a bunch of them; got them outside, keep them in the shade, and they ain't had hardly no shade."

Alonzo wondered when the rest of the people at St. Rita's were going to get to the jail; some had stayed at Beauregard, on Tuesday night, and he didn't know if they would join up together again.

"We see a truck coming through the levee, a garbage truck, and it's the rest of the ones from St. Rita's," said Alonzo. "That was some really sick ones in this truck."

Alonzo noticed his friend Jimmy's wife was in the truck, but he was not with her and that struck him as strange because she was in really bad shape.

"Where's Jimmy?"

"He just went walking through the road," someone answered.

That sounded odd to him; he never saw Jimmy show up at the jail. Some people had been going to the Chalmette Ferry landing on the Mississippi River, up the road from the jail past Chalmette Refining's massive plant. Alonzo and some of the people from St. Rita's, those who could actually walk to the ferry, were encouraged to go to Algiers. Alonzo grabbed his brother by the arm and guided him to Paris Road; they walked south toward the ferry landing and boarded a ferry; they sat on the hot deck of the boat, baking under the sun. Alonzo had on jeans and Carlos wore shorts. Alonzo did not like the look of his brother's legs.

"My brother's legs were red like fire. I never thought they was that bad, and his legs started peeling. My brother got second and third degree burns on his legs."

They crossed the river, and everyone looked at the New Orleans skyline as they left St. Bernard and docked in Algiers. Along with the hundreds of people who crossed the metal plank, there were hundreds more on land waiting for buses. You were left waiting if you did not move fast while the bus was loading. There was no one from St. Rita's who was going to outmaneuver the others trying to get on the buses.

"Everybody's trying to get on the buses; they don't care about the sick people, they getting on the bus," said Alonzo. "The young people gonna get on the bus first; when the bus would come they would get on. You trying to drag people and you ain't getting on no bus; that bus fills up in a second."

One of the St. Rita's nurses trying to keep the group together explained what was happening to an army guy.

"We ain't never gonna get on a bus," she said to the soldier. "We got sick people from St. Rita's Nursing Home; you gonna have to hold a bus for us to get on. We just can't jump on like these other people."

The military stepped in, and they helped escort the St. Rita's people onto a bus. The heat was inescapable; the jail was hot; the ferry was hot; and Carlos's legs were burning. It was Wednesday afternoon and they had already spent a painfully slow, hot day getting out of the parish.

"The whole school bus was jammed with people and they bring us somewhere in the city, under an overpass, Causeway and I-10 I believe that's where we were," said Alonzo. "We got out."

For Alonzo it was like going from the frying pan into the fire. They were dumped with thousands of people from all over the metro area, but it was mostly people rescued from their homes in New Orleans. They were lined up along the interstate in Metairie about fifteen miles from St. Bernard. Most tried to stay underneath the Causeway Boulevard overpass, but there were far too many people for the amount of shade available. The nearly all glass Galleria building was the dominant structure behind them, but it was too far of a walk for shade. Walking there would put them out of position to get on a bus if one came and too far away from food and water if someone started handing it out.

There were families with dehydrated kids, elderly people in wheelchairs, burning up, and compromised residents of St. Rita's Nursing Home, all trying to survive. The group had to stay close together for fear of losing someone in the dense crowd of evacuees, and these were people who could neither care for themselves nor afford to get lost. This also affected their ability to receive water and food being distributed by the first responders who were totally overwhelmed by the horrendous conditions.

"We're dying for water again, and the water's down the street, and we can't turn people loose."

Alonzo said people were drinking whiskey, but this did not bother him, because there was not much that could rattle a rough and tumble guy like Alonzo. But while they never caused any trouble for him, he felt uneasy about the way people were acting in that situation. He was not just caring for himself; he had Carlos and the others from the nursing home to care for as well. They had been through enough he thought, and he didn't want the situation they were in to become any more life threatening.

There was not much they could do except wait until it was their turn to get out. They thought it had been bad enough trying to get on a bus out of Algiers, but now there was no one to run interference on I-10 and people were wild, trying to escape the nightmare that had become the interstate. They knew they would not all be able to get on one bus together, so when night fell one of the nurses told Alonzo, "we're gonna divide up."

## Jail Break

Tuesday, Dr. Lee Domangue walked into the jail's hellish conditions. Nurse Barbara Warren was part of the wave of people that had left the hospital Wednesday. She felt relieved to be free of the overheated hospital. She and five patients had escaped by boat and went as far as they could up Paris Road before they transferred to a pickup truck and drove the short distance to the jail. She had heard they had electricity and hoped that meant cooler and more comfortable quarters. What she found was far from what she had hoped for.

"I was disappointed, and if you're going through a miserable situation you expect things to be a little bit better and it wasn't," said Warren. "There was nursing home patients just lining the hallway, just laying on mats at the jail. We had jail cells full of trash from the inmates, personal items and bags, garbage everywhere."

Wearing her white scrubs, Warren walked across wet and muddy floors, "just real nasty conditions." The first thing she did was clean up.

"I had to go through and clean out areas, so we could fit the patients in, get the debris out, and start assigning where to put the patients," said Warren. "What patients could tolerate a top bunk and wouldn't roll off and what patients to put on the bottom. [We] needed somebody coherent not to roll over and fall on the floor."

Warren was struck by just how many people were roaming around the jail inside and out and how many sick people there were to care for. After clearing out areas for patients, she assigned nurses to three different areas.

"Started diaper duty with the nursing home patients," said Warren. "We went around and changed the diapers, assessed the patients, every one of them was dehydrated. Keith [Bradbury] and I went through and started putting IVs and hanging fluids on each one of the nursing home patients; we brought stuff from the hospital. We had fire and sheriff's deputies, and they were dehydrated and vomiting and sick, and we didn't have fluids."

Dehydration became a major concern because they did not have their usual large bags of saline fluid. In order to give patients a reasonable amount, they squeezed small 50cc and 100cc bags of fluid into people.

"Ten to twenty of them, sometimes thirty of them into the veins of the patients," said Warren. "It was tough, stick them with the needle, hook them to an IV line and put a little bag on there, squeeze it, that ones empty, change it out, and put another one on there."

When they ran out of saline they had to use a substitute they would not normally use. For those who may have been diabetic and there were far too many, and with no way to figure out if someone was diabetic in advance of using the saline, the change of fluids was a real crapshoot.

"We started using, which is not a great fluid to hydrate with, D5 which is dextrose sugar water to re-hydrate," said Warren. "We didn't know whether they were diabetic, but we had to re-hydrate them, so we started using that."

Dextrose sugar is used to mix medications or if a patient's blood sugar is low. However, for them it was better than nothing.

"We were giving them volume and I was thinking of anything, some type of volume to put into the blood stream," said Warren.

It was this shotgun medical approach that was crucial for survival. There was no time for double guessing, no time to reinvent the wheel; they used common sense and a little ingenuity.

"We didn't write a thing down; there was no time to get physician orders for these patients; you just did what you needed to do to help the patient," said Warren.

Adding to the load were the nursing home patients from St. Rita's; Warren knew this was a bad situation for them to be trapped in.

"It was disheartening, normally you get nursing home patients who are confused and they kind of holler out and make noises and call names; they're kind of active verbally. But these patients didn't make noise, they laid on their mats and they didn't move. That was hard to see because nobody moved."

Dr. Domangue was also thankful for the calm that patients displayed. One young man was too calm and should have pressed doctors to help him because whether he knew it or not he was flirting with death.

"I saw a young guy, maybe twenty-five years old, who had massive bleeding from an injury to his forearm," said Dr. Domangue. "He had a huge wound and he had an arterial bleed as well, with multiple tendons injured. We got control of him quickly, probably lost a third of his blood volume and was still very calm about it. We put pressure on his injury and began to supply him with fluid, but we had no plasma or blood. He needed to go to surgery, and luckily enough we got this guy up and into a helicopter medevac transport system quickly"

Warren tended to one man having trouble breathing; she thought he was too sick to make it out of the jail and that he was dying.

"We lost one nursing home patient, a little, old, skinny, ema- ciated gentlemen that had a long beard, long hair, and he had what they call Kussmaul breathing," said Warren. "Just very irregular breathing, and you knew that he was on his way out. We just tried to make him comfortable, but there was nothing we could do for him, nothing at all."

The doctors and nurses had more work than they could ever handle at once and sleep was fairly non-existent. When the jail turned dark and became morning, she let some of her other nurses get rest at the BellSouth building where the firefighters had set up, but she refused to follow them.

"I did not sleep the whole time I was at the jail," said Warren. "I decided to stay because there was nobody to take care of the little people laying on the floor, the little, elderly nursing home patients that were full of stool and pee, so I stayed, and I made maybe three rounds throughout the night."

It was diaper duty for the most part and that was not made any easier after they ran out of Depend® underwear.

"We ran out of those, and there was some extra smalls, so it was more like a sanitary napkin to some of them because they were big women," said Warren. "We just kind of wrapped them between their legs to catch what we could and because they were tiny little diapers compared to the size of the people, and we just used that."

As difficult as it was for the nurses and doctors who had to look after thousands of people, Warren figured it was particularly hard on the elderly evacuees from St. Rita's and elsewhere but with age sometimes comes resiliency.

"A lot of them were demented, had Alzheimer's, and they would answer your questions if anything hurt like 'can I do anything for you' and most of the little old ladies would say 'no darling I'm doing just fine.' It's kind of like they accepted, they knew something really bad was going on, and they were just gonna sit there and be quiet, the ones that could talk would tell ya and wouldn't complain."

Dr. Domangue figured he and his staff saved countless lives.

"We saw I'm sure thousands of people, and if I had to esti-mate five to seven thousand people that we treated in that time span," said Domangue. "I have no idea how many people's lives we saved in the process. I think a significant number."

With an event of this magnitude, it is inevitable that people are going to lose their lives and many did.

"We had people actually die in the hospital prior to us moving patients out. Three of these people I think were do not resuscitate patients, elderly, disabled, debilitated," said Warren. "Once they expired you weren't gonna try to bring them back. One was not and I helped to resuscitate that patient, it was obviously unsuccessful."

Although the jail didn't have air conditioning, it had a huge walk-in freezer with meat and fish brought there by deputies. Dr. Domangue and Dr. Bertucci went in to chill their aching bodies early in the morning when most people were trying to relax under the cooler night sky.

"We stayed there for like two and a half hours it was comfort-able," said Domangue. "We were just sweaty and tired and beat to death, we stunk, no where to bathe. We were terribly chafed; you couldn't take care of yourself, and you were walking like John Wayne, and you tried not to walk very much; you wanted patients to come to you because you couldn't easily walk. Our nurse kept on checking on us to make sure we were surviving."

## CHAPTER EIGHTEEN

# Reel 'Em In and Get 'Em Out

## Wednesday, August 31

### Day Four

With more than forty people over the age of sixty-five with some sort of health issue and only fifteen airlifted out on Tuesday by the Coast Guard, St. Bernard High School was holding in the vicinity of four hundred people, Wednesday.

"We were starting to get desperate," said Ourso.

They had several helicopters come to the school to evacuate more people, but they were not coming often enough.

Lebeau: "The problem we had with the helicopters is the debris on the rooftops."

Ourso: "The roof insulation blowing everywhere."

Lebeau: "And these pilots flying the last couple of days, they can only fly for so many hours before they're mandated to have some down time. Once they'd leave, they'd say look we're coming back but it's not gonna be us but another crew. We'd wait and wait looking and listening."

When one did come back the tension subsided shortly, because it meant at least more people were getting out. The choppers would hover above the roof and lower the baskets down and if the occupants were small enough, they would try to bring two up at a time. Mitch McDaniel climbed onto the roof underneath the choppers.

"The winds felt like about fifty or sixty miles an hour; they had one of the wind turbines on top of the roof that someone

*Firemen Rodney Ourso and Michael Lebeau. Photograph by Mikel Schaefer*

needed to hold onto, so it wouldn't go flying off and hit somebody while the helicopter was hovering, so that's what I did,"
said McDaniel. "Actually holding that thing down, using my
body as a weight. It was a sheet metal turbine, industrial grade
similar to what you have on your own house but probably about
three or four times as big."

Those rescued climbed out of the window and onto the flat
asphalt roof of the school; the rescues were repeated until nearly
sixty or seventy people were taken out by helicopter. Because
people had to be lifted in a basket, some did not take to the idea
very easily.

"There was this one young lady who was afraid but both the
firefighters and the Coast Guard were able to talk to her," said
McDaniel. "They told her this was in her best interest to evacuate
now instead of waiting on evacuating later on."

One person they wanted out of there as soon possible was a
pregnant teenager.

"We had a fifteen-year-old girl due to deliver on Thursday; we
got her airlifted out; I was glad she left," said Lebeau.

With hundreds still inside the school, some sitting on the second floor windowsills with their feet dangling above the pool of

water below, the men figured they had far too many inside to wait all day for helicopters that may or may not come. Councilman Craig Taffaro and some others made it to the school and had heard the news that St. Bernard Highway had cleared. They thought if they could get the people to the highway, then they could get them out.

"We either had to make everyone walk through the water all the way to the highway, use the boats to get them up Randazzo [Drive] to the highway, or get a truck make it to the high school, and get 'em to the truck up to the highway," said Ourso.

Along with Lebeau, Ourso had decided to go back to the Violet Canal Bridge to see if they could get a few of the parish vehicles to load the people up and drive them the few blocks to the highway.

"We went there to see if the equipment had keys in it because water started to subside," said Ourso. "I think the first day it stayed eight foot for awhile until the next morning it was down about two foot, by the third day looking at four foot by the high school."

The men retrieved a parish dump truck and drove it back to the school through water high enough to stall the truck.

"We made a board with a mop stick on it, we had somebody ride on the front, while they're testing the water as we drove," said Ourso.

"Watching the depth of the water, so we wouldn't lose the truck to the depths of the water," said Lebeau.

They backed the dump truck up to the building and lowered a ladder into the truck bed and people climbed down. They checked to see who needed to board right away and held the healthier people back for a later truck. But the dump truck flooded out. Lebeau said thankfully, a former St. Bernard High classmate he knew as T-Bo pulled up with another dump truck. They lowered the ladder into the back of that truck bed and people carefully navigated the climb into the truck.

The people were on their way down the flooded street to escape the school. T-Bo then came back for load number two.

"We got half of it loaded and it died," said Ourso.

"We had to put those people back up on the roof again. Here these people had hope of getting out after three, four days," said Lebeau. "They were dehydrating with some problems still going on."

It was time to try something else; since by air and land had not worked well enough, it was back to leaving by sea.

"Luckily a couple of boats came by; we were able to evacuate everybody by boat," said McDaniel.

The men grabbed the ladders they used to get people into the dump trucks and placed them into the boats. Those who could climb down by themselves scaled down the ten feet or so into the boat; the ones who needed help like the injured and the elderly were secured with hoses by the firemen.

"We had to hoist people down from the top of the front of the school in the air down into the boats," said McDaniel. "We had several people who couldn't make it down ladders. The firemen came up with one of their fire hoses tied them around them and hoisted 'em down."

The boats made the short ride to the highway as the dump trucks waited to take the evacuees to the jail or Camp Katrina. A few stayed behind, such as Sergeant Hauck and McDaniel, to coordinate shutting the school down.

"We made sure we evacuated all of the civilians first; then a few of us had stayed behind to make sure that all the provisions were taken care of and make sure nobody was left behind," said McDaniel. "We had like two or three trips. Walked around made sure no one else was there, made sure any of the provisions we boxed up, all the food, that they can come back after and pick it up in case we needed it again in another location."

There would not be much rest for the firemen and deputies once they got out, but there was one hell of a reunion.

"We went to the courthouse first and dropped off a few of the deputies there, and then they brought us over to our guys," said Ourso. "That was the first time we saw any of our other firefighters."

"A lot of hugs and kisses and I haven't hugged and kissed so many men in my life," said Lebeau. "It was a happy sight."

Sergeant Hauck said he was the last man to leave the school, two days later, on Friday. A man of strong Catholic faith, Hauck and his wife run a Christian music dance school. Hauck tried to gather the boats scattered around the school they had to commandeer, trying to keep whatever he could in one place.

"I gave one final sweep of the school made sure there was nobody left and met up with the other deputies at the courthouse," said Hauck. "I was exhausted; I collapsed; I had infected legs, ant bites all over my body; I went under water a few times; I swallowed a lot of water and had infections."

## O Canada!

The firemen needed some relief, and it came from the second largest country by land mass in the world, Canada.

"The first bona fide rescue team to get to us in force, like big task forces, was Canadian Task Force One from Vancouver, Canada," said Stone.

This was Wednesday evening and Stone believed it was two more full days before any U.S. Search and Rescue Task Force teams reached the parish.

"It's like how can that happen? How can Vancouver, Canada, Task Force One get here before any U.S. task forces?" Stone said.

The trek from the great white north to the swampy bayous of St. Bernard started Tuesday. Tim Armstrong, the task force leader of the Vancouver Urban Search and Rescue Team, received a call from the head of Emergency Preparedness in the Province of British Columbia about trying to help Louisiana.

Armstrong remembered Solicitor General John Les asking him if there was anything that they could do for Louisiana and if their expertise could be put to good use.

"Definitely."

Armstrong said normally the red tape for such an operation would involve getting permission from Ottawa, Canada's equivalent to Washington, D.C., but the Solicitor General felt he had the power to cut through the bureaucracy.

Armstrong said Les told him he could make a direct offer to the Governor of Louisiana from the Province of British Columbia to aid the people of Louisiana.

Bob Bugslag is the director of the Provincial Emergency Program in British Columbia and asked Armstrong if he had any contacts in the area, and he said he did.

"I work closely with a company out of Baton Rouge, Louisiana," said Armstrong. "We did a lot of our training through a rescue training company called Roco Rescue Corporation."

Armstrong said a contact with Roco called the office of Governor Kathleen Blanco to work out the details. Eventually, the Louisiana State Police called Armstrong to find out information on the rescue squad. Once the checks were finished, Armstrong was told that the state would love for them to come but wanted to know what it would take to get the team to Louisiana.

"We're gonna have to lease an aircraft," said Armstrong.

"How much is that going to cost us?" someone asked.

"The Canadian government's going to pick up the tab," said Armstrong.

"Great come on down."

The next step was securing an airplane, which had its own set of challenges.

"Luckily we'd been working with a local airline that really stepped up to the plate and repositioned an air crew in Vancouver. They had an aircraft coming offline late that night; basically we activated a team, assembled the team, [and] got everybody going."

The plan was to fly to Baton Rouge as soon as possible, but Armstrong said the airport had run out of fuel.

"We thought we were gonna be shut down there, because we had a very small window for this aircraft, cause it had a regularly scheduled flight the next morning. They had to fly through the time that was slated for maintenance, so we ended up flying to Lafayette as an alternate airport."

The airport was closed but the airport manager opened the facility so they could fly in.

"It was only the airport manager and a handful of guys there at the airport to greet us. We got in there about four o'clock in the morning [Wednesday] and we headed to Baton Rouge to [State Police] Troop A headquarters."

From there they drove to Troop B in Kenner where they were informed all operations in the downtown New Orleans area were being halted because of violence.

"We were like oh great we've got all the way here and now they're not gonna do anymore rescue operations here," Armstrong said with a pronounced Canadian dialect.

Then Armstrong said two undercover State Police drug enforcement officers walked in and talked to him.

"Nobody's been in contact with St. Bernard Parish. We live in that parish and we haven't had any contact with anybody there."

After reviewing some information, they noticed that there were 911 calls from St. Bernard and then all communication was lost.

One of the troopers from St. Bernard said, "We need to get into St. Bernard."

Armstrong said State Police Captain Joe Lentini asked if they wanted to go to St. Bernard but said if so they wouldn't be able to get there by road because it was all cut off by water.

They entered by water as Armstrong and some of his Vancouver Urban Search and Rescue Team crew jumped into State Trooper boats and launched out of Zito's Shipyard outside of Kenner for a nearly hour trip down the Mississippi River to do an "initial recon" of the parish. They found Camp Katrina in full swing and pulled the boats into the Chalmette Slip where they met Sheriff Stephens among others.

"We told them we had a forty-six member USAR [Urban Search and Rescue] team from Vancouver," said Armstrong. "I don't think they knew what we were talking about. They were like whatever, great we'll take you down to the E.O.C. [Emergency Operations Center]."

It was there they met President Rodriguez.

"We're a forty-six member UASR team from Vancouver, how can we help?" Armstrong said.

"Oh hallelujah, the Mounties are here," said Rodriguez.

"No, no we're not the Mounties," Armstrong said.

"Oh, hey, everybody the Mounties are here from Canada."

"No we're not the Mounties. After that I thought whatever," Armstrong recalled fondly with a chuckle.

After explaining what he could do for the parish, Chief Stone walked in and Armstrong wanted to know how they could help.

"We've got people trapped in houses; they've been in there, it's totally under water; can you guys go in and start search operations?"

"We'll be back at first light," said Armstrong.

Armstrong and his recon team had to travel back upriver where they stayed at Lake Pontchartrain Elementary School in Laplace.

"There was nothing around Kenner; we were just sleeping on the floor of the elementary school there."

## Chalmette High Staff Plots Getaway

Wayne Warner found out people were being rescued out of the gym. He was happy they had unloaded the gym before they came to the school because for the last forty-eight hours he had no idea what had happened inside his gym or what condition it was in.

"I was really nervous about what was happening in the gym," said Warner.

The firemen rigged one of the flooded buses outside and they used it to move some of the hundreds in the gym. It took hours and hours, but the exodus had begun. With every dump truck, bus, or boatload of people leaving relieved, a measure of stress rolled off of Warner. But getting the sick people out of the gym was challenging as they had to physically carry people up and down stairs to get them to where the water was lowest, so the buses or dump trucks could pick them up. When it was time to get the school cleared out, the firemen came in and told every one they could start walking out.

"All the people capable of walking we told them the water's kind of low now you can walk up Palmisano [Boulevard] and get to St. Bernard Highway and walk towards Paris Road," said fireman Charles Liccardi, Jr. "At this point the water was low enough on Palmisano towards St. Bernard that some vehicles could make it, and we had a couple of vans come to get people in wheelchairs out."

Warner and the school administration could not stop thinking about the people who really needed help. They knew that getting them out of the school was the first step and that they were a long way from getting the desperate medical care that many needed.

"You're nervous for them that they're gonna be able to get their medical needs met soon enough to be able to make them comfortable and let them continue to live," said Mundt.

As they were getting the people out of the school, Warner's wife noticed that a man sitting in a chair had not moved for about an hour.

"She went to a fireman and said you need to go check him, and they were busy; they didn't get to him," said Warner. "She went back to him a second time and said 'you need to check him he hasn't moved.'"

Warner said they checked the man and found he had a pulse rate of around twenty.

"He was going," said Mundt.

"They did CPR; they shocked him; they did the whole bit," said Warner.

"I don't know if he died because they didn't want to tell everyone.

For the first time since Sunday, Warner and the others at the school were thinking about their own rescue and how they were going to get out of this mess. Lingering on Warner's mind was what everyone was going to do about his or her pets.

"We were told very explicitly that they weren't rescuing any animals, no animals were leaving," said Warner. "We had our animals, there were twenty-three of us left who had operated the shelters and that included their families. Twenty-three people and animals, and we had to get out of St. Bernard."

Warner figured there was only one way to get his people and their pets out at the same time and that was to arrange his own rescue, no government boats or buses, his own.

"I came up with a plan, I had a couple little connections with some people in the tug boat industry," Warner explained. "My plan was to get a tug boat to come to the river bank and we had a dock, maybe Murphy [Oil]. I had two people who had gotten tug-boats and our plan was to get on a tugboat and either go across the river where "Cookie" [Mundt] had relatives in St. Mary's Parish that were gonna get a school bus to come pick us up."

The plan was in full motion; the tugboat was on its way, and all they needed to do was get to the dock with their pets, and they were saved.

"Then I get a phone call; the Coast Guard has commandeered the first tug boat, went on with rifles and commandeered the tug boat," said Warner.

The Coast Guard had no idea this boat was set up for a civilian rescue. However, Warner had a back up, a second tug was willing to pick up the Chalmette High crew; the captain called Warner's middleman who had arranged the tugboat missions.

"He told the contact that the Coast Guard said the river was closed and if he went down there that they would take his license away from him," said Warner, who was pretty frustrated with not being able to take care of himself and his people. "This is the United States of America; we weren't asking for any help; we had made all these arrangements, which weren't easy to make, nobody had to do anything. I'm dealing through a phone that works sometimes and they got people doing the best they can. It was really a downer for us. We didn't have any government official help us, all we were gonna do is get on a boat on the Mississippi, which has been done for hundreds of years and go up the river, and we got shot down. I'm sure there were reasons; somebody said it was because they were shooting at the ships in the river or something like this; at that point we had been through hell."

They would stay at the school if they could not take their animals with them.

## One Man Band

Like Monday and Tuesday, it was much of the same at Andrew Jackson as Eric Colopy went out trying to rescue more people stuck in their attics.

"I probably got another ten to twenty more houses that had people still in the attics," said Colopy. "I couldn't get every single house; I was just going street by street and then I started picking up people and bringing [them] to the highway where they can walk up to the courthouse."

After a couple of trips to the Sav-A-Center on Judge Perez, Colopy had plenty of water with him to give out to the people he rescued. He crammed on as many people as he could fit in the boat.

"I even had times where I was pulling two, three boats behind me that had no motors on it, full of people just to get 'em to the highway," said Colopy. "I was making too many trips with just one boat by myself, and it was a little weird feeling."

Some sheriff's deputies made it to the school with more supplies and took with them a couple of elderly people that needed immediate medical attention. But after a few days they wanted to jazz up their food stock.

"After three days we got tired of eating tuna fish and chips, and we started scouting around in the school," said Colopy. "They had a cooking class upstairs, and they had a big commercial deep freezer full of chicken breast and sausage and hamburger meats; they had the pots and pans and all the seasonings. We started frying chicken that following evening."

Colopy then made an announcement.

"We ain't eating cold stuff tonight; we eating fried chicken with Emeril."

The feast was on. They had hit the mother lode and were going to enjoy a hot meal. They had hooked up a TV and were more comfortable than most.

*Eric Colopy with Emeril after finding food to cook inside of Andrew Jackson.*
*Photograph courtesy Eric Colopy*

"We had it set up pretty good, one of them had a portable TV with a cigarette lighter plug, so we had that hooked up to a boat battery," said Colopy. "We was watching the news; we had the lamps with battery and lights."

They also had more than enough to drink, because the second time Colopy went to Sav-A-Center he took more than water and Gatorade.

"I made sure we had plenty enough beers and stuff to make cocktails. I made some cherry bombs with Everclear and tequila. One of the older ladies [tasted one and] she came back with her spoon; she wanted four or five more. I said you want a cocktail?"

"What do you have?"

"What do you want?"

"What do you have?"

"No, what do you want?"

"I don't know?"

"How about a Margarita?"

So he broke out the Margarita mix, the liquor, and whipped up a drink.

"I mean it was hot; we didn't have no ice or nothing after so many days. We'd sit back watch the news, drinking Margaritas and frying chicken," said Colopy.

### Checkmate

In Baton Rouge, Bubby Bodden was one step closer to his goal; he was safe and out of St. Bernard, but he was still grimy and disgusting and wanted to see his family. Always thinking, always wondering what his next move was, it came to him. As he sat on the corner outside of the River Center, Bubby saw a Sheraton Hotel across the street. He went back inside to find Steve, the guy he ran into at the Andrew Jackson High shelter, to ask him if he wanted to check out of the River Center and into a hotel.

"We tried to use the pay phone and we tried to get a room," said Bubby. "First to take good showers, but it was booked up. Then it dawned on me my work has a store right outside of Baton Rouge."

He called the shop, told them not to close, and asked to have someone stay there and wait for him, because he was coming by cab. Steve was trying to get in touch with his wife who worked for a local union that also had a chapter in Baton Rouge, but he was not sure where it was.

"He decided to take the cab with me, drop me off, and then he'll go to his wife's place; wherever the local was," said Bubby.

When the cab pulled up to Bubby's company, two buildings away was the local union. It was yet another of Bubby's strange coincidences on this mind blowing trip.

"He went his way, I went mine, and I hadn't seen him again, other than him coming to the store saying he found his wife. His wife had already bought a trailer and she was coming to pick him up and we parted ways."

Bubby finally got a call in to his brother-in-law who said his wife, Connie, was being picked up in Mississippi.

"Then I contacted my family, my mom and my oldest sister. They came from Prairieville [Louisiana] to come pick me up, which was just an awesome feeling, gives me chills just thinking about it."

He was elated to see his family and they him because the last thing they heard him say Monday morning as Katrina was bulldozing St. Bernard was, "I've got to go, I've got a problem," and he hung up the phone on his sister.

"But there was still something missing, and I didn't want to sound mean to my family, but my wife wasn't there, and I was missing my wife," said Bubby. "I was pretty much half full, great to see my family but still missing something; I knew I had to get more information."

He slept that night with over a dozen people in Prairieville, and two days later that hole in his heart was filled.

"We all met at one of the houses and just eight hundred pounds loaded off of me, and I felt whole, very, very whole just a great feeling. When we got together it was like we were so happy to see each other that it wasn't ah you shouldn't have stayed in the situation; it was just damn, it's just good to be in her arms and feel her and talk to her. That right there said there's nothing that could happen to us that we couldn't over come, and I know she felt the same way."

### Bear Arms

Gunfire and fires erupted across New Orleans and they could be heard throughout the parish. With St. Bernard adjoined to the Lower Ninth Ward of Orleans Parish, there was a real sense of fear and urgency amongst the people and the sheriff's department.

"You could hear automatic weapon fire in the city and from the slip you really had a panoramic view of New Orleans in the evening, there was no lights," said Stephens. "There was no skyline in the city and all you could see was sporadic fires burning in different places it was really like being in a combat zone, and then when the automatic weapon fire started you really knew it was a strange situation."

Stephens knew something he would never tell to the hundreds of the people he was protecting at Camp Katrina — their tactical gear was flooded. They were able to piece together weapons, but what he was hearing on the streets made him feel extremely vulnerable.

"We got reports there were roving bands of people trying to get into the parish on the levees and there was gun fire in the Lower Ninth," Stephens explained. "We just started trying to rehabilitate what we had left. It obviously drives your anxiety level through the roof, particularly if you think that element could be contagious."

Stephens said they managed to scrape together eleven tactical elements, which included body armor and M4s.

"I mean we had a lot of old people on that slip and I think they could sense the urgency when they were swabbing them M4s, shaking water out that body armor. We had eleven armed components of a SWAT team."

As the top law enforcement official in the parish and more than forty-eight hours into Katrina, he knew a tragic event could turn even uglier if he didn't smash any threat that came in from the outside.

"We went to every sporting goods shop and pawn shop in the parish and confiscated all of the weapons," said Stephens. "We didn't want anyone better armed than we were, and frankly some of the weapons we confiscated were basically hunting rifles and shotguns we had to use to arm ourselves. We tried as much as possible to take out of the hands the potential looters and criminals deadly weapons."

Stephens sent his guys to the parish line to secure the boundary, but not every man he sent was a deputy.

"One of them was my son who is a Marine Corp veteran [who] served in Baghdad during the initial assault," said Stephens. "He's also a law student at Loyola, just a real stoic kind of kid. I told 'em, gentleman you have shoot-to-kill authority. Anybody does not obey your command the second time, you kill 'em, do not take fire."

It dawned on the sheriff that this was the second time his son had been given a mission that could end deadly after serving in Iraq.

"Are you ready for this mission?" Stephens asked his son.

"Dad, I'm ready to kill all f*#@ing night without remorse."

"That's gonna look good on your resume, son."

At the moment he gave the order he turned around to see a number of elderly women in earshot.

"There were like five old ladies in only their negligées and stuff, and they heard me say this. I went from shoot to kill to hey ladies, how y'all doing' how's the family and everybody," as the sheriff laughed about the sick irony of the situation.

They asked the sheriff what was going to happen.

"Well tomorrow I'm gonna make sure we've got more food and water, and I've got to get y'all some cosmetics because you can't go on television looking like you look."

"Sheriff, I wear Lancôme," one of the ladies said.

"I'm gonna call Lancôme and I'm sure they're gonna send a barge full of cosmetics down here."

Stephens said he wanted the ladies to worry about their

appearance and not about any possible danger. The men went to the city boundary on the levee to stop anyone trying to enter the parish.

"They did turn back a couple of groups of people that were armed and my deputies told me that your son said, 'If you do not stand down, we will kill you' and meant it from the very bottom of his heart," said Stephens. "I'm proud of him."

## CHAPTER NINETEEN

# My Brother's Keeper

## Thursday, September 1
### Day Five

The night air was the only refuge anyone had from the killer heat and inhumane conditions at I-10 and Causeway. Alonzo and one of the nurses from St. Rita's broke the group up in order to give them a better chance to get on a bus. The crowds were too big, too fast, and not in a mood to give up a seat on the way off of that highway. When a bus arrived people shoved the St. Rita's evacuees aside and these folks were in no shape to negotiate, especially the ones who could barely walk.

"It was everyone for themselves," said Alonzo.

The scene looked grim; there were thousands of people scattered all over the interstate. There were limited areas to go to the bathroom, so people were urinating and defecating anywhere they could. Some of the St. Rita's patients had on adult diapers and wet themselves. The nurses lain the elderly down in the crowd of people and changed them. They did this as the awful smell of the rotten trash, spilled liquor, and animal and human excrement permeated the air. There were people on top of people, and they watched as Chinook helicopters landed with supplies and more evacuees to add to the toxic mix of people and desperation. Ambulances loaded up evacuees and headed west out of Jefferson Parish to hospitals and shelters across the state and beyond.

The nurse asked Alonzo to take two people along with his brother Carlos and she would do the same. It did not feel right

305

and no one wanted to split up the St. Rita's residents, but they figured they had no other choice. Alonzo took control of his brother, a woman, and another man and walked over to an emergency medical area, with hopes of someone helping them onto a bus or into an emergency vehicle.

"I had Genie, a girl with diabetes, [and] I had Charlie," said Alonzo. "He was all right, scared of everybody. Genie could hardly walk; I had my brother, and I couldn't let him go; he'd go walking off and get lost."

Alonzo walked carefully through the crowd looking for a bus when he saw an ambulance; he approached the driver who offered to take only one of them. Alonzo felt uneasy relinquishing his duty to care for any of his crew because they might not fully understand what was happening to them. At least he was familiar to them.

"Man I hate to split up," said Alonzo.

"That's all we can do is take one person."

Alonzo allowed Charlie to go with them, and they took off without a word on where they were going.

"I don't know where he went."

Down to just Carlos and Genie, Alonzo managed to wrestle his way onto a bus in the early morning hours Thursday.

"We're sitting there on a bus and it never takes off. We never slept; we was really dragged out that night."

After a little time had passed, someone told those on the hot school bus that they were going to Armstrong Airport and that they would have food, water, and medical supplies. Alonzo said to himself, "Thank God."

The bus pulled away from the Causeway and I-10 hellhole, leaving people sleeping on unfolded boxes on the steaming hot asphalt and in the grass. Alonzo saw people looking at him, wishing they were in his seat. Behind him the wind whipped at the Galleria office building, and its blown out windows splattered on the I-10 service road below. Alonzo wondered if this ride through the depths of despair was finally coming to an end. The bus drove several miles to the airport. There were loads of busses with people on them at the airport, and the activity was buzzing with the landing of all makes of choppers. Alonzo did not feel the relief he expected. Everyone was told to stay on the bus, and Genie started to convulse.

"This pour girl is starting to shake," said Alonzo. "I got nothing to give her, no insulin; I don't even know what you do for a person like this; I figure you give them something to eat. I holler anybody got anything here for this girl? She's starting to go in a coma or something I guess with diabetes, so somebody had an orange, so I gave her this orange, peeled it for her and she said she felt a little better."

The yellow bus sat there for hours. There was no food, no water, no nothing. There was just a lot more of nothing.

"I can't take it, people's gonna die in the bus," said Alonzo. "A hot school bus in the summer jammed with people is hot."

Two bus drivers were arguing outside, and the situation turned ugly.

"Oh my God," said Alonzo. "They're arguing and fighting, cursing one another."

Then their bus driver climbed on board and said, "I'm taking y'all to Lafayette. They got an evacuee center."

A chorus of cheers erupted in the bus.

"Let's go!"

Alonzo would not feel truly comfortable until he arrived in a place where he and his brother could get medical treatment for Carlos's burns, a good meal, and a shower. Alonzo had no idea exactly where they were going in Lafayette until they arrived at the Cajun Dome, an arena where the University of Louisiana at Lafayette Ragin' Cajuns play basketball and where concerts and other events are held. As they unloaded the bus, they separated the people who needed special attention and those who did not. Those who did not stayed at the Cajun Dome.

"Everybody's looking really critical," said Alonzo.

He asked someone to take care of Genie.

"This girl gotta get insulin; I don't know what to do, and my brother's not getting the seizure medicine."

Alonzo and Carlos hopped onto an air-conditioned Greyhound bus for the short ride to the Lafayette Medical Center; the cool air was a tremendous stress reliever. As they were getting off the bus to go inside the hospital, Alonzo approached a man with a cell phone helping people off the bus.

"Can I use your cell phone?"

"Here I'll let you use it."

Alonzo reached into his pocket and gave the man the forty dollars he had to make contact with his family.

"I called my daughter and them. I called a bunch of numbers; I couldn't get them."

A call finally got through to one of his daughters; she then called his nephew Ronnie Alonzo, who had evacuated near Lafayette, to go get them. It was a phone call the Alonzo's were not sure they would get. Reports had been released about the deaths at St. Rita's, and there was no word on who exactly was trapped. The Alonzo family was exhilarated about finally hearing from Gene and Carlos.

"I was glad to make that phone call; I never even thought we were gonna make it," said Alonzo. "Even after we survived the hurricane part; I said we gonna die trying to get somewhere we could be with our family."

The medical staff found out what seizure medication Carlos needed and gave Alonzo his heart medicine. They were safe, and Alonzo said if it were not for some of the sacrifices of the nursing staff who had stayed at St. Rita's, who knows how many more deaths they would have had.

"The nurses was amazing," said Alonzo. "They had their own families too, but they stood to help these people; they put these people first. They was some brave people, heroic; they went through a lot staying with these people."

Alonzo's praise was generous but when it comes to Carlos, he is truly his brother's keeper. Carlos probably would have died if Alonzo had not gone to the nursing home to make sure he was safe. For Alonzo, blood is not just thicker than water, it is an unbreakable chain. This was not the first time he saved his brother's life.

About sixteen years ago, Alonzo and Carlos were dredging oysters in Lake Coquille around Black Bay. It was a cold day in March around two in the afternoon when on the ride home in their large twenty-three-foot flat boat they hit a wave head on. The boat filled with water instantly and sunk.

"Just went straight down and water came and one second we're just floating in the water in the middle of the lake," said Alonzo.

A piece of the plywood floor floated out of the flat boat and Alonzo and Carlos grabbed on to it. The lake was cold and empty of other boats. They could see the marsh bank, but they had a good ways to swim. They stayed in the frigid water for a couple of hours, using the plywood to keep them afloat as they kicked and used the waves, which pushed them toward land. Carlos was getting over the flu and his weakened body was having a tough time handling the reduced temperature.

"We got to the bank and we said a prayer," said Alonzo. "Thank God that we made it."

"They gonna come find us, but I don't feel good," Alonzo recalled Carlos saying.

"We gonna walk down the shoreline; you'll warm up a little."

The water was over the marsh grass. They walked for no telling how long and how far in about a foot of water, and the temperature was still dropping.

"We stopped, then he couldn't walk no more," said Alonzo. "Then he couldn't see no more; I said walk slow."

"I can't see," said Carlos.

"What? You can't see?"

"I'm weak, weak, weak, and I can't see."

"We ain't got far; we got a levee over there."

But Carlos could not walk, his legs gave out, and he collapsed in the marsh.

"I drug him to that levee and that's where we stood. It was a little dry on this levee, all the way to Bayou Bernard levee."

When the men did not return, the search and rescue was launched out of Hopedale.

"The Coast Guard passed; I could see the guy in the helicopter; I could see his helmet and everything," said Alonzo. "He was looking for a boat; we in the grass, and I'm waving, and he kept going. They looking for a boat and they don't see it."

Carlos was burning up with fever, unconscious, and had slipped into a coma. Wet and freezing from the cold, they huddled up to keep as warm as they could as night fell. Then it started raining, and they had nothing to protect themselves from the freezing precipitation. They would have to survive the night in the marsh if they were going to make it at all. When the morning came Alonzo had to do something drastic to get them out; he could not carry his brother, but the sooner someone got them out of there the better chance he had of saving Carlos.

"The gnats were so bad, so I said I'm gonna walk to Hopedale; it's all I could do; he was out," said Alonzo. "When I lay him down he quit breathing, so they had some mango bushes, I hooked him to a mango bush sitting up, and I put a belt holding him up. I tried to swim this bayou and I couldn't, so I found a gallon jug and I crossed the bayou; I had that jug holding me up, and I crossed the bayou, and I was walking to Hopedale on the levee and that's when an outboard motor came."

One of Alonzo's friends found him walking on the levee, and they rushed back to get Carlos.

"When I got back to him, it looked like an ant nest on his head from the gnats; he was just black with gnats in his nose and everywhere. I'm wiping his face and he could hardly breathe."

They motored back to the boat launch at Pip's Place, and a helicopter landed to take Carlos to West Jefferson Hospital. They put Alonzo in an ambulance and took him to De La Ronde Hospital in Chalmette.

"He never did come out right; he almost died . . . from a lack of oxygen; he's been in St. Rita's ever since."

Carlos was a fireman, with a wife and three daughters.

Like with Harold Kurz at St. Rita's, Alonzo carries guilt, asking did he do enough for his brother Carlos that rigid March afternoon. He wonders what would have happened if he would have walked to the levee the night before instead of waiting until daylight.

"If I would have done that that night I might of saved him from getting a brain injury. I didn't know. I was just waiting for somebody to find us; I didn't think about leaving him. I had to cross the bayou to get to the levee down to Hopedale. They had a lot of people out."

This is how those with unconditional love think, not about the truly miraculous things they have done, but about how they could have done more. This is from a man with a heart condition who needs shots of nitroglycerin to keep him out of danger. Alonzo's selfless love for Carlos may come from the fact that they lost a younger brother a few years before the boating accident.

His name was Alex. Alonzo and Alex had finished dredging oysters that day as well. Only twenty-three years old, Alex had been tired and hungry, so he drove down to Paris Road to pick up a pizza.

"They had a dump truck parked right there by that Lutheran church there and he run into the back of the dump truck that night," said Alonzo. "The truck broke down, and he must have fell asleep; [the] dump truck [was] parked on the side of the road, and he veered off and ran into it. He got killed right there."

For Alonzo it's heartache he won't ever get over, two handsome brothers, one dead, the other in a nursing home with brain damage. Alex and Carlos both with him dredging oysters before their tragic accidents; Alonzo wishes he could have been there to save Alex too. He probably would have, but the powers that be had selected him as Carlos's guardian angel.

## CHAPTER TWENTY

# Divine Intervention

## Thursday, September I

### Day Five

Donald Colletti and Jim Pitre made quite a formidable duo taking care of just about anything that needed to be done in St. Bernard. The two men along with Colletti's cousin, Ricky, were walking in the water back to the boat parked near Pellegrini's barber shop on Judge Perez when Colletti asked, "What is that?"

"Cous, this don't look good, that's crude," said Ricky, who works for an offshore oil company.

"Before we could even make it to the boat this slop surrounded us," said Colletti. "Once we made it through the oil, we got into the boat; I came off my feet my elbow hit, my knee hit; I hurt my knee cap really bad, my arm really bad; I chipped a bone in my elbow, and I lifted my knee cap up and tore some fibers and ligaments in my knee."

They went back to the courthouse to get some medical help; then Colletti and Pitre were split up.

"The district attorney here for the parish Mr. Jack Rowley, he's the one who got me a bandage and a knee brace, by the time that was over I lost track of where Jimmy was," said Colletti.

Meantime Pitre was walking back to the boat from the courthouse after trying to check on the body of his mother. When he turned on a street behind Lehmann's Bar on St. Bernard Highway, which is directly across the street from the jail off Paris Road, he saw two men holding another young white guy who was badly beaten against the wall. Out of the corner of his eye he saw the motion of someone going down to the ground. Someone's feet were slopping around in the wet mud, and it was ominously violent.

"Hey what's up guys," Pitre said.

"Go about your own business," one of the men shouted back.

He looked down the alleyway where he saw a black girl, around his daughter's age, in her early twenties underneath a man on the ground. Two men were trying to conceal what was going on behind them. He walked toward the men.

"Whoa no, not today guys; there's no way!"

One of the men started walking toward Pitre.

"Who the f… you think you are?"

Shirtless, Pitre reached into his shorts pocket and pulled out a nickel-plated .32 automatic and pointed it at the five men. He said three were white, one was black, and one looked Hispanic.

"I'm God, and I'm getting ready to take your life!" Pitre said.

They had to notice Pitre's obvious affection for the Lord. On one arm the forty-six year old has a tattoo of the Blessed Mother, and down the inside of his right forearm he has a tattoo of Jesus and his wife's name, Nora, along with his daughter's names, twenty-three year old Jeanne' and twenty-two year old Jennifer. On one leg he has the Blessed Mother holding a baby in honor of their first child, a baby boy they lost in the seventh month of Nora's pregnancy. On the other leg he has Jesus with the Sacred Heart. He has a tattoo of his sister's face because she died of cancer and on his back he has the Blessed Mother with two angels with his wife and daughter's names. The guys wanted to take off, but Pitre didn't flinch.

"Man don't move, don't even think about moving!"

The men did not want to press the tattooed apostle.

"I already told that one guy I was gonna kill him. Pulling a gun on them is not really a good situation to be in. It's a situation I didn't want to be in, but it was either that or they was gonna ruin this girl for the rest of her life. They was probably gonna ruin this guy too. You could see the corruption that was right there."

Pitre told the girl to move behind him and his pointed pistol, and he told the beaten fellow to go around the building to the corner and grab some of the firemen to take these "cling-ons, clings to society, loaded thugs" off. This all seemed so out of place for Pitre who had spent three full days saving lives and all these guys wanted to do was destroy life. Pitre took the two to an apartment where he, Colletti, and others were surviving.

"We've got to walk about six blocks; you'll be well protected there until I can get you over to the evacuation place."

He gave them something cold to drink and ice for the woman's neck out of a working refrigerator they had hooked up to a generator. He gave the woman his shoes and some clean clothes out of the apartment as well.

"I'm gonna get y'all something to eat."

When he got back to the apartment the others were there as well.

"After we fed them, we all got together, getting ready to send them out to the evacuation people. We got in Ricky's boat with the guy and girl and brought her to Paris Road where they did have a police officer, and he picked them up. Whatever money we had in our pocket we gave to her. I gave her my address and told her if you want to come back and get a job."

The woman, whose name Pitre did not know, grabbed him and hugged him firmly.

"I never did anything any normal man wouldn't have done; they would have stuck their neck out too."

Pitre and Colletti went to retrieve the boat they were using and found that it had been stolen. They had already parked the *Big Fish*, opting to ride around in a neighbor of Colletti's smaller six-teen- to seventeen-foot boat. They had it stocked with the food, water, and medical supplies they were bringing to Chalmette High School. The men jumped in Ricky's boat to find the thief.

"We heard shots going off and we were following, kept asking boat after boat did y'all see a blue and white boat," said Colletti.

The gunshots frightened the men, so they went to Colletti's house and collected more pistols from his attic. Then Colletti told Ricky that the boat was coming directly toward them on Missouri Street.

"I took my camera and started playing like I was taking pictures; Jimmy put a hat on so he wouldn't see it was us," said Colletti.

Colletti just pointed that camera and took pictures until they got closer.

"When we get close you get right in front of him, and I'll get in the boat, and I'll take the boat back," Colletti told Ricky.

The thief slowed the boat as Ricky pulled alongside, and the men acted as if they were going to have a friendly conversation when Colletti, hiding an aluminum bat behind his back, hopped on the boat. Colletti saw the shotgun on the floor of the boat with shell casings spread all over and whipped the bat around. The man backpedaled, "Don't hit me. I didn't steal nothing."

"You're in our boat; all our stuff's gone," Ricky yelled.

He kept moving backward and fell out of the boat.

"He was frightened that I was gonna hit him with the bat," said Colletti. "When we grabbed hold of the boat, his hand got caught between a stop sign that was barely out of the water and the boat, and it ripped his hand wide open. I put the bat down, told him I wasn't gonna hurt him; we got him in the boat."

The only thing they had in the boat to clean the cut with was HotDam, an alcoholic drink appropriately named. Colletti bandaged up the man's hand. They brought the injured man, who they think was around fifty years old, back to the parked *Big Fish*. Colletti could have really used some of the medical supplies the man had stolen from the boat, because the medical supplies in the *Big Fish* were wet; then they dropped him off.

"I told him the best thing you can do is go back to where you're staying, gather your family up, the next boat that passes tell 'em you want to be rescued. Go to Jack Stephens tell him you cut real bad and have them bring you to Baton Rouge, because if you let that cut go too long it's gonna get infected and you gonna lose your hand."

Instead of gaining a bit of retribution, they rescued the man and tended to his injury.

"We brought him back to where he was staying, never laid a hand on him," said Colletti. "Needless to say he got all the supplies and everything we had in the boat."

As for Colletti's theory on the shooting spree the man had gone on, "Don't ask me what he was shooting at, but he was shooting that shotgun pretty good. I don't know if he was just looting or what he was doing, but he looted me."

## Finding Mama

Having been rescued two days before from the maintenance yard and having rescued dozens of others, Martin Onidas received a phone call he never dreamed he would receive. One of his family members told him, "You gotta find mama."

"I was in shock then cause I had told them I know I was essential personnel and my wife was too, she was at Baptist

*Maintenance yard supervisor Martin Onidas. Photograph by Mikel Schaefer*

Hospital [Memorial Medical Center]," said Onidas. "I told them, look y'all go get my mama; I told them a couple times; in my mind my mama was going with them."

The burly Onidas caught a boat that dropped him off on Colonial Drive in Violet. He jumped out and walked to the levee and jogged a mile east toward his mother's house on Goodwill Drive in Violet. There he saw nothing but water. Onidas flagged down a family in a boat and asked them if they would pass his mother's house.

"I was yelling and yelling, nobody said anything," said Onidas. "I was in this guy's boat, and I didn't want to go look in there by myself."

He thought his mother might have taken refuge in the Greater Mt. Olive Missionary Baptist Church on Goodwill Drive as well. He looked around but no one was inside of the church. The next place he thought to check was St. Bernard High School, but she wasn't there either.

Onidas went back to the Violet Canal Bridge and grabbed a trash truck and loaded it with some people from the bridge. As they were driving toward the river levee, Onidas spotted someone he recognized.

"Did you see my mama?"

"No."

"Where you come from?"

"I walked from Goodwill; your little nephew and a guy named Alvin Johnson gave me a ride in a boat to the levee."

Onidas believed God was with him on these hectic and harrowing days, and this was the sign he had been looking for.

"When he said Alvin Johnson and my little nephew, Melvin Onidas, I knew I had a good strong mind that my mom and them was safe, cause I know my nephew he's a hard worker, and I know this guy Alvin Johnson, he's a good guy, and I know they'll take an elderly person to safety."

He saw another man on the street as they journeyed down to Goodwill.

"This guy used to play the organ in our church; I spot him from like a mile away. I said man that looks like Lamont cause he's got a funny stance."

They drove the trash truck in his direction.

"Lamont how you doing? You seen my mother?"

"Yea they home."

"I had a truck load of people; I left the people; I told them I'd be right back. The water was still kind of high; I ran through the water yelling and yelling, and I was so happy. I grabbed my mama, hugged my mama with tears coming out."

"Mama what made you stood?" he asked.

"If you woulda been here you woulda got me outta here huh?"

"Yea."

"I was so happy when I seen her because I wasn't sure what went on," said Onidas. "I hadn't heard from them; and I was like so devastated; I didn't know what I was gonna find when I get there. Then I was able to find her, and it was a big release, and when the phones started picking up, I was able to call my brothers and sisters some of them was in Memphis, some in Houston, and it was a big release to everybody."

The reunion was as sweet as it could have been considering he had a truck load of people waiting for him. He did not have time to hang around and eat some of his mama's cooking. She was frying chicken; he grabbed a piece and headed for the door.

"After I drop this load off, get y'all stuff ready; they want everybody out of the parish."

"I'm not going," she replied.

"I'll be back for you."

Onidas dropped off the truck full of people at the jail and went back for his mother.

"I picked her up in the trash truck along with two other old ladies, and I had a lot of other people in the back of the truck. We was picking up people that needed [to be] saved. At that point they had a smell out there and stuff, and we were trying to get everybody to safety."

He drove his mother to Camp Katrina where she evacuated and was eventually picked up by other family members out of town. Onidas said his older brothers and sisters tried to convince their mother to leave, but he would have handled it a little bit differently if she would have disagreed.

"If my mama woulda stood, I woulda stood; I wouldn't left and left her here. If we had to all pick her up, she's a big lady, I woulda found a way to get my mama outta there. Ain't no way in the world I woulda left."

## Fill The Breach

Workers and people trying to escape St. Bernard were running their boats right over the levee near pumping station #7 at Bartolo Drive in Meraux. But as the water level dropped to near the top of the 40 Arpent levee, boats started jumping it. The wheel wash caught the top and eroded the levee so much that water flowed back into the parish. People were taking their boats through the locks and getting out of St. Bernard. Wednesday evening Russell Gelvin and his men realized a breach had developed and they had to do something to plug the breach.

"The part where we got across the levee I had to back the boat up into the canal and put both motors down and gun it to jump over the levee in a little cut they had," said Gelvin. "By the time we got there Wednesday evening the little cut they had was washed away, and it was deep; you could just drive right through it. The water's coming in, just eroding it even more. So they couldn't crank up pumping station #7."

Gelvin and two trustees, Steve Edgett and Tarrance Armstrong, took it upon themselves to close that breach the old fashion way after they awoke Thursday morning. They motored over to the hole and found water rushing back into the parish, defeating any pumping they could do there. They talked about the best way to attack the problem; the men saw a log and some pilings. Edgett and Armstrong jumped into the water and tried to stop the waterfall by hand.

"We drug logs and pilings that were floating over to the breach in the levee, and we were trying to jam them in the breach," said Gelvin.

The water rushed through the breach, making it difficult for Edgett and Armstrong to maneuver the heavy log into the force of the water without it pulling the debris out of their hands.

"Be careful!" Gelvin yelled at his crew.

"We had about a twenty-foot log," said Armstrong. "Rapid water flowing through enough to push us anywhere. We shoved a log in there and we try to put stakes down, but I mean the water was coming too hard."

The men knew what they were doing was dangerous and there was nothing to stop them from being swept away in the water.

"They didn't really care if they were gonna get hurt," said Gelvin. "All they wanted and had on their mind was getting the levee fixed."

Armstrong and Edgett pushed and shoved until they wedged that twenty-foot log into the levee, but their effort wasn't enough to stop the water from flowing back into St. Bernard.

"We took a part of a deck that was up there with two-by-fours and we're trying to drive the two-by-fours in the ground to stop the logs from being floated away," said Gelvin. "After we worked on that for a few hours we realized that wasn't gonna work."

That's when they got in touch with someone with the parish; this person told them that they did not have anyone who could bring them the sandbags that were stored in a warehouse at the port.

"But if we got up there we could go to the sheriff's office, get a truck, and go get the sandbags," said Gelvin. "The guys got the truck, went over to Kaiser Aluminum [the port], got in the sandbag barn, loaded it up."

Gelvin was worried about parking his boat and leaving it filled with the supplies they had for the pumpers to go get the sandbags.

"We had some supplies on the boat and I knew that if we left the boat unattended when we came back our supplies were gonna be gone because it was happening all over," said Gelvin.

One of the men unscrewed the hatch to store some of the supplies inside and out of sight.

"I didn't realize they had the hatch open, and when I turned around, I fell through the hatch," said Gelvin. "I dislocated my knee; I thought I broke it at first, but I got up, snapped it back in place."

Some deputies and firemen showed up to check Gelvin out, but he needed immediate medical attention. Armstrong and Edgett felt obligated to plug the breach, and they vowed not to let the parish down.

"I had to stay, I had to. We asked Russell can we stay?" said Armstrong. "So he called Bob Turner and said these guys want to finish doing their job, so Bob said cool."

However, Gelvin said the sheriff's department wanted to lock Armstrong and Edgett back up, since he was heading to the hospital. Gelvin talked them into leaving the trustees with Turner.

"That's when I took charge of the two trustees," said Turner.

The truck, loaded down with sandbags, drove to Paris Road until the water was too shallow to go any further. They could only load the boat up with so many sandbags before they carted them to the levee. It took many trips to get enough sandbags to the breach.

"We went and got the sandbags, jumped back in the water, and filled the breach up," said Armstrong.

It was gutsy work by a couple of men who could easily have left the parish before the storm began. Armstrong and Edgett not only saved people, they took a chance with their own lives. This was not asked of them but neither saw any other way.

"I'm not gonna let nobody die; I had to help; I had to be there," said Armstrong. "I risked my life for other people's lives."

Gelvin was transported to the jail around two o'clock that afternoon to see a doctor.

"The doctor checked me out and said I needed an MRI and an X-ray, and I was outta there."

Gelvin tried to make himself as comfortable as possible at the jail; he joined the walking wounded and the sickest of the sick in line for a ride to the ferry, the slip, or a helicopter straight out of the parish. The doctors and nurses would treat people and get them out of the jail, only to have others replace them. The medical staff could only hope the people would stop coming. They did not think there were that many more people who had stayed behind because they had seen thousands.

The nurses, totaling about forty at this time, had all been at the jail anywhere from twenty-four to forty-eight hours, and since Sunday they had undergone one unnerving experience of survival after another. There were still nurses at Chalmette Medical Center as well, and Albert Schell along with his parents and his dachshund, Oscar, was one of the first nurses to leave Chalmette Medical Center on Thursday. Schell had decided to leave for the jail when none of the plans to evacuate the nurses seemed to come together.

"Since it was my boat, I was one of the first loads to get out of there," said Schell. "When I finally got over to the jail they had just airlifted the last patient from that point out. All the nurses, we went over to the ferry, and we were gonna catch a ferry and go across the river, but at that point it seemed like it was a long wait. A ferry never did come to pick us up."

They walked back to the jail to meet up with the other nurses, and then they all got in the back of a pickup to be taken to the BellSouth building.

The plan to get the nurses out of the BellSouth building sounded a lot like the plan to get them out of the hospital.

"When I first got to BellSouth one plan was some type of cruise ship was gonna pick up all of us and bring us out; that fell through," said Schell.

"At this point they're at their wits end," said Dr. Domangue. "They were really distressed and overwhelmed. They had no sleep for long periods of time. They had weathered the storm in the hospital; they had weathered the aftermath in the jail, taken care of all these people under the worst of conditions; and they desperately wanted to get out."

With the lack of communication, many had had no contact with their families, who had no idea whether they were alive or dead. The unsolved question: how would they get these people out? For the doctors and nurses it was emotionally difficult to treat people and ship them off with their chart or whatever was left of a chart, without ever knowing the outcome of their condition. They wanted to get the nurses out as a group and prospects were extremely limited.

"We had a guy Mike Trosclair, who was a pastor with United Pentecostal Church out of Madison, Mississippi, who happened to arrive by boat," said Dr. Domangue.

Trosclair had spoken with Larry Ingargiola by phone to let him know he had crossed Lake Pontchartrain and had come into the parish through the floodgates, and he could get a lot of boats and move people out.

"Lee, what about the nurses?" Ingargiola asked Dr. Domangue.

"This is ideal," said Dr. Domangue.

There were no weather issues, and the lake was calm, so they decided to offer the nurses a ride on Trosclair's boats out of the Violet Canal onto buses to Madison, Mississippi. By Thursday night the last of the nurses were spending their final night at the BellSouth building they shared with the firemen, and Schell's coworkers at the Medical Center had finally left by helicopter.

The medical catastrophe that had hit St. Bernard was moving into a manageable state.

"We had three areas we were treating patients in," said Dr. Domangue. "One was still at the jail with Dr. Bertucci. I went to Exxon-Mobil; Dr. Lemerande had left with his family by this time. We had some paramedics by the riverside Camp Katrina at the slip. Three areas treating patients at the river was minor first aid. The one by the jail and Exxon were more advanced."

Dr. Domangue, Dr. Bertucci, and two nurses, Barbara Warren and Keith Bradbury, stayed behind.

"I couldn't leave Dr. Domangue and Dr. Bertucci; I knew my children were fine," said Warren. "I didn't know about my house; I thought it was gone [in Slidell]; I decided since my children were fine and well taken care of by my family that I would stay and help them because they had no other help. Keith did the same thing."

It would be two and half weeks before Warren saw her teenage son and daughter and her house. It was not damaged.

At 10:30, Thursday night a helicopter airlifted Gelvin out of the jail. With his leg bandaged up, he was headed to a MASH unit at Armstrong International Airport.

"Can you get off the helicopter because there are no wheelchairs?" someone asked Gelvin after they had arrived.

"No problem."

Gelvin hobbled to a FEMA MASH unit set up inside the airport and said he met a man who introduced himself as an emergency room doctor and wanted to know what had happened to his leg.

"I dislocated my knee, and they told me I needed an MRI and an X-ray."

Without looking at the knee, the doctor told him, "Well you're walking on it, so it can't be broke, leave."

"What do you mean leave?"

"Get outta here there's nothing we can do for you."

"Let me explain something to you, I just got flown out my parish; I have no money, no phone, my cell phone's not working, and where do you want me to go?"

"Get back on the helicopter and go back to your parish."

"If they'll let me back on that helicopter, I'll go right now. I didn't want to be flown out to begin with."

He pointed over to the wall and said "there's payphones on the wall" and walked off.

"I went and found a detail deputy at the airport with Jefferson Parish; I explained to him my situation; I'm in uniform the whole time," said Gelvin. "I had my gun on my side; they brought me down to the command center; they told me I could use their phones to contact somebody. If I could not get somebody they would bring me to Jefferson Parish headquarters and take care of me."

Gelvin contacted his youngest brother, Keith, who works for a major tugboat company and was on his way to Houston at the time.

"He said he was trying to get in touch with me and his cell phone wouldn't work, and it was a miracle his phone worked at that time."

"I'll send a crew change driver in; I got one in Hammond to pick you up at the airport," said Keith. "I'll have him bring you to Baton Rouge."

The driver was going to take Gelvin to his brother's father-in-law in Red Stick. A deputy told Gelvin, "I don't think they're gonna let him through the road block; go talk to the State Police."

Gelvin walked outside of the airport and found a couple of "big shots" from the State Police and explained his predicament.

"I need to either get this guy through the road block or if you all can drive me to the road block and he can pick me up."

Unfortunately, they said they could not do anything for Gelvin.

"They wouldn't even help me; it was fellow law enforcement officers from Louisiana, and they would not give me a hand," said Gelvin. "They told me nobody was coming through the road block and they couldn't bring me to the road block and that was it."

A SWAT team from Caddo Parish was checking out at the airport in the command center, saying they were going to Gonzales when the Jefferson Parish deputy asked them if they would give

Gelvin and another St. Bernard deputy a ride. Gelvin pulled out of the airport pretty upset at what he felt was rude treatment from fellow officers and for being forced out of the parish at this time. He did not want to leave, but he was no good to them until his leg was treated, and he knew it. Gelvin's ride was waiting for him in Gonzales.

## The Whitfields Get Out

Wayne Whitfield had spent a few days piled up with friends in two bedrooms on the second story of a house in Chalmette close to the school administration building near Paris Road and St. Bernard Highway. Whitfield counted twenty-five people holed up with four dogs and two cats. Chris Whitfield, Wayne's brother, knew it was time to move out.

"We didn't know if we was coming or going," said Chris. "Then everybody started breaking down, had a pregnant girl over there. We was going crazy and your feet being waterlogged the whole time it was like the bottom of my feet was pulling all together and it was bruised. I could barely walk. Everybody was drained."

When they ran out of food and water, they walked to the Chalmette ferry. As they walked past the jail, they saw people still needing to be moved from there. The barbed wire fence juxtaposed with the chaos almost made sense to Whitfield. Like thousands of others fleeing St. Bernard, they ferried over to Algiers and then bused to Causeway and I-10. Whitfield said they were told they were going to be there for twenty minutes before heading to Houston. When they unloaded the bus onto the highway, he knew they weren't going anywhere soon, especially after a few hours of terror.

"The worse case was I-10 and Causeway, way worse than the storm," said Whitfield. "To me I was more scared on I-10 and Causeway than I ever was during the storm."

"That was a killer," said Chris. "I'd rathered die in St. Bernard than spent one minute over there. I would have rathered the storm, shaking with the wind and rain hitting in the boat for an eternity than spending any time there. We was all going crazy, but I'd a still stayed in St. Bernard than go to the interstate."

Like Alonzo who had left I-10 before they arrived, Whitfield could not fathom the hardships people endured on the side of the road. He saw someone dying and became pissed.

"We saw people die, some elderly people mostly," said Whitfield. "I think we saw three ourselves."

Three full days after Katrina hit, food and water were precious commodities on the interstate, and Whitfield, Chris, and Danny had as much trouble as Alonzo getting something to eat or drink off of the military choppers, and they were not hauling around infirmed people.

"They were throwing the water back because they didn't want to get involved in the crowds," said Whitfield. "They were understaffed, undermanned. They were tossing the water; if you didn't catch it, you didn't drink. The old people in the back couldn't fight; they had hundreds laid out and as the hours went by some were dying and people with little kids stayed behind in the back. We fought for every little thing we had, food and water, and I was mad."

With that many people under stressful conditions, Whitfield said it was getting violent and dangerous.

"They had fights; the cops weren't breaking up fights," said Whitfield. "There was guys punching women just to get in front of the line [to get on a bus]. It was mass confusion, and in order to get to the front, you had to fight your way to the front, and I watched people get beat up; I was more afraid for my life for those two days then I ever was for the six or seven hours riding the storm out."

The violence nearly pushed Chris to commit a criminal act to escape.

"I wanted to get outta there. I don't know how to hotwire a car but I was wanting to try anything to get off that interstate. I wanted to walk; I kept telling my brother let's walk; he's like stay here we gonna get on a bus."

"I was afraid I was gonna die," said Whitfield. "I was afraid I was gonna get killed. They had weapons; they had death threats."

After sleeping on the concrete and suffering alongside thousands of others, the men fought their way onto a bus headed to Texas Friday evening. Chris passed out from exhaustion. When the bus stopped at a truck stop in Baton Rouge, the men jumped off, and Whitfield called his wife.

"That was the first time I heard my wife and mom in five days. They thought we were dead; they had listed us on the Internet as missing or dead," said Whitfield.

His wife picked him up in Baton Rouge, and he was reunited with his three children. Danny had lived for days not knowing whether his pregnant wife had given birth or not. He made it back just in time for the birth of his baby boy.

Whitfield lost his truck and his boat when he had to leave it on the side of Paris Road; his boat along with hundreds of others littered the streets of St. Bernard.

"We lost ninety percent of our pictures," Whitfield recounted. "I was a baseball and soccer coach, pictures are gone, trophies, plaques that were given to me as a coach. Everything that you take for granted, everything that doesn't mean anything at the time, it means everything now."

## The Maple Leaf

After a long trip from Vancouver and some sleep on the floors of a Laplace elementary school, Canada's Task Force Team One was ready to do what they were trained for, save lives. They had been to New York after September 11, and nearly four years later they were back in the States. Their first stop was State Troop B in Kenner where they picked up some police protection because they were worried about violence spreading out of New Orleans. They also met a couple of guys from Wildlife and Fisheries.

"We know a couple of back roads; we think we can get in there," one of the Wildlife agents said.

"We'll follow you."

They traveled east to I-510, which turns into Paris Road heading south after you cross the bridge over the Gulf Intracoastal Waterway.

"We went through miles and miles under water, two to three feet deep water, in trucks. It was a little touch and go there but we managed to get to St. Bernard, but it was totally under water still, and we couldn't get to the EOC where we were the day before," said Armstrong.

They started from the new base of operations set up at the Exxon-Mobil building, and right away they began pulling people to safety three full days after Katrina hit.

"We had some boats, a lot of abandoned boats; our mechanics got the boats running right away; helicopters came down; we started a medical evac plan," said Armstrong. "We started plucking people out; got about seventy people out that first day."

The Canadians provided St. Bernard firefighters with the rest they desperately needed.

"They were just physically exhausted, and they needed relief, and we were the relief for them," said Armstrong. "But that's the thing we've done over and over again; if anything is to be learned from these things, you need government agencies to realize you've got to get trained professional people to devastated areas quickly to give local responders relief; because we saw it at 9/11, all these rescue workers are suffering as a result of it mentally. They had them engaged too long and it starts to create mental health issues later on. Same with these guys they were engaged probably too long; they needed relief quicker. They were working day and night, and even after we were gone they were still working. Everybody pulled together it was phenomenal."

Chief Stone said other crews made it there after the Canadians, a team from Escambia County, Florida, with around twenty members and another crew from St. John Parish with another twenty people.

In honor of the Canadians, firefighters converted a ladder into a flagpole and raised the Canadian Maple Leaf flag.

"We actually had some American's come in and say what is that flag doing flying up there," said Stone.

"We didn't want to offend anybody," said Armstrong.

"Our guys jumped on them and said that flag's up there flying because those were the first people that got here to help us," said Stone.

But Armstrong could sense that a few did not like the idea and told the chief to raise an American flag as soon as he could.

"They ended up scrambling around looking for an American flag, but they couldn't find one. Finally they got one and we put that up side by side. It's a pretty dramatic picture," said Armstrong.

One hundred nineteen people were glad the Canadians took it upon themselves to travel to Louisiana. They saved that many people in the four days they were here. If it were not for a couple of State Troopers who lived in St. Bernard, the Vancouver Urban Search and Rescue may not have known about going there. It was another example of St. Bernard helping St. Bernard.

Meanwhile, the St. Bernard Fire Department began detaining the people they rescued. Anyone they found walking or swimming in the grimy, heated, stagnant water was brought to a decontamination area.

"We had some portable tanks, and we had a decon shower set

up," said Stone. "We had some soap and water and brushes, and we tried to be as gentle as we could."

Under normal circumstances they would have made the evacuees disrobe completely, but there were no clean clothes for them to put on.

"Some people were taking off some of their clothing," said Stone. "We were trying to find shirts for some people and stuff."

Some of the shirts came from a T-shirt printing shop they had found. They confiscated the big box of shirts and most of them said New Orleans Mardi Gras. Due to the lack of clothing many of the firefighters changed into the dry shirts. This new clothing took away some of their authoritative appearance. They definitely wanted replacement uniforms.

"They wanted uniforms; they were upset because they didn't have anything to wear," said Stone.

The T-shirts were a welcome relief from the dirty uniforms, but there was one shirt Chief Stone did not want the men wearing.

"Some of the shirts said "F... milk got pot," said Stone. "We told the guys you've got to turn them inside out. They understood and they turned them inside out."

### A Fresh, Cold Shower

The Exxon-Mobil building seemed like the Ritz-Carlton compared to the flooded parish complex, yet it still did not have electricity, water, or communications. One of the most underrated and under appreciated perks of modern living is taking a shower. The stench emanating from the human flesh was unbearable and the pungent aroma was tough to inhale. Every one wanted a shower, but no one could find one.

"One of our evacuees actually was a boyfriend of my former secretary," said Ingargiola.

The man thought he had a solution to the showerless days and nights, saying there might be a shower in the plant. It was going to be an outdoor shower with cold water.

"Go set it up; let's see what we can do," Ingargiola said.

The man walked into the area he thought might give everyone the primitive creature comfort. He found a shower head with an emergency release; all they needed was some soap and a lot of nerve to stand in the middle of an oil refinery without a shower curtain. Lack of a shower curtain certainly didn't stop the steady flow of people. Men and women took turns, showering separately. They took off their filthy, wet clothes, and underneath the steel machinery and sounds of hissing refining oil, they poured the cold water over their aching bodies.

"When you go three days without a shower, especially when it's hot, I don't care what kind of water it is," said Ingargiola.

The evacuees showered mostly at night to avoid being seen in the nude.

"You take your golf cart because they had golf carts, and if the golf cart was gone, you know somebody's taking a shower, so you didn't go back there," Ingargiola said.

Ingargiola and his wife, Brenda, used one of the carts and drove to the area together.

"I was one of the lucky guys. I had my wife with me. The water felt good."

If anyone snuck up on Ingargiola and his wife while they showered in the night air, Ingargiola said, "They did some good sight seeing."

## Moving on Up

After a couple of nights sleeping in the back of a car or wherever he could, Tony Guerra's son, Troy, suggested they go to the Crew Boats Incorporated dock off of Paris Road to see if the owner Pat Pescay's yacht was still around. It would be an oasis in the waterlogged desert.

"I think I saw Mr. Pat's yacht, and I think it's at the dock," Troy said.

"There's no way that boat's at the dock," Guerra said.

"I tell you I saw it; we gotta go take a shower."

The dirty, tired, hungry men decided to ride to Bayou Bienvenu with hopes of going from the farmhouse to the penthouse. They drove back to the government complex to salvage some of their clothes and arrived at the dock around eleven o'clock that night.

"The boat was here."

The yacht looked as if someone had parked it that night; it had no visible damage. Right away they could tell they were not the first to climb aboard the beautiful yacht; some people had broken in and had spent some time there. Not quite believing their luck, they were relieved in knowing that they would bunk in clean sheets with soft mattresses and lay their heads on pillows instead of car door handles. The men wanted to take a shower and clean their filth-ridden bodies, but there was no water coming out of the shower.

"The water pump was burnt up, and we had to go fix it," said Guerra.

They may have been delayed but certainly not deterred. After a few hours, early Friday morning about two o'clock, the sweet smell of clean water and the tingling sensation of running soap over their skin became a reality. Never before had they realized how much they had taken for granted the simple pleasure of a shower.

The yacht's generator also gave the men the full luxurious treatment; they had air conditioning, a cold refrigerator, washer and dryers to clean the few clothes they had left, and clean blankets to sleep under.

"It was like a godsend to be able to take a shower and lay in a bed," said Guerra. "We had no clothes; we had to take our clothes off and wash it and dry 'em."

Lying down for the night, Guerra still had not spoken to his wife to let her know he was alive.

CHAPTER TWENTY-ONE

# The Long Way Out

## Friday, September 2

### Day Six

Sitting in the Violet Canal with his boats, Doogie Robin wanted to get his crew out of there and into Bayou Bienvenu in Chalmette. Katrina tossed boats docked at The Pope Launch in the Violet Canal into a huge mangled mess. A shrimping boat was thrown out of the canal across the shell road into some trees. Also a sailboat had been lifted out of the water and dropped on the dock. Some of the big boats like the *Mr. Schlitz,* which sat alongside the *Master Trey* survived, as did *Invincible Vance, Lil Rick,* and *Honey Sucker,* which were all tied next to each other. Farther up the canal, they wanted to get their boats to a place where it would be safe to dock them, so they could leave the parish.

"They had so much going on in Violet Canal; we couldn't afford to stay there; it was a mess," said Doogie.

At one point they thought about going out through the Mississippi River.

"We had friends that were river pilots," said Doogie's son, Don Robin. "We couldn't go with the big boats because all of the bridges were out; plus we couldn't go through the locks because they weren't working. We knew we would have to go with the smaller boats to get out."

Those thoughts ended when longtime friend and former resident of St. Bernard Parish Mike Trosclair made it into the parish from Mississippi.

"Thank God for him, because it was like the light," said Don. "We knew we could get out; it showed us the way."

They decided they would move Friday to Crew Boats Incorporated. Doogie's son, Pete, had already taken a party barge on a recon mission to see if they could go through the inside canal from Violet into Bayou Bienvenu. He found the path littered but passable despite the boat and animal carnage.

"They had boats scattered; all types of boats," said Doogie. "Whatever you want; they had all kinds of boats and animals."

"Friday morning when we woke up, way before daybreak, we started moving boats around and fueling them up, stealing gas basically from other boats that were docked there," said Don. "This particular one that we got fuel from it was a small yacht and it was full of gas, and the guy who owned the boat wasn't there, but the guy who owned the dock was, and with the dock owners approval, we took the fuel."

While they had some small boats to run around with, they needed to move the big oyster vessels out of the canal. They fueled them up with diesel the dock owner had. When others saw Doogie and his sons making their move, "naturally they

*Boats thrown all over the inside of the Violet Canal. Photograph by Mikel Schaefer*

started doing the same thing." Then they got a radio call about nurses needing a way out, and "the boat people" agreed to help. The nurses caught a ride down to the Violet Canal.

The word of the rescue also made it to Wayne Warner at Chalmette High. After the Coast Guard shut down the tugboats, Warner tried to evacuate the parish. He found out a church group led by Trosclair was getting people out by boat to Lacombe, north of Lake Pontchartrain, and then by bus to Madison, Mississippi. However, if they did not include animals, Warner wanted no part of it. Fortunately, he was told animals were welcome. He was skeptical, but they accepted the offer.

A fireman, who was obviously a very good mechanic, fixed a school bus that was used to evacuate people out of Chalmette High on Wednesday. He rigged another flooded bus and school board van to get Warner, his crew, and the pets out of the school.

"We asked the firemen if they would take us to the Violet Canal, and we'd give them the bus," said Warner. "The van we were able to put the [pet] carriers in."

The animals got the better end of that deal, because the van was air conditioned. The idea was to leave the van for the parish

*Chalmette High gym after everyone had cleared out. Photograph by Mikel Schaefer*

to use after the drop off. Around 11:30 A.M. they boarded the bus and van and went to the canal.

"We pull up; we got all our dogs and cats, and I'm saying to myself five steps have to happen; we actually have to get on the boat; the boats have to bring us somewhere; we have to get a ride to where we can get to other people," Warner said.

At the Violet Canal small boats maneuvered around the tossed boats and wrecked dock. The smaller boats then brought the evacuees to a larger boat.

"We're hauling these animals around, and half these people go on a small boat with these animals, and they get put on a big boat," said Warner. "If we can get to Lacombe we don't need to get on a bus; we can get people to meet us in Lacombe. I kept saying how are they going to get us across the lake to Lacombe. On the boat there's this young lady, and I asked her where are we going?"

"Where were you told you were going?"

"We were told we were going to Lacombe."

"Well we can't get you to Lacombe; we're gonna go to Bayou Liberty."

"Where is Bayou Liberty?"

"Across the lake by Slidell."

"Is there a highway where somebody could come and pick us up?"

"Yes."

An hour later Frank Auderer came back and told Warner that there was a problem.

"They're not taking us . . . to the North Shore [the north side of Lake Pontchartrain]; they're taking us to Paris Road."

The "boat people" of the Violet Canal did not mind taking the Chalmette High people, and Don Robin had no problem transporting some of the nurses that had loaded onto his oyster boat either. The problem was with the communication about where the boats were going and where the evacuees had to go to find the buses for Mississippi.

"They did not know we were going to Chalmette," said Don. "They were coming from Chalmette and trying to get to Highway 90 [in New Orleans East] where Mike Trosclair had arranged to have some buses pick them up. That's where they thought they were going with us, but our boats couldn't make it there, and when they started boarding the boat that I was on, before long my boat was full of people, and then I had to break it to these people that we were going to Chalmette and that's where we're gonna park. Two miles from where we were bringing them is right where they came from, and they said 'wait we got a problem.'"

A Coast Guard vessel with five guardsmen made their way over to find out what was going on.

"I told them we were getting out of here and we were going to Chalmette and we did have a problem that these people wanted to go to Highway 90; we couldn't make it there," said Don. "I'm sure they had to be a little skeptical about who they were talking to, because they had one fellow had his hand on his machine gun, and that's where his hand stayed. Believe me; my eyes looked at him only when I talked to all the rest of them."

After they left, Wildlife and Fisheries Captain Brian Clark pulled up to see if they could help out. After Don explained the Trosclair arrangements and that there was no way for any of the boats there to get to the buses on Highway 90, Clark said he would be right back.

"He went to talk to Trosclair to see what they could arrange," said Don "Then about fifteen to twenty minutes later Brian [Clark] called me on the radio, and he said just go ahead and bring them to Chalmette; he had everything taken care of."

Brian made arrangements to get the buses from Highway 90 to Paris Road. Unfortunately, this word had not yet reached Warner as another boat pulled up to pick up the rest of the people from Chalmette High. Warner and company grabbed their pet carriers and started boarding the boat.

"We don't take animals," the boat captain said.

Flabbergasted, Warner said, "I was told we could take the animals, and we have half the people here with their animals."

"We were told we can't take animals; I'm sorry we're not gonna take animals."

Another boat came, and it was the same story; they weren't transporting animals.

"That got us hacked off, so I tried to get in contact with somebody at the [Chalmette] refinery who was trying to help us get out," said Warner. "Parish officials were over there; I couldn't phone them. I stopped a police car in Violet and asked if they would call them. We're sitting there thinking this isn't gonna work."

Warner was on the dock with half his people there and the

other half on a boat. Mundt, who was already on a boat, was getting a little crazy about being split up.

"My phone says no service at this point," said Mundt. "The boat owner is talking with the guy who's driving our boat, which is attached to three other boats. They're gonna go up the Violet Canal and go someplace, and my biggest worry was that we were separated. We couldn't get answers; it changed every minute; it was a different story; a different destination; a different time schedule; everything had changed, and we were separated."

Warner had made contact with his nephew and asked him to pick them up in Lacombe. Mundt had talked to her sister as well. They were trying to coordinate getting everyone where they needed to go.

"My sister was on standby and her husband to come in vehicles to pick up like fifteen people and fifteen animals," said Mundt. "I called her that morning and said it looks like we're going to the North Shore, but we decided don't leave because plans are changing. I can't even call them and tell them the plans are changing, because I have no service on my phone, and we're separated from him [Wayne] and Frank [Auderer] at that point, and we don't know what's going to happen. It was just the worst hours waiting to find out. I told the boat captain eventually I can't get separated from my other people. It was one for all and all for one."

They had decided they were not leaving anyone or any animals behind even if that meant they had to go back to Chalmette High School.

"I was ready to go back," said Mundt. "I'm not leaving until I get everybody together."

"I told the people on the boat I'm not leaving without my animals," said Warner. "That was the ultimate thing. I would have gone back to Chalmette and just stayed by myself and taken care of the animals. I wasn't afraid; I didn't fear for my life or anything. It would have been miserable."

When it seemed as if they would just pull back to the school, Richie Campo pulled his boat up. He had brought the first Chalmette crew out to a big boat, and he was back to take the rest of them. They found out they were not headed to north of the lake; they were heading to Paris Road to the dock of Crew Boats Incorporated. This was a six hour trip instead of the normal ten to fifteen minute bus ride to Paris Road.

"I figured we were going to wind up at Chalmette High again," said Warner.

Mundt had made friends with the captain of her boat; his name was Earl. He had just gotten out of Poydras and was trying to get to his daughter in Lafayette. While talking to Earl, Mundt heard what she had hoped for since she stepped on that boat.

"I could hear on the radio that the other people were on the same owner's boat fleet, and we were all going to the same place, which relieved my mind dramatically that we were going to hook up with Wayne and Frank and them again."

Mundt told Earl, "If you can get us to wherever we can get a ride, then I can get you to Lafayette tonight, cause my sister was from the Lafayette area."

## Doogie Leads the Way

Doogie untied the *Donna Ann* and his captains followed behind creating a flotilla of Robin's boats. Sort of like E.F. Hutton—when Doogie moves, so does everyone else.

"When one moved away, they all followed me down there; I don't know how many boats followed me to Bayou Bienvenu," said Doogie.

"There was a train of boats going through," remembered Don. "We had our own plus maybe twenty more that were coming with us.

The boats cruised out of the Violet Canal into the inside canal.

"When you get to one point where it's close to the MR-GO, they had a bunch of camps that used to be there in the Violet area, and all of those camps are, needless to say, demolished," said Don. "They had debris in the water at that point; you've got to dodge all kind of stuff."

It was a tight fit for some of the bigger boats. Don estimated the canal may have been about fifty feet wide and some of the boats were twenty-five to thirty feet wide.

"It got kinda hairy there," said Don. "We had smaller boats that were actually helping us get through these spots. My dad was in one; Chris [Don's brother] was in one, and they were kind of like assisting us to get through these tight areas, cause at one point it's a little snaky canal, and once we got through that area, then it was pretty much open, because then the canal runs right alongside the MR-GO; it's about five hundred feet off of the ship channel."

The boats made it into the open area of Bayou Bienvenu. It resembled a boat cemetery.

"It was like a war zone," said Don. "You had crew boats up on the bank, yachts up on the bank, tugboats, and everything was a wreck. The businesses, naturally, some of them were there, some of 'em wasn't. Bayou Bienvenu took a beating pretty bad too."

Nurse Albert Schell was on one of the workboats and said they took a wrong turn when they got to Bayou Bienvenu.

"We got screwed up and got the wrong message that we were going to some place back up Chef Highway," said Schell. "This gentlemen ended up driving us through the locks, and at this time there was a lot of water pressure flowing out, so it wasn't hard to go through the locks."

But the man driving the large boat with twin engines came flying back up saying, "Oh no, I'm sorry; I gave you the wrong story; they are starting to bring them to Bayou Bienvenu and putting them out on Paris Road, so you're gonna have to go back through the locks.'"

The driver of the workboat said, "I'm sorry; I've got all these people and all their luggage and all; there's no way I can get back through the locks."

The man in the smaller boat announced, "Everybody in the boat, except animals and luggage leave in that boat; everybody else get in my boat."

The man apparently did not want any animals in his boat. Those with pets had to stay on the big workboat.

"The rest of us got in this high powered boat, and he just gave it the gas, and the boat came out of the water and everybody started screaming," said Schell. "We go flying through the locks, and he brings us all the way down Bayou Bienvenu, and he dropped us off at Paris Road."

Before they could get to Crew Boats Incorporated, the nurses and Chalmette High evacuees had to exit the big boats and load onto smaller ones to get to the dock. When they walked onto the shell dock, there were two school buses waiting from North Louisiana. The Chalmette High crew boarded the buses with their animals; they put their pets in the back of the bus. The Department of Wildlife and Fisheries placed some of the dogs in the back of their trucks.

"I don't know how many boat loads of nurses they had

taken," said Schell. "We were all in different boats; it was at least three or four boats. We had to wait for everybody to get to the buses, and then we loaded up in the buses."

"They escorted us out of St. Bernard Parish," said Warner.

They drove north on Paris Road and over the "Green Bridge," which isn't green at all and crosses the Gulf Intracoastal Waterway. They kept going until Paris Road ran into I-510, and then exited onto Chef Menteur Highway in New Orleans East toward I-10.

"Went down Chef; you would hear high pressured gas lines blowing flames up in the air; it was a mess," said Schell.

From there they drove up the opposite ramp to get on to the "high-rise" on I-10. They were able to view a dramatic picture of New Orleans. St. Bernard was ninety-nine percent devastated. This was the evacuees' first chance to see what had happened to everyone else.

"We passed the people on the interstate, and the people were carrying black garbage bags, probably everything they could get out, and they were walking," said Warner. "There were huge stretches along that interstate where there are no exits for miles, wondering where they were going. We passed people downtown who were living on the interstate; it was really heart wrenching to see your city like that."

They crossed the Crescent City Connection to the West Bank and from there they came back across the Mississippi River over the Huey P. Long Bridge, ending up in the industrial and shopping area of Elmwood in Jefferson Parish.

Wildlife and Fisheries supplied food and water for everyone. The plan was to get them to a staging area at Clearview Shopping Mall in Metairie then on to Madison, Mississippi. The Chalmette High crew had not planned to go to Madison, but they changed their minds.

"We said the hell with it; we went through all this already; we'll just go and let people pick us up in Mississippi and spend the night," said Warner.

So they waited and waited and waited.

"The buses never came," said Warner. "Then we were told we were going to Dallas. I said we're not going to Dallas; we don't have to go to Dallas. All we gotta do is get somewhere where somebody can come pick us up. Then the plan changed to Gonzales [Louisiana, just south of Baton Rouge]."

Warner called his nephew again while Mundt called her family to tell them of yet another change and another drop off destination. In order for everyone to get picked up together, they created a phone chain, which kept everyone informed about the final destination. Once there was a change, Warner's nephew called someone. The Chalmette High crew was also there with others who had evacuated St. Bernard. Someone with Wildlife and Fisheries told the group that they could not just leave them there on their own, and along with the two buses, they had only three Wildlife and Fisheries' trucks there. They would not be able to fit everyone and their animals.

"I'm standing out there with my three dogs, and there was another gentleman with a dog, and there was no room," Warner said.

Warner told them to leave him some water. He wanted to stay behind with his three dogs and wait until someone could pick him up the next day. Luckily Wildlife and Fisheries was able to retrieve another truck. They had everyone in Gonzales at the Tanger Outlet Mall at one o'clock Saturday morning. A trip that began at 11:00 A.M. and should have ended around 1:00 P.M. took nearly fourteen hours.

Schell joined up with his sister in Donaldsonville while Mr. Warner's ride was waiting for him.

"When we got there the people who we had contacted were waiting there and, it was just super," said Warner. "Saturday morning I had to go back to Covington, and I got to Covington about 2:30 A.M. The other part of the group went to Baton Rouge and Lafayette; Earl got to Lafayette."

## The Robins Finally Fly

Doogie Robin did not lose any of the boats he rode out the storm with, but he did happen to lose two other boats. He had one in straps at Pescay's place that they were copper painting. He thought that was as safe a place as any to leave his boat. The other one was a converted Lafitte Skiff he used for trawling and oyster dredging that he tied up on a trailer in Yscloskey, but it still ended up in the bayou.

Saturday morning, Doogie and his family left St. Bernard, took some smaller boats, and crossed Lake Pontchartrain to Bayou Liberty in Slidell. For Doogie, it did not matter that he was near eighty years old. As the patriarch of a fishing family that has made its living on the water and whose name conjures up thoughts of fresh seafood in St. Bernard, he would not even consider riding out Katrina outside of his boat. He has ridden them all out including Betsy, which had been considered the mother of all hurricanes in Louisiana before Katrina.

No one thought it wise for him to stick with his boats, not his nine children or his "twenty-four or so grandchildren," but just like you can't teach an old dog new tricks or break a man set in his ways, you won't get Doogie off his boats.

"I could have, but I wouldn't have been satisfied somewhere else and didn't know what was going on over here," said Doogie. "No way in the world I could. I couldn't visualize myself leaving this place behind with the hurricane coming like that, regardless. I'll do it again; I'll do it all over again. Katrina was rough; I only thank God, one thing, that I didn't stay down in Yscloskey for this one, because if I'd a stood in Yscloskey I wouldn't be here talking to you I'm sure."

And if Doogie were ever going to go, that would probably be his perfect farewell ride.

## Sanchez Gets Out

Glenn Sanchez spent the entire Thursday on his wooden plywood plot from Asia. For a man used to taking two or three showers a day, he felt somewhat rejuvenated when a friend came in with a bag and gave him a brand new shirt, a toothbrush, and a brand new pair of underwear. He put the underwear on and brushed his teeth, but he did not put the shirt on until Friday.

"I just smelled that shirt for a whole day," said Sanchez. "I didn't wear it for a day; it smelled so good."

After having to suck on a button because he was so thirsty, he never went without water again.

"Anytime they said they were giving out food and water, I was in that line; I wasn't going without water any more," said Sanchez. "I stashed water. Water was a big commodity; I needed my water."

It was around eleven o'clock Friday morning when Sanchez finally boarded a ferry to Algiers. His mind was somewhat at ease; he had contacted his family prior to leaving thanks to an acquaintance who had visited the slip on Thursday.

"Lt. Governor Mitch Landrieu walked up, and he fishes down

here [in Hopedale]," said Sanchez. "I know him and I asked him if he could just maybe call my daughter and let her know I'm alive. My daughter worked at a hospital and her phone rang and somebody picked it up, cause she didn't have it on her, and he said 'this is Mitch Landrieu looking for Jennifer Sanchez.' They said hang on, and they said 'how do you know him?' He said 'your dad's alive and safe.' I thought that was real cool, taking the time out to do that in the middle of all these problems."

When they arrived at the ferry landing in Algiers, Sanchez said in order to get on a bus the military asked if anyone had any drugs or weapons. So Sanchez pulled his trusted Leatherman from his pocket and put it in the bucket.

"I wasn't missing the bus," he said with a laugh.

The buses went up the West Bank Expressway to I-310, and Sanchez figured they were heading to Baton Rouge; however, they took the exit that went back toward Armstrong International Airport in Kenner. Like Gene Alonzo found out, they pulled alongside other buses waiting for orders.

"We sat in the airport for five or six hours in these hot buses," said Sanchez. "They said if you got off you couldn't get back on."

When the bus finally took off, much to the relief of everyone onboard, instead of turning onto Airline Drive in the direction of Baton Rouge, the bus turned toward New Orleans. Sanchez thought that was fine because there is an airport exit road that will take them to the interstate. When the driver passed that exit, Sanchez thought he would turn on Williams Boulevard and catch I-10 out of town there. The driver passed up the Williams turn.

"They taking us back towards the city," said Sanchez. "Everybody starts panicking. That's when I was more fearful than any other time throughout the whole ordeal, right then, cause the city was pretty corrupt at the time."

These people couldn't believe it; then the bus driver stopped and turned around. The panic attacks ended immediately as the bus drove westward.

"We got to St. Charles Parish, [which borders Jefferson Parish past the airport] and they [the police] stopped us, and we had to stay in those buses until eleven o'clock at night, sitting on the road," Sanchez said.

Eventually they let the bus leave. Farther down the interstate they saw buses stopped at a trucking weigh station in Laplace. They were transfering people onto other buses heading to Texas.

They did not need or want to go to Texas; they just needed to get to Baton Rouge.

"The people I was with, Danny was a student in Baton Rouge, and he had a dorm. We had a place to go; we're just forty miles too short," said Sanchez. "We asked the cops if we could sit on side the road until somebody came and picked us up."

"Go ahead."

They borrowed the officer's cell phone and called Danny's brother who worked at the Marriott in Baton Rouge.

"We stayed on the side of the road for maybe an hour and [Danny's brother] showed up with a taxi cab and with another vehicle and they brought us to the dorm. Danny didn't have the keys, so they had to break the window; so we got in the dorm. They had four cold beers in there and I drank one of them; best beer I had in a long time," Sanchez laughed. "Then I was the fourth one to take a shower or fifth and that was a wonderful thing."

## Evacuating the Manor

Paul Borden, Jr., also known as Taco, and his family spent four full days in the aftermath of Katrina in the second story of his uncle's home on Landry Court in Meraux; it was time to get out. Since Monday, Borden and his Uncle Earl had been taking the boat out during the day and rescuing people. They had two boats, an eighteen-and-a-half-foot bass boat that they used for shallow water and a twenty-three-foot flat boat. Borden guided his boat to a house and helped some people.

"One girl, once we got her and her friends in the boat she started crying," said Borden. "I didn't know her, at first I thought it was cause she was happy, she was being saved."

Then she told Borden, "When we went to leave the house Monday, when the water was rising, me and my sisters and [their] boyfriends were leaving, and all of a sudden some current swept my sister away and, I haven't seen her yet."

"She believes her sister drowned and that really hurt; can you imagine leaving and all of a sudden seeing a family member being washed away," said Borden.

And there were the animals. When Borden and his uncle passed dogs on the roofs, they'd bark at them until one decided he was tired of being on a roof. Then they passed a dog on their way to Winn-Dixie to get some food and water for rescues.

"It was a black lab; he jumped off the roof and swam behind us until we got to Winn-Dixie," said Borden. "My uncle felt sorry and put him in the boat with us, and we brought him and put him off on the levee. When he seen that land he took off. I guess he was so happy he was saved."

There was one rescue he remembered most of all. The sheriff department's duck boat passed his home, and they could not go deeper into the neighborhood because the power lines were down. So they docked at the house while Borden took his smaller boat around the neighborhood, scoping for any last holdouts.

"By then it was evening time, and we'd kill the motor, blow the horn, and listen real good," said Borden. "It was so quiet in the neighborhood you didn't hear a bird or nothing. We heard somebody holler, so we went to the house and we tapped on the roof and heard voices. We hurried up and got a pry bar, a hax, [and] mauls and made a hole in the roof."

They found two elderly ladies sitting in the sweltering attic. For three and a half days they sat in there, waiting for someone to hear them. Borden went to get some friends staying nearby in a two-story house to help pull the ladies out and by Thursday evening the ladies had finally gotten out of that hot, dark, dingy space.

"We brought them to the sheriff's duck boat and unloaded them," said Borden. "Them ladies there, it was a miracle that we heard 'em. Because in that area the water didn't actually go down to seven-foot to maybe Friday, and I'm sure they would have been nervous to come down because the water was still high."

With his work seemingly done, Borden loaded up a few things; he wanted to move his family out.

"We had to get out the parish; we didn't know where we were going or where they would take us. We left early; by the time we got to high ground it was eight o'clock [in the morning] and I saw some friends, Alan Abadie and our councilman I know him real well, Craig Taffaro."

"Taco, you're not leaving?" said Taffaro.

"Yea, I'm leaving with my family."

"Man we'd appreciate it if you'd stay back and help us, you and your uncle; but especially you, since you know how to operate boats. We got about [sixty-eight] elderly people at the [St. Bernard Manor]; we need to get them out.'"

"Well I got my family."

"We'll take care of your family for you."

They loaded up Borden's family, and he sent a friend to help take care of them while he and his uncle went on another rescue mission.

Firemen Rodney Ourso and Michael Lebeau had been on rescue missions ever since leaving St. Bernard High School, and they were also assigned to evacuate the St. Bernard Manor, which is a place for retired people. While some were trapped there after the storm, others who did not live there were dropped off there after rescue missions. The manor consisted of three five-story buildings that were dry above the first floor and filled with dozens of people, and the parish wanted to unload them.

The firemen's plan involved using a carport entrance that was ten to twelve feet high. They placed a ladder in the bottom of a boat, which they tied very tightly to the building; then they put the ladder up to the carport, which went into the window of a second story room.

"What we did is went to each room," said Lebeau. "They told us not to enter any room unless you hear a voice, so we're knocking on doors, and we got them over to the ladder and got them down the best way we could."

"A captain with the fire department stood with me, and the first unit I went in I had to bust the door down, because they never had a breezeway to get in through the second story," said Borden. "I went up the stairs and up to each door, banging on the doors, making sure, asking if anybody's there, and they had a few people."

The able bodied people were the first to climb down the ladder, out of the second story window, and into the boat below. Then they were shuttled a few blocks down Archbishop Hannan Boulevard to National Guard and sheriff's personnel to load them on buses. This was by no means a quick evacuation; it took the men time and patience. After moving those who could scale the ladder, firemen used a technique that enabled them to get evacuees who needed help out of St. Bernard High. They hooked up a nylon strap around a person's torso area, and they lowered some of them down the ladder.

"That worked well," said Lebeau.

For extreme cases, a fire truck carrying wooden stretchers showed up. Borden and his uncle loaded the stretchers onto their boat and hauled them over to the manor. They handed wooden stretchers up through the window and firemen laid people who were in wheelchairs, had amputated legs, or were too obese onto the stretchers. They strapped the people down and the firemen picked them up and balanced them on the ladder.

"They started sliding these old people down about a twenty-foot ladder with a rope tied to them and the expression on their faces," said Borden. "They were hollering and screaming, which you couldn't blame them because you see nothing but water down below you, and they're sliding you down. No one's up there guiding it down; it was a rope tied, and they'd slide it down and luckily it stood on the ladder till they got to us. Me and my uncle would grab and put it down and untie it, and they'd pull it up. We'd stack them up in the boat, and they'd pull the ladder up, and I'd take off and go to St. Bernard Highway."

Ourso kept track of the people they unloaded from the three buildings of the Manor; they rescued sixty-eight total. Ourso said the tedious task lasted most of the day. Still if there was any daylight left that meant more possible rescues, so Lebeau and Ourso took off around the neighborhoods near there and the destroyed Archbishop Hannan High School, which sat directly across the street from the manor.

"We went out to the neighborhoods into Lexington, Cypress Gardens, and Jumonville," said Lebeau. "In all of those areas still getting more people off, still finding people there that didn't want to leave yet."

### Insult To Injury

Not far from where the manor rescues were going on, President George W. Bush was flying over St. Bernard Parish in his helicopter, *Marine One.* It was an "impressive" sight for those on the ground. Captain Brian Clark of the Louisiana Department of Wildlife and Fisheries was one of those people scanning the sky looking at the president. It was Bush's first visit to Louisiana since Hurricane Katrina. Brian, along with State Senator Nick Gautreaux from Abbeville, another Wildlife agent, and the air-boat driver were on a rescue mission on Lena Drive near the Murphy Oil Refinery. Brian asked the driver to shut off the motor, so they could take in the president's visit.

"When he did, I looked at the wake of the boat, and I looked at the water wash up on somebody's house," said Brian. "This looks bad. The water hit on the side of the house, and I seen the oil film and right then you could smell it. You could just see it at that point; it was just a slick everywhere."

The moment of the president's visit to St. Bernard was when parish officials found out about a second disaster to hit St. Bernard; this one an environmental catastrophe. Something must have happened at the Murphy Oil Refinery.

"I got on the radio, and I notified the Office of Emergency Preparedness," said Brian. "We backed out; it was bad; you could barely breathe in it. It burned your nose. We knew it wasn't right to be in there; we made our round and were pretty certain all the people were outta there."

The head of the Emergency Operations Larry Ingargiola got a second piece of bad news — a possible oil leak at the refinery. His thoughts were about the same as when the hurricane hit.

"Oh, shit! Basically the same thing I said when I seen the water coming up; oh, shit!" said Ingargiola. "Is it gonna catch on fire? At that time I didn't know it was crude oil. I'm worried about a fireball; worried about my rescue workers that are in this shit. How dangerous is it?"

He figured it had to be as bad as he could have imagined

*A Murphy Oil tank moved, releasing nearly a million gallons of oil. Photograph by Pete Tufaro*

348                                         LOST IN KATRINA

because people started showing up at the parish government's commandeered home at the other refinery in the parish, the Exxon-Mobil facility. They came in to see the doctors they had at this makeshift medical center.

"Almost immediately after we heard about it, we started seeing rescue workers, not just firemen or policemen, people going out there to rescue people," said Ingargiola. "They were coming in with golf ball-sized blisters on their arms, their bodies. You could smell the Benzene on them when they came."

Ingargiola could hardly believe what was happening to St. Bernard.

"It's the kind of experience you don't even have a nightmare about. You feel like your hands are tied, and you don't know where you're gonna get help from."

Brian had also put a call in to Sheriff Stephens after talking to the EOC.

"Sheriff, they've got a two-foot oil slick on top of this water back here."

"What!"

"They've got a tank that ruptured."

"Just when you think things can't get any more screwed up you get something like that and that would just take the wind out of you," said Stephens.

The sheriff and fire department went into a different kind of crisis mode, and there were still people that needed to be rescued. When they reached Murphy Oil, they found a heavy oil slick with strong fumes. If the men breathed in too much, they would get headaches. One of the 250 thousand barrel tanks between Judge Perez Drive and the 40 Arpent Canal holding crude oil had shifted off of its foundation and was leaking hundreds of thousands of gallons of oil. The tank had a retention levee around it, but when the water went down low enough, the oil poured out and over the levee and into the neighborhood.

"We had to mobilize sandbags, send volunteer deputies and firemen, and emergency personnel back there with three hundred sandbags on different airboats to re-stabilize that retention levee around the tank or there would have been more oil," said Stephens. "Can you imagine how funky that duty was; you've got nothing to clean up with around here, got no water."

Ingargiola realized they could only assist in something of this magnitude, and "according to our plan, now it's become the

Coast Guard's problem. We tried to put some barriers up, tried to contain its area. Anybody we can find; by this time I may have had twelve workers," said Ingargiola. "I had the fire department doing what they can with their retention equipment. We couldn't call on anybody; they all evacuated."

Murphy Oil spokesperson Mindy West said the floodwater moved the tank nearly thirty feet at the vacant refinery. She then added, "When the tank was sat down it buckled and in the buckling a leak developed." On Saturday they notified the EPA, DEQ, and the Coast Guard to clean up the spill.

The EPA said [tank #250-2] was holding sixty-five thousand barrels of mixed crude oil and a little more than one million gallons leaked out. Murphy Oil said there was a logical reason; it may have taken ninety-six hours before someone discovered the slick.

"If there's some water in the tank, oil and water in a tank is going to separate," said West. "Since the leak was at the bottom of the tank, the water would have escaped first, which is probably one of the reasons why the oil was not apparent earlier than it was. If there was oil and water in the tank, the oil was going to float above the water. If the leak was at the bottom of the tank, then the water was going to escape first."

The oil had flowed into more than seventeen hundred homes, filling nearby canals like the 20 and 40 Arpent. Animals left behind were running around with oil on them. The EPA and Coast Guard divided up responsibilities for the clean up, which reached out about one square mile.

Within that square mile, Brian was almost to his sister's house when he noticed the oil slick. For him it was more of the same for his entire family who lived in St. Bernard. They all got wiped out. Brian had seven feet of water in his home; his brother Chad's house had been flooded as well. The homes of Clark's other brother, mother, and sister, who had oil in her home, were also destroyed. Katrina did a clean sweep of the Clark family.

CHAPTER TWENTY-TWO

# All Over but the Crying

## Saturday, September 3

### Day Seven

*Colletti and Pitre after saving more than two hundred people. Courtesy Donald Colletti & Jim Pitre*

By Saturday most of the parish had been evacuated, except for the people who had to be there, like government officials and first responders. Donald Colletti and Jimmy Pitre were also still there.

"The hardest thing for me in this whole hurricane would be Mrs. Joyce passing away; the second hardest thing is I sent my family away to safety, but they had no idea I was [safe]. I knew they were gonna see pictures of St. Bernard completely under water, and I had no way in my mind to get in touch with them," said Colletti. "Day after day it was killing me. When it would turn dark and I would take some of my family pictures out of the totes and put them in the boat and just sometimes cry myself to sleep."

A friend told Colletti to be thankful that he had not bought his wife the Cadillac he wanted to get for her because it would have been flooded.

"He was just rattling on about all the features the Cadillacs had and one of them was OnStar®," said Colletti. "A light lit up in my head; a friend of mine works for the water board, Jason Liccardi, told me if you can figure out a way to get in touch with your wife, I can get you to a phone. His friend had a satellite phone that worked on and off."

Colletti found Jason, "I know how to get in touch with my wife."

"Tell me, and we'll all know how to get in touch with our families," Jason said.

"You gotta promise I'll be the first call."

"O.K."

"Get in touch with directory assistance get the number for OnStar®."

"OnStar®!"

"My daughter just bought a brand new Yukon and it's got OnStar®."

Jason tried but could not get a signal for the phone at that time. He promised to get in touch with them later. After some time, Jason was finally able to talk with a representative at OnStar®.

Colletti's wife Rita and his daughter, Natasha, were driving in their Yukon in Texas, listening to her wedding song on the radio, "It's Your Love" by Tim McGraw, when Colletti said a voice came over the radio.

"Natasha Guerra?"

Rita and Natasha were surprised by the voice from out of nowhere.

"Yes, this is Natasha."

"This is [name] from OnStar®, and we want to let you know your father is alive and well and loves you."

"They totally just flipped out right then and there," said Colletti.

"My wife had got on the internet looking for me. Everybody in this parish knows me; I own an outboard motor shop in this parish and know everyone. She got on the internet 'did anybody see Donald Colletti from A-1 outboards?' One guy said yes, he was trapped in an attic. Another guy said yes, I seen him; he was trapped on a roof. Another guy said, I saw Donald; he was rescuing someone, and he drowned."

For three days Rita had heard that her husband was dead, but Colletti's son and daughter convinced her the information was unreliable and kept her spirits alive.

"My son, my daughter kept telling my wife they ain't no way in the world daddy drowned, no way."

Jason drove a tractor to find Colletti to let him know his family knew he was alive.

"I turned to Jimmy, Jimmy we've only been here six days; I can do two months now; I'm relieved now; let's get to work."

Pitre also got in touch with his family that day.

Colletti said the men finally left St. Bernard Tuesday, September 6 to be reunited with their families. Colletti estimated they saved 230 people. These people could now be reunited with their families.

## Final Departure

Charlo, Chuck Thurman, Frankie Asevado, and B.B. were still in lower St. Bernard Saturday morning. For three nights they slept at Sebastian Roy Elementary School in Reggio. Wednesday morning they moved to the school after Constable Tony Guerra, Eusevio Garcia, and Kenny Campo arrived at the substation in an airboat. They told them there were no rescues from officials in this end of the parish yet, and they were on their own.

Because the school is prone to flooding from Lake Borgne and Breton Sound, the parish built the circular structure on concrete columns ten feet off of the ground in 1968, so while it suffered wind damage the facility was not flooded. When they got to the school, the windows had been blown out. They climbed the debris-ridden staircase that was also filled with debris riding rattlers.

"There were little bity rattlesnakes everywhere," said Thurman. "Ground rattlers, every piece of debris you seen floating just had snakes and all kind of stuff on top of them."

However, one important find at the elevated school, the walk

*The remainder of the home Charlo was in before it was destroyed. Photograph by Mikel Schaefer*

in freezer, was untouched. The school was stocked with plenty of canned goods and meat. When they fried shrimp, they now had the fixings to go along with it.

"Trays of ham, different stuff like that," said Thurman. "We had everything to go with it once we was at the school."

They only wanted to survive, but Charlo longed to talk to his family.

"I wanted my wife and daughter to know I was alive," said Charlo. "I knew they was freaked out."

Everyone had watched the horror unfold all around the New Orleans area on the television. When they saw the violence in the city, Thurman and Asevado went for protection.

"They got a little nervous; they went in a trailer around Kenilworth and got their hunting guns in case," said Charlo. "Seem like people was going crazy; we knew we couldn't go no where with the dogs, and I couldn't walk no more."

All Charlo could do was rest. His body had been whipped something fierce by Katrina, "My feet was at least twice, maybe four times bigger than what they normally would be."

Charlo had grown much more comfortable and fond of Thurman, Asevado, B.B., and the six pit bulls.

"They were lap dogs if you pet them."

B.B. treated the cuts all over Charlo's body and nursed him along. Saturday would be check out day. Thurman and Asevado hung on, because they didn't want to leave their dogs; but they found out parish officials wanted St. Bernard emptied. After meeting up with Thurman and Asevado Tuesday, Thurman said Ricky Robin had gone back to his vessel in the Violet Canal and talked to the men at Sebastian Roy over a VHF radio. Robin had told them supplies were low on the boats docked in the canal and the boats were filled with people; meanwhile, there was far too much food and water at the school.

Thurman and Asevado hot-wired a van, and when the water had receded enough to try to get to the Violet Canal, they made a run up Judge Perez. As they got just past St. Rita's Nursing Home, Thurman and Asevado ran into Mitchell Roussell with the sheriff's department.

"They had a big trash truck, and we tried to get them to come down there and take a bunch of supplies from the school and bring it up to Ricky in Violet; but he said we can't do that right now," said Thurman.

The men said Roussell had told them to go back to Sebastian Roy and pick up the others, so they could leave with him. Thurman drove back to school to get B.B. and Charlo in order to rendezvous with Roussell, but when they got back the deputies had already left.

"So we got this far, go back, fill this van up with what we got, and we'll bring it up there ourself," said Thurman. "I ran into Tony [Guerra] and Eusevio [Garcia] again. He says they have a truck. They came over there, we loaded their truck up with water and sacks of food and rice and toilet paper and Germ-X, and they left and came down here. They didn't go by Ricky and them."

They loaded the van with whatever they could and left the school for the last time. The wheels were about to pop; they had so much in the van, but they knew this would be their last trip. They wanted to get as many supplies as they could to the Violet Canal. They said goodbye to the pit bulls.

"We left the dogs at Sebastian Roy," said Thurman. "We can't go somewhere with pit bulls; we didn't have leashes for them; we didn't have kennels; you can't do that. We put the food out; they had plenty food and water; we figured as soon as we can get back, we'll come back and get them."

"They cried to leave them dogs at Sebastian Roy," said Charlo.

Driving down Judge Perez one tire went flat, then another, then another until they had four flat tires. It was hang on time because they weren't stopping. They kept riding with sparks spitting off the metal rims.

"As long as you didn't stop you was alright," said Thurman. "We got right to the street above the Violet Canal; we got all the way back almost to the levee where we were gonna bring Ricky the supplies, and the van wouldn't go no more; that was as far as it went."

"When we got there the people wasn't there, just the fisherman and others we knew in the Violet Canal," said Charlo. "We knew the people on the boats. There wasn't a bunch of people up in there."

They started talking to an old man sitting on his porch. They asked him to leave with them and told him they were heading up to the highway to catch a ride out of the parish.

"Come on, go with us; wherever your family's at we'll make sure you get to there," Thurman said.

"Oh no, I'm not going anywhere; I could use some water and supplies though."

They gave him food and a five-gallon bucket of water. Then they unloaded some of the stuff in the van and gave it to those staying on the boats. Barely able to walk in shoes, with his feet wrapped with ACE® bandages, Charlo walked out to St. Bernard Highway and flagged down a dump truck.

"I brought the dump truck back for them, so we could all get in," said Charlo. "The dump truck went all over picking up other people."

They tossed the rest of the supplies from the van into the dump truck full of people. They drove in the packed truck to the Chalmette Ferry, and Charlo and the gang walked onto a big tugboat, which took them to Camp Katrina. When they arrived at the slip, they saw other animals there with their owners. It upset them, but Thurman knew they only had one decision to make and that was to leave the pit bulls until they could get back to the school. In Algiers, the military was still searching everyone for weapons before they were allowed on the buses. The foursome had already hopped aboard one.

"We was supposed to be going to the airport," said Charlo. "Once we got across the Luling Bridge onto I-310, they put us on a tour bus. They said they couldn't fly us to Houston, so we're going over there on a bus."

Charlo had borrowed Thurman's cell phone when they got to Algiers. He called his family for the first time.

"They heard my voice, and they're screaming and started crying, 'he's alive!'"

He told them they were going to Houston, and his family began driving that way. Thurman also got through to his family, who had evacuated to Columbia, Louisiana, around the Monroe area, and he told them as soon as the bus stopped somewhere, they were going to get off and have them come pick them up. Unfortunately, as quickly as decisions were made, they were changed. The four were now on their way to Dallas. When the bus stopped in Alexandria, Thurman, Asevado, and B.B. got off and begged Charlo to come with them. Charlo decided to ride it out.

"I'm gonna need tetanus shots and antibiotics with all these cuts and bruises," Charlo said.

The guys worried about Charlo going it alone, but pride pushed him on his own path home.

"I carried my own weight once I got a little groceries in me; I got the dump truck; I was hustling myself," said Charlo.

After four days in lower St. Bernard together, the men and B.B. exchanged phone numbers and went their separate ways. On the way to Dallas, Charlo said they heard that they didn't have anywhere to stay once they got there, and since the bus driver had been on the road for so long, they ended up in a big parking lot in Mesquite, Texas. People got off the bus to stretch their legs, but Charlo said they didn't walk far away.

"When State Troopers tell you to get up and go, you go, especially the mamas; they were holding them youngins by the neck, fussing at 'em," said Charlo. "They didn't want to lose their kids in whatever town."

Someone walked on the bus with a brand new pair of tennis shoes and that caught Charlo's attention.

"What did you pay for them tennis shoes?"

"They on sale for $9.99."

"I'm gonna get me a pair."

Charlo did not have a penny on him; he had lost his wallet, cell phone, and bible when he was hanging in a tree. His ID was in his wallet. Once the storm had calmed down and when he was stuck in the hackberry tree, Charlo pulled off his ID, which was taped to his leg, and put it back in his wallet. His wallet, phone, and bible were probably still near the tree he had climbed out of. The bible was something he had owned for a long time.

"Somebody gave it to me when I was hitchhiking, when I was a hippie in the middle 60s," he recalled. "I don't know why I still had it, and I don't know why I took it with me, but I still had it."

Walking very, very slowly, on two swollen feet, to the store, he received a little of the treatment many evacuees would receive around the United States. A lady stopped to ask him if he was an evacuee. When she realized he was, she tried to give him all of her money.

"No mam, I don't want your money; I want a pair of shoes."

She started crying and said she needed to help him.

"Take it easy; it's gonna be O.K. I'm gonna be O.K."

"Let me drive you to the store," she insisted.

"I can walk there."

But after more prodding, he gave in and caught a short ride in her SUV.

"I go in there and she wants to buy the shoes and before you know it the people in the store give me my shoes," said Charlo.

*Charlo holding the life ring that saved him after he was thrown in the marsh.
Photograph by Mikel Schaefer*

His feet still wrapped in bandages, Charlo wanted shoes big enough to go around the bandages. He went in and found himself a pair of $9.99 white shoes with a purple tongue called Rebound, size twelve. Normally, Charlo wears a size ten and a half.

"I kept telling them I'm gonna miss my bus. I didn't want to hurt her feelings, so she puts me back in the car and sure enough the bus is gone. Here I am in Mesquite, at least fifteen to thirty buses, and I'm watching them, and they're taking off."

"If I could use your cellular phone, maybe I could call my daughter and my wife, and they'll come and get me," he asked his new friend, Sharon.

He caught his wife and daughter on the road to Houston. They turned around and drove towards Mesquite. Charlo told Sharon the reason why he split up with his crew was so he could get a Tetanus shot. Sharon brought him directly to the emergency room.

The hospital treated his wounds, gave him a Tetanus shot, and started him on antibiotics. He also received a pair of pants and a shirt. Finally enabling him to take off the grungy, ripped clothes he had worn for the past week. Before he was released from the hospital, his wife and daughter had made it to Sharon's house. When he saw his family again, he couldn't remember experiencing anything else quite like it, with the exception of the birth of his daughter. He realized it was the anticipation of this moment that had kept him alive. For the rest of his life, he will know that he cheated death in the worst kind of way.

"I don't know why I'm here; nobody knows what goes on, until I guess it's all over with," Charlo reflected humbly. "When I get depressed, angry, mad, or disgusted, I put in my head I'm not alone in this. They've got a lot of people, hundreds of thousands, hurting; it's not personal. Together we'll build our country back; that's being a good American. I know I ain't going no where; I love St. Bernard."

# AFTERWORD

The streets were finally drained of floodwater, only to have Hurricane Rita flood parts of the parish again later in September 2005, dramatically slowing the recovery process. St. Bernard Coroner Dr. Bryan Bertucci lists the final body count in St. Bernard at 154, which includes people who died within a month of the storm. However, without the rescue efforts from first responders and civilians the death toll would have been much higher, especially if the flooding would have occurred in the dark.

Sixty seven thousand people called St. Bernard home before the storm. Around the second anniversary of Katrina officials reported that more than a third of the population had returned. The number is staggering either way you analyze it. It is easy to see the negative effects with forty thousand former residents away, yet with such complete devastation, it is quite a statement to have so many return to fight through the rebuilding pains and reclaim their homes.

One of the parish's saving graces has been the school system. Superintendent Doris Voitier, along with many of the dedicated staff, brought in trailers weeks after the storm and opened up a school on the campus of Chalmette High on November 14. More than three hundred students, ranging from kindergarten to twelfth grade, showed up for an emotional reunion. This occurred before New Orleans opened any schools, including those in areas that had minor damage. By the end of the school year, nearly 2500 students had attended the newly coined St. Bernard Unified School. In the fall of 2007, St. Bernard will reopen five schools for approximately four thousand students. Before Katrina, the school system served nearly nine thousand students at fifteen school sites.

Soon after Katrina, the U.S. Army Corps of Engineers began repairing the destroyed levees along the MR-GO and eventually admitted that the levees had been poorly designed, built, and maintained. Miles and miles of levees have since been rebuilt up to twenty feet high. Leading the rebuilding efforts were a number of Corps workers who also lived in St. Bernard before the storm. They, along with a number of their families, were devastated by the floodwater. For the most part, the Corps has accomplished its goal of restoring the main hurricane protection levees to pre-Katrina levels by June 1, 2006. They also fixed the breach along the Industrial Canal in the Lower Ninth Ward, which was also responsible for flooding the parish. While there is still more work to be done to protect St. Bernard, many do not feel comfortable with the levees' ability to survive a similar type of storm without further improvements.

Thousands of residents, who not only suffered the flooding from Katrina but were also covered with oil from the Murphy Oil Refinery, have received badly needed funds for homes damaged by the oil in a lawsuit settlement. Many homes in the oil zone have been demolished and some closest to the spill are being bought by the refinery.

Many businesses have returned, and those who have set up shop in conditions that for months seemed like the old frontier have profited. There are a couple of major grocery stores and fast food chains that are reopening, and many mom and pop establishments are filling in the gaps. The two major oil refineries in the parish, Murphy Oil Refinery and Chalmette Refining, were back online almost immediately after the storm and helped serve as a catalyst for the industry. The St. Bernard Port also rebounded quickly and is at one hundred percent capacity and is helping to drive the economic engine as well. Long defined for its fishing industry, St. Bernard and its fishermen were dealt a major blow by Katrina. Most in the industry still struggle to get back to their trade.

The ranks of the first responders like police and firefighters have diminished due to a smaller population and less tax revenue for pay. The police force has seen nearly half of its once four hundred officers return. The fire department has roughly ninety firefighters; before the storm, they had 116.

The parish's can do attitude has been on display as it held a Carnival parade, the Krewe of Nemesis, just months after the storm, while there was still debris all along the route. They followed that up with another successful parade in 2007, this time with the trash gone.

Life is tough, but residents say it's getting better. Despite the threats of another possible Katrina, they don't want to live anywhere else. Many of the people interviewed in this book are still in the parish and plan to stay no matter what, even outside of the hurricane protection levee. Charlo has a trailer on his lot in Hopedale, in the same spot he was swept away into the marsh; his wife refuses to come back and lives patiently north of Lake Pontchartrain. Gene Alonzo is rebuilding a small home on his land in Yscloskey, and Glenn Sanchez still runs his marina in Hopedale. Some, like Chuck Thurman and Frankie Asevado, have moved inside the levee system.

However, returning has brought with it many forms of heartache. When the parish reopened, about three weeks after Katrina, Asevado returned to Sebastian Roy School to find only one of the six pit bulls barely alive. Someone had shot four of the dogs; one of the young ones had died naturally. The one dog that survived had given birth to three puppies, all alive. A little more than year after the storm, Eric Colopy found out Mr. Billy had passed away, and he finally learned his last name at the funeral service.

"Redding, had a card with his name on it. W.W. Redding, everybody called him Billy. W.W. Redding born 1937, died 2006," said Colopy.

Some lifelong residents have not come back like Bubby Bodden. He moved north of the lake along with David Griffin and Mitch McDaniel. Thousands of former residents will not come back. Many have settled for selling their plundered homes for bargain prices and have moved away, foregoing the emotional stress it takes to live in a place like St. Bernard. Many homes remain untouched, while thousands have been demolished with thousands more to go.

Many say until the levees are rock solid, they're never coming back. While few have experienced a new lease on life in new areas, no one I've talked to would have traded leaving St. Bernard to find that new way of life. It was a parish with one degree of separation, just like most of the metropolitan New Orleans area. For too many, there's no more going next door to visit mama or granny or down the street for dinner with a brother, sister, or cousin. This is what made St. Bernard so unique and rich and the most disastrous outcome of Katrina. As a lifelong resident so aptly described, "Katrina was a people bomb," scattering friends and family all over.

About a week after Katrina, I wrote down some thoughts in a control room at Louisiana Public Broadcasting, working for WWL-TV. We were broadcasting nearly non-stop. It was a piece that inspired me to preserve St. Bernard's story. St. Bernardians have proven they have guts, determination, and heart and will fight for their homeland. Nothing, not even a disaster like Katrina, will change that, ever.

Modern day Atlantis, sounds quite dramatic. Sounds quite improbable. Sounds quite real. I'm still having trouble describing the reality of what is now St. Bernard Parish. It's a blue-collar workingman's community, where they love their women and their fish and not necessarily in that order. A community wiped clean by Hurricane Katrina. More than forty thousand homes and businesses flooded by Katrina. Sixty-seven thousand people's lives destroyed by Katrina. Rooftops whipped by the high winds and sent sailing, scorched by tornadic activity. Cars and boats flipped and tossed over on their sides, raised and dropped on the tops of trees and roofs of homes. Forty-, fifty-, and sixty-foot shrimp boats tossed onto highways and turned upside down in the bayous and marshes.

It's a place I once called home; a place that many friends and family once called home. A place where best friends once roamed, played, kissed girls, and grew up to be men. A place I've buried my own blood, my oldest brother John. A place that is now frozen in history.

There are no neighborhoods to return to; schools are in ruin; parks are destroyed. Some will return like their parents did during Hurricane Betsy in 1965, Flossy in '47, or the great flood of 1927, and some will remain as if this God forsaken tragedy was just a bump on the highway. But far too many cannot return, will not return, and don't want to return. The bulldozers will come and will level the estimated twenty-seven thousand homes ravaged during Katrina.

The water spilled in from every direction. From the south as the storm surge from the Gulf of Mexico rushed in, overtaking the roads like they were designed to be tributaries for the rising waters. From the north as the Industrial Canal levee broke free, leveling homes in New Orleans' Lower Ninth Ward neighborhood. From the west came the water that reportedly flowed over the Mississippi River levee in a small section down in Violet, and from the east as the levees along the MR-GO providing the main hurricane protection collapsed under the pounding blows of Katrina and her reported over twenty-foot storm surge.

Reports say when the levees broke, the water rose a foot a minute, giving people just minutes to get to high ground, which in many cases meant people scrambled inside of their attics, then axed, sawed, or busted their fists through the roofs. A south Louisiana attic in the dead of summer with ten feet of water nipping at your heels is a sobering unrealistic thought turned into reality.

I just can't get my head around the fact that St. Bernard, my long time home, my friends' home, my family's home, and my history is gone, as I know it at this moment. Good people with good work ethics, good hearts, and overwhelmed with the good life. It is not oversimplified glorification; it is the truth and Katrina put a dagger right through their hearts—our hearts.

Will she rise from the floodwater and the debris to live again? Yes. Will it be next year? Who knows. Will it be ten years? Who knows. But she will be again. The spirit is tattered and worn and splintered, but she is not broken. Some just may be tempted to put an asterisk on her tombstone. St. Bernard 1780-2005*, but she'll pick herself back up and will live again. For those who suffered through the horrors of Katrina and still suffer today, the pain will fade and the parish will rise again.

# Index